STEVE McQUEEN

Steve McQueen

A TRIBUTE TO THE KING OF COOL

Marshall Terrill

Steve McQueen
A Tribute to The King of Cool
Marshall Terrill

© Dalton Watson Fine Books Limited

ISBN 978-1-85443-240-7

Dalton Watson Fine Books
1730 Christopher Drive,
Deerfield, IL 60015,
U.S.A
glyn@daltonwatson.com

www.daltonwatson.com

R Boys Republic

This book is dedicated to the selfless men and women who have worked for the Boys Republic in Chino, California, an organization that Steve McQueen credits with turning his life around. It is also dedicated to the young boy and girl residents who had the courage to examine their lives and work hard to become productive members of society.

A portion of the proceeds of this book will go towards the Boys Republic and I encourage readers to generously donate to this wonderful organization that Steve McQueen supported his entire life. For more information about the Boys Republic or how to donate, visit www.boysrepublic.org.

Marshall Terrill

Contents

Contents

Acknowledgments

Authoring a book is very much like directing a movie—it could never get off the ground without a supportive cast and crew. So I'd like to thank my cast and crew for their selfless and giving natures, and unwavering support of this project.

The Cast:

Zoe Terrill	Wife and Computer Widow
Mike and Carolyn Terrill	The Parental Units
Barbara McQueen	Down-home Diva
Glyn and Jean Morris	The Publishers
Mark Osborne	The Sponsor
Cheryl Hosmer	The Editor
Ben Gibbs	The Designer
Kandee Nelson	Literary Grease Monkey
Donna Redden	Ace in the Hole
Pat Johnson	Ass Kicking Friend
Sue Johnson	Everybody's Mom
Dave Friedman	Talented Photographer
Hilly Elkins	The Prince of Cool
Adrienne McQueen	The Germanator
Veronica Valdez	Nancy Drew
Michael Manning	Comic Relief
Mike Jugan	The Pilot
Darren Wright	Master of His Domain
Will Smither	Son of a Beech

The Crew:

(starring in alphabetical order):
Andrew Antoniades, Andy Armstrong, Tom Askew, Daniel Baggs, Jean E. Black, John Bruno, Ellyn Cole, Beth Davey, Karen Bruno Hornbaker, Lynn Howard, Scott Howard, Liz Ingersoll, Steve Kiefer, Sandi Love, Brian Mayfield, Brian O'Mahony, J. Stuart Rosebrook, Cathy Rosera, Hikari Takano and Loren Thomson.

Steve and Barbara McQueen,
Chicago, 1979.

I didn't fall in love with a movie star. I fell in love with a man who loved motorcycles and flying as much as making a great pot of mashed potatoes and having a beer with friends.

So whenever I open any book about my late husband, Steve McQueen, I usually only read about the years we spent together. It's not a matter of being self-centered. It's simply that I never read about Steve before he met me because that was a man I didn't know. To this day, I've not seen most of his movies—only *The Blob, The Towering Inferno* and *Tom Horn* in their entirety, and some snippets of *The Thomas Crown Affair, Bullitt* and *The Getaway*. Strangely enough, my grandparents never missed an episode of *Wanted: Dead or Alive* and that's the one show I risked getting in trouble for to watch. I'd sneak behind the couch in the front room when I was little, mesmerized by the blue eyes and big gun of the man I would marry nearly twenty years later.

I got Steve at a good time in his life.

Over the past few years, my friend and co-author Marshall Terrill has been educating me about the man who was my first love. Although I don't really want to know about his past because not knowing makes the three-and-a-half years we were together even more special, sometimes I need some background information when I'm prepping for an interview or about to give a speech. And what better resource than Marshall? He has dedicated the last twenty years of his life to Steve's history and is without a doubt the most knowledgeable person I know on the subject.

Marshall's heart is also in the right place because he tells Steve's story with great compassion and understanding. Many books and articles have taken on a tabloid-style slant, but Marshall is a seasoned journalist who gives both sides of the story and lets the reader form their own conclusions. The greatest compliment I can pay Marshall is that Steve would have liked him because he's a straight shooter.

I have come to love Marshall, who is now my little brother, protector, confidante and close friend. Don't be fooled by his stoic demeanor and polite exterior—behind those spectacles and intellectual facade is a person who possesses a wicked sense of humor and is a loveable goofball. It's been said that writers are failed actors and Marshall pretty much lives up to that stereotype.

As for this book, it has made me break my own rule in only reading about my years with Steve. I laughed, cried, sympathized and cheered for my husband in these passages. To have learned so much about him through the eyes of others and to see how Steve reached their lives, touches my heart.

Below left: A porcelain ashtray that McQueen took a liking to and 'liberated' from a hotel in Bologna, Italy. He used it as an ashtray at his home, The Castle, in Brentwood, California.

Below right: McQueen's Persol sunglasses from *The Thomas Crown Affair* fetched $70,000 at the Steve McQueen Sale in November 2006 hosted by Bonhams.

Introduction
Mark Osborne

Below left: A porcelain ashtray that McQueen took a liking to and 'liberated' from a hotel in Bologna, Italy. He used it as an ashtray at his home, The Castle, in Brentwood, California.

Below right: McQueen's Persol sunglasses from *The Thomas Crown Affair* fetched $70,000 at the Steve McQueen Sale in November 2006 hosted by Bonhams.

It is certainly an honor to be invited to write an introduction for a book about one's idol, particularly as this wonderful book explores new territory in such an innovative and creative fashion. It is a 21st Century look, if you like, at one of the most charismatic personalities of the 20th Century.

I have been a fan of Steve McQueen for most of my life, since my father first sat me in front of *The Getaway* at a tender age—that was the beginning. McQueen was compulsory viewing in our household, from the annual and patriotic showing of *The Great Escape* at Christmas time through to McQueen's last movie, *The Hunter* in 1980.

In the last several years, my involvement with McQueen has been of a more commercial nature, so I will focus on this aspect, as it provides continuity with the pages ahead.

In 2006, in my role as Head of the U.S. Motoring Department at Bonhams Auctioneers, I was approached via an intermediary to meet with Barbara Minty McQueen, Steve's widow.

Barbara had "one or two" mostly motorcycle-related pieces belonging to Steve that she was prepared to consign, in the hope that a wider audience could appreciate them. My visit then saw me inspecting a vast array of not only McQueen motorcycle-racing gear but also hunting and personal items—plus collectible Americana. It became clear that the property had the makings of an entire Sale featuring more than 200 pieces, reflecting his diverse hobbies and interests.

Our subsequent Steve McQueen Sale proved to be an enormous success. In fact, to this day we still receive inquiries for the sold-out catalog—and many of the copies in circulation have changed hands for staggering sums. Active buyers at the sale ranged from the British aristocracy to avid Japanese collectors; from fans of McQueen's movies to followers of his two and four-wheel exploits; from well-known memorabilia dealers to a lady from Wales who owns a Bed & Breakfast and who just had to have McQueen's egg basket as a conversation piece to amuse her guests.

During the lead-up to the Sale and afterwards, I was asked by those in the media and prospective buyers why McQueen is still relevant —what accounts for his broad appeal some thirty years after his sadly premature death? I thought about his service as a sharp-shooter in the Marines and his famed attempt to create the 'McQueen Super Tank' by porting and milling the heads of an obsolete tank. That's certainly intriguing for a start. Was it that he represented the United States in the sporting arena as part of the 1964 International Six-Day Trials team, or that he competed at the top levels of motor racing? Was it that he flew his own vintage airplanes?

I think it was all of the diverse interests and endeavors to which McQueen committed himself so fully, taken as a whole, that secured his indelible status as an American icon—not forgetting of course that at the same time he made some of the most memorable movies of the sixties and seventies.

In short, McQueen was the real deal.

He was a genuinely cool, self-made, original guy, and this resonated with people during his lifetime and continues to do so today. In my experience, he is one of the only true 'stars' who commands near-fervor from people of all ages and from every walk of life when pictures of him or his possessions appear on exhibition or at auction.

Steve McQueen: A Tribute to The King of Cool provides a wonderful insight into this great man's enduring legend. It is a uniquely fresh and a highly collectible addition to our bookshelves for all of us who continue to be captivated by the utterly charismatic Steve McQueen.

Mark Osborne
U.S. Motoring Department
Bonhams Auctioneers

Author's Note
Marshall Terrill

Am I obsessed with Steve McQueen? That's a fair question given that this is my third book on "The King of Cool".

Countless hours of my life have been devoted to research, locating sources, correspondence and photographs, buying up memorabilia, and the agonizing torture of transcribing taped interviews. All because I have a healthy respect for the man, where he came from, and what he was able to accomplish in his fifty years on this earth.

I have been to Steve McQueen's home in Slater, Missouri, where he was raised as a youth, and visited the clinic in Juarez where he died in the recovery room on November 7, 1980. Of course, it's the journey in between those two places that sustains my fascination with the actor and continually moves me to ask: *Who was Steve McQueen?*

A complex individual to be sure. He was a movie star. He was a boy from the wrong side of the tracks. He was a loving father and husband. He was a male chauvinist. He was notoriously cheap and tightfisted. He gave generously and anonymously to charity. He was mistrustful to the point of paranoia. He was a loyal friend. He could be cruel. He had a weak spot for old people and children. He hated men in suits. He was ashamed of his lack of education. He outsmarted every movie executive in Hollywood with his Ph.D. from the streets. He was apolitical yet FBI Director J. Edgar Hoover kept an active file on him and he was placed by Richard Nixon on his famous "enemies list". He was anti-authority and anti-establishment. He was patriotic. He was disciplined and hard working. He created havoc on movie sets. He paid regular visits to the Boys Republic in Chino, California, in hopes of inspiring them to become productive citizens.

In the sixties and seventies, Steve McQueen was the biggest movie star in the world and the alpha male of his generation. He riveted audiences in countries as disparate as Britain, Japan, Germany, Russia and France with his tough guy persona. His style consisted of an unlikely combination of willfulness, unpredictability, strength and vulnerability. And yet, no one—let alone himself—could have predicted his staggering worldwide success in films such as *The Magnificent Seven*, *The Great Escape*, *Love with the Proper Stranger*, *The Cincinnati Kid*, *Nevada Smith*, *The Sand Pebbles*, *The Thomas Crown Affair*, *Bullitt*, *The Getaway*, *Papillon* and *The Towering Inferno*. McQueen had a ninth grade education, and his alma mater was a reform school. His mother was an alcoholic who abandoned him repeatedly through childhood, and he never knew his father, who was also an alcoholic and died of cirrhosis of the liver at the age of 52. McQueen had nothing going for himself. Amazingly, it proved to be enough. Steve McQueen built his fortune on Steve McQueen. He was his biggest ally. At times, he was also his own worst enemy.

How did a man who seemed destined to live his life on the margins of society rise above his circumstances in order to become one of the greatest icons of cinema? The fact that McQueen managed to become an actor in itself is astonishing. By all accounts, he fell into acting in order to escape menial jobs. He did not choose his profession for the love of the craft or to fulfill some high aesthetic ideal. He was not seeking fame or immortality. McQueen picked acting simply because it beat having a nine-to-five job and so that he could "meet chicks." And yet, he came to master his craft and know the camera like nobody else, and achieve great fame and wealth. All in a profession he didn't consider "a real man's job." In his own words, acting was "candy ass." Still, he worked hard at it and had an immense drive to succeed. Otherwise, how could McQueen have become so good in a field he didn't particularly respect?

What Steve McQueen respected were cars, motorcycles and the men who excelled in racing them. His first passion was machines, and he had a natural affinity for them. McQueen was mechanically adept, fiercely competitive and completely fearless. He drove many a car to complete destruction. On the set of *Hell is for Heroes*, he wrecked three rental cars—the count would have been higher if the studio had not told him the next one would be put on his tab. On another film, he drove a brand new car until the engine caught fire. McQueen jumped out of the burning vehicle like a seasoned stuntman and laughed about it moments later with a friend. When not on film sets, McQueen competed against the best race car drivers and bikers in the world and held his own. Many of these men formed McQueen's close-knit group of friends, tough guys who did not give a damn about Hollywood and kept life real for the movie star.

McQueen was a complex, contradictory man who lived the same way he drove his motorcycles and cars: fearlessly, ruthlessly and at top speed. He may not always have known where he was heading, but he always made sure to take himself as far as he could.

This is not your typical "tribute book", but Steve McQueen was not a typical man. His unparalleled spirit, multidimensional image, contradictory behavior, uncensored desire, bravado and puckish humor is hopefully captured in this 360-degree perspective from his family, friends, co-stars, business associates, acquaintances and adoring fans from around the world.

His legacy, I believe, is worth keeping alive.

Steve McQueen Family Tree

Paternal side:

Dugal McQueen
Born: late 1600s/early 1700s in Corybrough, Scotland
Died: 1747 in Baltimore, Maryland
Married: **Grace Brown**
Children: William, Ruth, Sarah, Thomas and Francis

Thomas McQueen
Born: 1731 in Maryland, United States
Died: 1763
Married: **Elizabeth Berry**
Children: Joshua, Elizabeth, John, Benjamin, Thomas II and Daniel

Thomas McQueen II
Born: 1761 in Maryland, United States
Died: 1823
Married: **Sarah Wilson Vaughn**
Children: Mary, Uriah, Joshua, Benjamin, Joseph Wilson, Thomas III, Elizabeth, Sarah Sally, Jennie Jane, Deborah, Nancy and John

Uriah McQueen
Born: 1787 in Virginia, United States
Died: 1853
Married: **Elizabeth Betsy Tanner**
Children: Belinda, Rev Joshua, George, William R.T., Thomas, Joseph Tanner, Uriah, Elizabeth, Catherine and Indiana

Joseph Tanner McQueen
Born: 1820 in Indiana, United States
Died: 1859
Married: **Catherine Cook**
Children: Jacob C., John S., Albert M., Mary Victoria, Laura Kansas and Joseph T.

Jacob C. McQueen
Born: 1845 in Indiana, United States
Died: 1919
Married: **Elizabeth Aikin**
Children: Hattie F., Louis, Lillian, Jane, Sarah K.C., Harden R. and Herman

Louis D. McQueen
Born: 1 October, 1869 in Illinois, United States
Died: 1919
Married: **Caroline Culbertson**
Children: William Terrence

William Terrence McQueen
Born: 15 March, 1907 in Nashville, Tennessee, United States
Died: 1958
Married: **Julia Ann "Julian" Crawford**
Children: Terrence Steven

Terrence Steven McQueen
Born: 24 March, 1930 in Beech Grove, Indiana, United States
Died: 7 November, 1980
Married: Neile Adams, November 2, 1956
Children: Terry Leslie and Chadwick Steven
Married: Ali MacGraw Evans, July 12, 1973
Married: Barbara J. Minty, January 16, 1980

Maternal side:

Samuel Thomson
Born: 31 Dec. 1691, Blair Manor, Ayrshire Scotland, emigrated 1717
Died: 28 Aug. 1753 in Fredricksville Parish, Virginia, United States
Married: **three times**
Children: William plus ten others known

Captain William Thomson
Born: 1727 in Spotsylvania County, Virginia, United States
Died: 1778
Married: **Anne Rodes**
Children: Anne, (Major) Rodes, Mary A., William, Clifton, Asa, John, Eunice, Elizabeth, Lydia, (Brigadier General) David and Sarah

Asa Thomson
Born: 25 January, 1764 in Louisa, Virginia, United States
Died: 1842
Married: **Dianna Quarles**
Children: Mary, Roger, Martha Ann, (Captain) John William, Nancy, Asa Quarles, (Rev.) Robert Yancey and George Q., Robert Thomas

Captain John William Thomson
Born: 19 March, 1794 in Kentucky, United States
Died: 1822
Married: **Nancy Ellis**
Children: Pike Montgomery, John Milton, Nancy Ann and William Ellis

Captain Pike Montgomery Thomson
Born: 20 August, 1819 in Fayette, Kentucky, United States
Died: 1902
Married: **Elizabeth Eleanora Goodwin**
Children: John W., Lloyd G., Lucian M., Pike M., Jr., Ruth, Laura, Polly Jane

John William Thomson
Born: 21 January, 1845 Fayette, Kentucky, United States
Died: 1916
Married: **Julia Franklin Graves**
Children: Claude William, Emmett, Emma, Lillian, and infant who died at birth

Lillian John Thomson
Born: January, 1879 in Slater, Missouri, United States
Died: 1964
Married: **Victor L. Crawford**
Children: Julia Ann

Julia Ann "Julian" Crawford
Born: 10 April, 1910 in Slater, Missouri, United States
Died: 1965
Married: **William Terrence McQueen**
Children: Terrence Steven

Terrence Steven McQueen
Born: 24 March, 1930 in Beech Grove, Indiana, United States
Died: 7 November, 1980
Married: Neile Adams, November 2, 1956
Children: Terry Leslie and Chadwick Steven
Married: Ali MacGraw Evans, July 12, 1973
Married: Barbara J. Minty, January 16, 1980

A period photograph of the Thomson homestead, Slater, Missouri.

Porkers or Pork Rinds?
Loren Thomson

No matter what kind of stock you have in life, most people would choose fun over fleas.

Take my distant cousin, Steve McQueen. He is widely known as a great actor who overcame a tough childhood. But who knew that he came from downright good stock? Let me take you back briefly to the early days of the nineteenth century. It's quite a story, full of war, compassion, sibling rivalry, hog farming, and a hint of showgirls. I am a second cousin on his mother's side and this is our family history. Captain Pike Montgomery Thomson was the first in the Thomson clan to venture into Missouri, and settled in Foster's Prarie in Howard County around the age of twenty. He married Elizabeth Eleanora Goodwin of Kentucky, and they homesteaded approximately 1,700 acres of prime farmland.

Pike was in his forties when he answered General Claiborne F. Jackson's call for men and enlisted in the Missouri State Guard. He served under George K. Dills' staff, Parsons' 6th Division of the Missouri State Guard, and fought in the battles of Dry Wood and Lexington, Kentucky in the Civil War.

Ascending to the rank of Captain in the Confederate Army, Pike was captured by the Union and set for execution. However, a compassionate Yankee captain spared his life but "banished" him from the country. Pike was allowed to take his wife and child to her parents' Kentucky home before he left. Had he been executed, neither Steve McQueen nor I would have been born. The war ended soon after Pike's banishment and he returned with his family to Saline County, where he later served as the president of the Slater Bank and raised his children: John W., Lloyd G., Lucian M., Pike M. Jr., Ruth, Laura and Polly Jane.

John William Thomson married Julia Franklin Graves and was an expert stock breeder. He didn't do so bad on the human side, either: he was the father of Claude W., Emmett, Emma, Lillian and an infant who died at birth. Lillian was Steve's maternal grandmother.

I never knew Claude, the man who practically raised Steve, but from what I gather, he was a shrewd and acquisitive businessman. A prosperous hog farmer, he eventually squeezed his siblings out of the ownership of the family farm.

Steve's mom, Julia Ann, was born in 1910 to Victor and Lillian (Thomson) Crawford. "Julian," as she was called, was a problem child and didn't adjust well to adult life. My father, James Lucian Thomson, didn't like her although he never specified why. I suspect it was because she was spoiled.

At nineteen, Julian married Bill McQueen. Their union didn't last long, but it did produce a son, Steve, who was born in Beech Grove, Indiana, on March 24, 1930. When Julian returned to Slater, Claude offered to look after the boy.

Claude genuinely loved Steve and would have let him stay for as long as he wanted, but make no mistake, Claude had a hog farm and he put Steve to work. Based on my own limited experience, raising hogs is a hard, dirty, 24-hour-a-day business. The stock has to be fed, moved, and watered regularly, as well as providing birth assistance and castration. Hogs are not clean animals and they are usually infested with fleas if kept in the open.

Why Steve McQueen ran away with the carnival at fourteen would have been a no-brainer for me back then. Traveling with a bunch of "dancing girls" and carnies would certainly outdistance nursing a bunch of half-wild porkers to a teenage mind.

Loren Thomson is a distant cousin of Steve McQueen. He is a retired attorney and resides in Bloomington, Illinois.

St. Francis Hospital, the birthplace of Steve McQueen.

The home of Victor and Lillian Crawford, Steve McQueen's maternal grandparents. McQueen lived here until the age of three.

Searching for Steve McQueen
Will Smither

I had lived in Beech Grove, Indiana, most of my life before hearing that Steve McQueen was born there, and wondered why no one was talking about it. I went to the public library and found only one McQueen biography on the shelf and there in the first paragraph of the first chapter was my hometown. Was Steve McQueen, the famous actor, born in Beech Grove? My search for the truth began at that moment and has continued for over twenty years.

Beech Grove is a self-contained city, but it is completely surrounded by Indianapolis, the largest city in Indiana. For the most part, Beech Grove has maintained its autonomy and identity with its own mayor, police and fire departments, school system, and library, as Indianapolis has spread to the boundaries of Marion County.

In 1930 when McQueen was born, Beech Grove had a population of 3,552 and was quite rural with several farms in and around the town. Fields and wooded areas would have existed in places now covered with neighborhoods (many not built until the fifties or later). The city owes its existence to the railroad repair shops prominently sitting at the east end of Main Street. For years, the shops were the largest employer in the town, but though they remain, over time the number of employees has decreased considerably.

The railroad shops have given Beech Grove some local notoriety, but few outside central Indiana have heard of the city (unlike Speedway, another independent town in Marion County, which is home to the Indianapolis 500). I have often wondered why anyone would say that Beech Grove was McQueen's birthplace if he was not born there.

Some biographies state that he was born in "Beech Grove Hospital". However, a hospital by that name has never existed in the city, the local establishment being called St. Francis Hospital since 1914. It is also unclear whether McQueen ever lived in the city. Reports that he went to elementary school in Beech Grove or to another school five miles southeast of the town have not been substantiated. In the 1931 Indianapolis City Directory, a Julian McQueen is listed as rooming at a house on North Drexel Avenue in Indianapolis, approximately four-and-a-half miles from Beech Grove and it is likely that St. Francis was the closest hospital for Julian to have her baby. Ultimately, that may be the only connection that McQueen has to the town.

My interest in Steve McQueen began with Beech Grove, but I have become more than a casual fan. As long as there is some aspect of his work to see and more information about his Indiana roots to be discovered, I will be searching for Steve McQueen.

Will Smither is a librarian at the Westfield Washington Public Library in Westfield, Indiana. He resides in Indianapolis, Indiana. He moved to Beech Grove when he was one-year old and lived there for thirty-two years.

MARION COUNTY
HEALTH DEPARTMENT
making a difference

NON-CERTIFED COPY OF BIRTH

Marion County Health Department records show:

NAME AT BIRTH	TERRANCE STEPHEN MCQUEEN
DATE OF BIRTH	MARCH 24, 1930
PLACE OF BIRTH	MARION COUNTY
PARENTS NAME	WILLIAM & JULLIAN MCQUEEN (CRAWFORD)
FATHERS STATE OF BIRTH	TENNESSEE
MOMS STATE OF BIRTH	MISSOURI
FILE DATE	APRIL 3, 1930
CERTIFICATE NO.	187
DATE ISSUED	Tuesday, November 01, 2005

A copy of Terrence Steven McQueen's birth certificate issued by the Marion County Health Department in Indiana. Note the incorrect spelling of McQueen's first (Terrance) and middle (Stephen) name. He continued to spell his name a variety of ways throughout his life.

Hooky

Bob Holt

Top: The Thomson homestead in 2007.

Bottom: The headstones of Claude Thomson and his wife Eva Thomson, later remarried to John Simmermon.

"Ornery little bugger" is the best way I can think of to describe Steve McQueen as a kid.

Steve was raised across the street from me on his Uncle Claude's farm. Claude Thomson was one of the biggest hog farmers in the area and always wore an old cowboy hat. His wife, Eva Mae, was a former showgirl and a little on the wild side. She used to buy cigarettes from my dad.

Even though Steve was seven years older than me, we attended Orearville School together. It had eight grades and probably held twelve to fifteen students at a time. Steve was smart but he did not like to go to school. We often walked along the old dirt road together, and many times he walked past it, right into Slater. He loved playing hooky.

As I said, he was an ornery little bugger.

Bob Holt is a retired steel worker at Standard Haven Glasco. He currently lives in Slater, Missouri.

Last Tango in Slater

Thomas Allen Ryan

Right and bottom left: Farming and the former Chicago & Alton Railroad were Slater's biggest economic engine for decades.

Bottom right: Slater Depot, 2007.

Slater was a rough, agricultural railroad town. Many troop and prisoner-of-war trains rumbled through its center in the post-Depression and World War II days. Times were tough. The people even tougher. That's where Steve McQueen comes to mind.

When I was a kid, I was in a fistfight with Steve. Even though he attended Orearville School, he had ventured onto the grounds at Slater Elementary one afternoon. I can't remember how or why it started, but I had my hands full with this blond-haired, blue-eyed kid. The fight seemed to last forever until it was broken up by one of the teachers who unceremoniously banished Steve once it was discovered he wasn't a student there.

He sure could fight.

Thomas Allen Ryan grew up in Slater, Missouri, and is a retired member of the United States Air Force.

Bricks from Claude Thomson's fireplace.

Kids, Trees and Broken Appendages
Fred McBurney

My father, Alexander McBurney, was a country doctor who practiced in Slater, Missouri, for nearly fifty years. He kept meticulous records of all his patients and one labeled Steve McQueen ended up in his file drawer when he broke his arm.

Dad was friends with Claude Thomson, Steve's great-uncle. Steve had fallen out of a tree and Claude brought him to dad's office on the second floor of the general store on Main Street. He took a few X-rays and determined that the arm was broken. He set it back in place and put Steve in a cast. Six weeks later, the cast was taken off and the arm was good as new.

When I was growing up, just before World War II, most everything was rationed, especially gasoline, and because Steve was raised in the countryside, hardly anyone in Slater knew he existed. I later discovered that Steve and I were the same age and we would have attended high school together had he not left town for the circus. As

it turned out, he attended elementary school in Orearville while I was schooled in Slater, so we never met.

Yet Steve and I probably sat in the same movie house on several occasions, which was typical of a Saturday afternoon in Small Town, USA. The Kiva Theatre on Main Street held close to 200 people and Saturday matinées were strictly for kids. They'd show cartoons, a couple of serials and then the main feature, usually *Hopalong Cassidy* or the *Lone Ranger*. Many of the kids wore their cowboy hats and shot their cap guns at the villains on the screen, whooping and hollering it up.

It was that same sense of adventure that brought Steve McQueen to my dad's office.

Fred McBurney lives in the home where he was raised and is a life-long resident of Slater, Missouri.

An original window frame from the Thomson home.

Nothing to Lose

Charles "C.H." Hines

The first and only time I ever met Steve McQueen, I got into trouble.

Steve grew up a few miles from the farm where I was raised. We lived in an area that locals referred to as "The Blackberry Patch". In other words, we were country hicks.

Steve's great-uncle Claude Thomson used to visit our farm a few times a year to buy coal. On one of these visits, he brought Steve with him. Steve was about three years older than me and had curly blond hair and bright blue eyes. I thought to myself, *Man, that is the ugliest kid I have ever seen in my life!*

We attended different country schools and I hardly spent any time with kids my own age, so I naturally gravitated toward playing with Steve for a time while Claude loaded up his GMC flatbed truck with coal. He was one of our biggest buyers and told my step-dad that he used it to feed his hogs. When pressed further, he revealed that he fed the coal to the hogs to put weight on them before they were sold. He was feeding them with two-cent coal and selling them for ten cents a pound. Smart guy.

I don't remember exactly what happened, but Steve and I were in trouble before the day was over. My mom lit into both of us, but it was worse for me. She pulled me inside the house by my ear. I could hear Steve chuckling the whole time. That was the end of our playtime.

Even though I was the one who was worse for wear that day, Steve didn't have an easy life on the farm. Claude was a slave driver and work is the name of the game when you have a farm. I'm sure Steve labored from sunup to sundown and I am certain Claude would have continued working him hard if he had stuck around. Steve knew there was a bigger world out there that extended way beyond that farm on Thomson Lane.

The way I see it, Steve McQueen had nothing to lose by leaving Slater.

Charles C.H. Hines retired from Kraft Foods and is a resident of Slater, Missouri.

Orearville School, the one-room schoolhouse where Steve McQueen was educated. Today it is Abbott's Chapel on Front Street in Slater.

The Red Berri

Janice Sutton

That red baseball cap caught everyone's eyes.

Steve McQueen went by his mom's remarried name back then. I only taught the young Mr. Berri for about six weeks in 1942, but what a memorable time it was. I was his teacher at Orearville School, a white frame, single-room schoolhouse on the outskirts of Slater. At the time, I was known by my maiden name, Janice Jones.

Steve was a feisty twelve-year-old sixth-grader. Usually just ten to fifteen students attended the kindergarten through eighth grade school, so Steve was not hard to miss, being the only blond-haired,

blue-eyed boy in the class who was a bit of a smart aleck. Then there was that red baseball cap that made him stick out like a banner for America's favorite pastime. The country kids thought that was pretty neat. Unfortunately, Steve and his red cap relocated with his mother to California about a month-and-a-half later.

I have to wonder what Steve would have been had he stayed the center of attention in Slater.

Janice Sutton taught in Slater, Missouri, until 1947. She now lives in Kansas City.

Above: Main Street in Slater, Missouri, probably in the forties.
Right: Postcard of Broadway Street in Slater looking north.

Ice Cream Social
John Berlekamp

Steve McQueen used to come to town on Saturdays and buy ice cream. I know, because I sold him the ice cream at the City Pharmacy. Saturdays in Slater were no doubt the biggest day of the week, when everybody came to do their shopping and to socialize.

I didn't know who Steve was at the time other than a "farm kid"—slang for someone who lived outside the Slater city limits. Because he lived in Orearville, he went to the country school, and we city folk didn't know many of these farm kids, since they did not come to Slater until ninth grade and then you'd just see them out on the street.

The city at the time consisted mostly of the main street drag, which had about forty merchants. There was a train depot on one end and the Kiva, Slater's only movie house. Every merchant was a mom and pop concern.

I worked as a soda jerk at City Pharmacy and did a little of everything. I stocked the shelves, swept the floors, scooped ice cream and everything the manager didn't want to do. Steve, dressed in blue jeans and a T-shirt, came in every Saturday. I imagine it was one of the few pleasures he had in life at that time. He was quiet, withdrawn and kept to himself. He usually bought his ice cream and left to go stand out on the corner.

In the late fifties, I moved to Kansas City after a stint in the service. When *Wanted: Dead or Alive* became a big television hit, a co-worker of mine realized that I was from Slater, told me that the star of the popular Western was also from there. I made sure to watch the next episode. Even though he was older, that face was unmistakable.

How about that? Serving ice cream cones to Steve McQueen is my claim to fame.

John (J.W.) Berlekamp is a retired school superintendent. He lives in Springfield, Missouri.

Steve McQueen at the carnival in the 1953 movie *Girl on the Run*. This photo appears courtesy of Steve Kiefer, who has one of the greatest McQueen memorabilia collections in the world.

Of Jigs, Fleas, Carnivals
and Last Handshakes William Kiso

Steve McQueen knew how to land the best jobs. Even at seven-years old he seemed drawn to the world of entertainment.

My first vision of Steve was of a young boy dancing the jig in a flatbed wagon. I met him through his great-uncle, Claude Thomson. Every year I'd go to the Thomson farm to help Claude and his son, Mac, thresh wheat. Claude was considered wealthy for that time. He had a large farm, close to 1,000 hogs and twice as many fleas. I remember once I had to lead a bunch of hogs into a barn because it looked like it was going to rain. The fleas were so thick in the barn that I could hardly see. Later on, I had to burn my clothes.

Claude called on me to help with the threshing of the wheat because he and Mac didn't get along so well. I acted as their go-between. Steve was our entertainment. When he came out into the field and danced that jig in the flat-bed wagon, he sure made his shoes talk.

Later that evening, I went back to the Thomson farm. Some of the women had put together a dinner for the threshers, which we ate in the backyard. I was sitting on the ground with Steve, right beside me. Suddenly, he moved his body to where I thought he was moving forward; instead he tumbled backward, did a somersault, and landed on his feet. I tried that once when I was younger and about broke my neck.

I'd see Steve every now and then; but, the last time I saw him was when a traveling carnival came to town in 1944. I remember the date because it was the same year that I joined the service. The carnival featured a big Ferris wheel, rides and tents. There was also a boxing ring, which was off to the side of the street.

Steve hollered out to me and walked over to watch a bout, excitedly telling me that he had taken a job with the carnival as he shook my hand. I watched him disappear under the boxing ring canvas and never saw him again.

William Kiso is a retired farmer and a lifelong resident of Slater, Missouri.

Above: Stealing hubcaps on the set of *Somebody Up There Likes Me*, something McQueen had practiced on city streets in real life.

Left: Steve McQueen with Ted Petersen, Santa Paula 1979.

He Fought the Law and the Law Won
Ted Petersen

Buddy Berri and the local law enforcement didn't exactly see eye-to-eye back in the forties. "Buddy", as he was known to everyone back then, was actually Steve McQueen.

Buddy's step-father was Hal Berri and even though they never cared for each other, Buddy was forced to take his last name. They often locked horns, which is why Buddy spent a lot of time on the streets of Silverlake, a suburb of Los Angeles.

As a matter of fact, Buddy at the time didn't have much respect for any type of authority. I remember once walking home from a movie in Hollywood when he spotted a police bike parked outside a restaurant. The policeman was inside but had left his helmet and gloves on the seat. Buddy's eyes grew wide. He put them on before throwing his right leg over the seat and hopping on the bike. He placed both hands on the throttle and arched his body forward. "Vrooooom! Vrooooom! Vrooooom!" Buddy said as I panicked, thinking the cop was going to come outside and arrest the two of us

at any moment. He finished by throwing the helmet and gloves down on the street and breaking off the back antenna. He must have been angry as hell about something because back then, that lack of respect towards law enforcement was quite uncommon.

Not much later Buddy was caught by police for stealing hubcaps. His mother had him sent to the Boys Republic, a reform school in Chino, California. Even though Buddy hated his step-father and the idea of going away for eighteen months, he later credited the place with turning his life around. I would have to concur.

When we met up later in life, Steve had mellowed out and had become a good, law-abiding citizen. We were especially amused by the fact that he was best known for playing a police detective in the movie *Bullitt*.

Ted Petersen was a World War II veteran, a Navy pilot and owned the famous race car Old Yeller. He died in 2001.

The 1946 Boys Republic baseball team. Steve McQueen is seated on the top row, fourth from the right. Roommate Robert McNamara is front row, first on the left.

Roommates for Life
Robert McNamara

Those piercing blue eyes met mine for a split-second as I dropped my belongings on the floor of the John Barnett Dormitory at the Boys Republic. He had the aura of a loner. His body language spoke volumes: don't mess with me.

I was sent to the Boys Republic in Chino, California, in early 1946 when my parents moved to Holland. My step-father was a research chemist for Shell Oil and was asked to help with the reconstruction of a refinery that the Nazis had blown to pieces. He took my mother with him, and they decided that I could use a little discipline, because I was a handful.

I did not have much in common with my new roommate, Steve McQueen, except that we were both sent to the Boys Republic by our mothers. We never had what I would call a friendship.

Steve had been there almost a year and was hardened, like most of the kids in the place. He was cut off emotionally and guarded, just like me. Had I asked him a question, most likely I would not have received an answer. Steve was the one who did the approaching if he wanted something. He didn't have to tell me much about himself because at sixteen, I was going through the same thing and did not need or care to delve into his life or business. Reflecting back, he was mentally in pain. When I saw Steve later on the screen, his independence and anger were real.

We played on the same baseball team. He was a backup player and didn't seem to care much for the sport. We did share sneaking off to smoke cigarettes under the bridge leading into the Republic. But we never had what I would call a friendship.

The two of us had something else in common. We both ran away from Boys Republic, but not together. He went solo, and I ran with three other boys, although we were all caught eventually. I was apprehended in Long Beach, about forty miles away, while Steve was found underneath the bridge where we used to smoke. We were the recipients of a spanking from Boys Republic administrator, Frank Graves. He used a 20-inch long, wood paddle filled with little holes to express his frustration with us. After Mr. Graves was finished, we both walked a little funny for a few days.

Our experiences at Boys Republic were sometimes painful, but life-changing. I know that Steve credits the place for turning him around.

In reading one of McQueen's biographies, I was amazed to discover that we became Christians within months of each other. That brings me great happiness because I know that we're going to see each other again, and then we'll be close friends.

Robert McNamara is a retired businessman and resides in Irvine, California.

Boys Republic students raking leaves for Della Robbia Christmas Wreaths, which is a fund-raising mechanism for the organization.

Don't Mess with McQueen

Arden Miller

Even as a kid, Steve McQueen was a force to be reckoned with.

I knew Steve because we were roommates for three months at the Boys Republic in Chino, California. I was there for driving my father's Buick off his car lot when I was fourteen. Steve ended up there because he didn't get along with his step-dad.

Neither physically intimidating nor athletic, he was nonetheless as tough as nails. If anyone messed with him, he would find a way to retaliate.

I remember one time a couple of students in the cafeteria did something to tick off Steve, and he ransacked their rooms when they weren't around. Nobody knew it was Steve, but I suspected he did the dirty deed. I commended him in private, "You did a good job on their rooms." He smiled and said, "Yeah, those guys will never mess with me again."

Numbers didn't matter to Steve. One time he took on the entire Boys Republic court, our version of a student council. Court was held every Monday night and it comprised a judge and jury of kids, as well as a prosecuting and defense attorney. Whenever there was an infraction, students went before the court. Once, Steve committed an infraction and was given a penalty, and he promised one in return.

"I'll get back at ya," Steve warned everyone in the room. That was Steve, and he made good on his promise. He found a way to retaliate against the judge, jury and the two attorneys. He'd ransack your

room, lock your door, turn over your bed, put shaving cream in your shoes. He dealt in street justice, which meant he could strike anytime, anywhere.

Because I roomed with Steve, I saw a different side to him. He looked out for me because I was the new kid. He'd tell me, "Don't do this. Don't do that. Watch out for that kid." Or, "If you want to go into town one night, I'll show you how to break out." Then we'd sneak out and walk into Pomona.

Life at Boys Republic was not easy. It was a 288-acre dairy farm with a large herd. Our daily routine included rising at 4 a.m. to milk the cows, eat breakfast, attend class all day, then milk them again. Everything was discipline-based. It wasn't a jail and we could leave anytime we wanted, but if we did, we headed back to court and took our chances with a judge. Steve and I decided to stay and I can honestly say it changed both of our lives.

I saw Steve again at a Boys Republic fundraiser in 1963. We shared some laughs and he told me about a movie he just completed called *The Great Escape*.

"You've gotta see it," Steve said with a glint in his eye. "It was just like escaping from Boys Republic on those nights when we went into Pomona."

Arden Miller was a Marine, successful businessman and served on the Boys Republic's Board of Directors for a decade. He died in February, 2008.

December 5, 1968

Frank Graves' Office
Boys Republic
Boys Republic Rural Station
Chino, Calif. 91710

Attention: Joan Van Eaton

Dear Joan:

Per our telephone conversation of today, enclosed is the list of people who should be sent Della Robbia Christmas Wreaths. With all wreaths, please send a little card saying: "Seasons Greetings from Neile and Steve McQueen" (except those going to Mr. and Mrs. Steve McQueen and to Solar Productions).

All wreaths should be billed to:

Solar Productions
% Guild Management Corp.
10203 Santa Monica Blvd.
L.A. California 90067

Thank you,

Betsy Cox
(Steve McQueen's Secretary)

bc/

Please send regular (small) size Della Robbia Christmas Wreaths to:

Mr. Gordon Stulberg
CBS Studio Center
4024 Radford Avenue
North Hollywood, Calif. 91604

Steve McQueen
% Solar Productions   (no card attached)
4024 Radford Avenue
North Hollywood, Calif. 91604

Mr. & Mrs. David Foster
1120 Angelo Drive
Beverly Hills, California

Mr. & Mrs. Lou Jordan
11352 Thurston Place
L.A. California 90049

Mr. & Mrs. Bob Hope
10346 Moorpark Street
North Hollywood, Calif.

Mr. & Mrs. Robert Schiller
Guild Management Corp.
10203 Santa Monica Blvd.
L.A. Calif. 90067

Mr. & Mrs. Steve McQueen
27 Oakmont Drive   (no card)
L.A. California 90049

Mr. Rupert Allan
Allan, Ingersoll & Weber
1901 Avenue of the Stars
L.A. California 90067

Colonel & Mrs. Benton
27 Oakmont Drive
L.A. California 90049

Mr. & Mrs. Herbert Ritts
29 Oakmont Drive
L.A. California 90049

Mr. & Mrs. Leslie Bricusse
1106 San Ysidro Drive
Beverly Hills, California

Mr. & Mrs. David Hemmings
28 Malibu Colony
Malibu, California

Mr. Neil Sloane
326 S. Beverly Drive
Beverly Hills, California

Also please send 2 large Della Robbia Christmas Wreaths to:

Mr. & Mrs. Steve McQueen
27 Oakmont Drive   (no card attached)
L.A. California 90049

You Don't Walk Alone
Max Scott

Above: A letter from McQueen's secretary, Betsy Cox, ordering Della Robbia Christmas Wreaths.

Opposite: Steve McQueen with a Boys Republic student, 1962.

Opposite inset: McQueen paying a visit to the Boys Republic in Chino, 1975.

Steve McQueen's kinship with the students at Boys Republic revealed a depth of understanding that only a man who has stumbled in those same shoes knows.

After he became famous, Steve visited the main campus in Chino Hills once or twice a year until his illness kept him from making the trip. He would call and ask if he could come on a specific day but since he never stopped by my office, I rarely met him. Instead, he went straight to the cottage, to the very room that he was assigned while at the school. On one occasion in late August, he and Ali MacGraw sat on the floor of the room which was jammed with students while the temperature hovered close to a hundred degrees.

He also enjoyed the Activity Center, shooting pool with the students, fielding their questions about whether he worked on the farm or if he had been assigned to the kitchen, what he liked most or least about the program, etc. Almost immediately, Steve would turn the attention back to the boys, asking what they were currently doing and if they were making the experience a positive one in terms of their futures.

Once he ventured over to our print shop where the students had been making turquoise Indian-type bracelets. Steve purchased over $1,000 worth although the jewelry was quite poorly made and of little value. They were thrilled.

I also remember Steve driving around campus in an old Jeep that had been donated to Boys Republic. He drove up Reservoir Hill and around the farm laughing and joking as students surrounded the vehicle.

Following his visits, they would write to him; and, without exception, he answered their letters. Steve would call me asking for information about the letter-writers so he could write a meaningful personalized response.

I have limited information on how Steve related to adults, but I do know he was very paternalistic with our students. He showed uncommon interest and sincere concern in each individual, extending himself to a number of them following their graduation from Boys Republic. One of those was Frank Hill. Steve served as a father figure for Frank, offering employment opportunities and support for a number of years.

He was sweet and gentle with our students and seemed to understand their struggles with family rejection and abandonment, legal issues and peer relationships, and the program structure at Boys Republic.

Max Scott has been the director of the Boys Republic for more than two decades.

PLATOON 53
S/SGT. ALESHIRE
SGT. ANDERSON
CORP. MCMARTREE
PARRIS ISLAND, S.C.
JULY 1947

Top: McQueen's Marine Corps platoon, Parris Island, South Carolina, July 1947. McQueen is sitting in the middle row, fifth person from the left.

Left: The flip side of the photo, signed by all the members of McQueen's platoon.

Above: McQueen with his arm around an unidentified female.

Left inset: Close up of McQueen's Marine Corp platoon photo.

Opposite top: A shirtless McQueen working the water hose to keep the enemy at bay.

Opposite bottom: Sharing a laugh with Marine buddies Joe and Don.

Soldier in the Dark
Cliff Anderson

Steve McQueen, the Marine, left much to be desired. Steve McQueen, the friend, had no peer.

I served in the Marines with Steve in the late forties in Quantico, Virginia on the Potomac River. He was billeted right across the hall from me in the Brownfield Barracks. We discovered early on that we were both from Missouri—he was from Slater and I was from Kansas City. You were always looking for somebody close to home to buddy with as it made the time away easier. Despite this common bond, Steve often tested our friendship to the limit.

I was a First Sergeant and a Company Commander, McQueen was a Private First Class. At least his military jacket marked him a PFC when he graduated from boot camp at Camp Lejeune but I don't ever recall seeing a stripe on McQueen's arm the entire time I was in the Marines. Steve wholeheartedly earned his reputation as an incompetent soldier, and was constantly in trouble. There were times when I had to reprimand him even though we were friends.

At first, I thought Steve was gung-ho. Everybody had a job to do from sweeping floors to cleaning the blinds to picking up cigarette butts on the grounds. The absolute worst job was cleaning the latrines, but one morning McQueen came to me and asked specifically for that duty. I gladly gave it to him because no one else was lining up for the job. McQueen worked like hell the first few days. The floors, the toilets, and the stainless steel knobs looked spic and span. Eventually I learned that he took the job because he could lock the door for the first hour, bundle up his jacket and sleep on the floor.

At that time, the war was over and soldiers could wear civilian clothes on base when off-duty. Steve had a girlfriend in Baltimore, Maryland, and he dressed up like a "Pachuco" from Los Angeles to impress his gal. He wore peg pants, a gold chain around his neck,

a black comb in his back pocket and a duck-tail haircut. He would get into fights and was disciplined quite a bit because of his hair. I remember a Sergeant Major screaming, "McQueen, God dammit, you're not getting any liberty until you cut off that duck's tail. I want the barber to cut it back to how it was in boot camp!" Did McQueen comply? Hell no. He'd rather be disciplined than cut off that hair because he wanted to look smart for his lady admirers.

McQueen caught it quite a bit because of the opposite sex. He did his job during the day, but couldn't wait for liberty to get the hell out of there. Baltimore was about eighty miles away. Complicating the fact was that McQueen didn't have a car, so he'd usually catch a ride into Washington, D.C., to a place called Thompson's Restaurant near the White House. From there, Steve would have to hitch into Baltimore.

You could always tell when Steve had spent the night smooching because he would come back late at night or early in the morning with his lips rosy from lipstick. I've no clue what was in it, but it was hard to remove. I would usually cover for him, but sometimes it was so late that I had to discipline him or risk losing the respect of my men.

Ten years later, Steve played Josh Randall in *Wanted: Dead or Alive*. I followed the series without realizing that it was him. It never entered my head that my military buddy and the actor on the screen were one and the same. Anyway, in the Question and Answer section of *TV Guide* a fan wrote in and asked about him. The editors answered (incorrectly) that Steve McQueen was born in Slater, Missouri, and that his real name was Terrence S. McQueen. Then it dawned on me. That is "Tough Shit McQueen." The back of his military clothes had read "T.S. McQueen" which stood for Terrence Steven "Tough Shit" McQueen. Only I and a couple of others could get away with calling him that.

In July 1973, I was on a hunting trip with some friends and saw in the newspaper that Steve was getting married at Little America in Cheyenne, Wyoming. So I checked into the same hotel, and gave the bellhop a tip to take a note to Steve saying that I was in the lobby, and signed it "Swede Anderson from the Quantico days." Steve came down a few minutes later and we exchanged greetings, had a drink, talked about old times and caught up with each other's lives.

Steve was one of a kind and someone special in my life.

Cliff Anderson is retired from the Marines and lives in Liberty City, Missouri.

Star Attention with a Side of Ham and Cheese on Rye
Theodore Mann

In Greenwich Village, New York, McQueen is sitting on a motorcycle that was his normal mode of transportation in the early acting days.

Steve McQueen knew how to stand out in a crowd, even in a cramped New York City bar.

I knew Steve in the fifties when he was trying to make a name for himself. I ran the Circle in the Square Theatre on Broadway and 50th Street and pretty much knew every actor and actress on Broadway. Steve had auditioned for a part in *Summer and Smoke*, a Tennessee Williams' play. He had an aura about him but he just wasn't right for the part. He shone much brighter at Louis' Tavern, a bar located next door to the theater.

Louis' was a small place, but a popular watering hole for actors, singers, entertainers, writers, artists and the avant-garde. Bob Dylan, Jack Kerouac, Peter Falk and Lee Marvin all came. But none of them, for my money, stood out like Steve McQueen. He usually rumbled up on his motorcycle around 10 p.m. with a rather sensational entrance, even for an actor.

Steve never failed to find a stage and hold court. He was always the one in the middle, always the center of the attention. I can see it so clearly in my mind—even today—Steve telling stories with a beer bottle in one hand and a ham and cheese sandwich on rye in the other. He was so handsome, so full of life and lived every minute as if it were his last.

Theodore Mann has been the artistic director of the Circle in the Square Theatre School in New York City, since the fifties. He divides his time between New York City, New York, and Carmel, California.

Supreme Confidence
David Hedison

Actors for the most part are an insecure lot. Not so with Steve McQueen. The man had an over abundance of confidence and was sure that stardom was just around the corner.

I knew McQueen from the early fifties when we studied together at the Neighborhood Playhouse under the tutelage of the legendary Sanford Meisner. It was more or less basic training for actors. I attended from 1951 to 1953, but was known as "Al Hedison" at the time.

For size reasons, Mr. Meisner divided the class into groups "A" and "B". Steve was in a different group from me with actress Joanne Woodward, who of course, later married Paul Newman. We combined when we put on showcases and plays at the Neighborhood Playhouse. Agents would attend our performances to see who they might be interested in representing.

Steve was an agreeable fellow, joking around, having a good time, generally pleasant. He always came to the studio on his motorcycle. I lived down the street from the Neighborhood Playhouse in a $5 a week rented room, and we went to class everyday just as in college. We studied Monday through Friday from 9 a.m. to 4 p.m. It was one class after the next with a few minutes in between. We took voice lessons from Carol Veazie, acting lessons from Wynn Handman, and dance lessons from the legendary Martha Graham. There was a lot of dance and ballet so that we could learn to move well, especially important in Steve's work where his fluidity stood out.

Steve's big strength was his self-confidence. I wouldn't call him a character actor because he had star quality just being himself. All movie stars essentially play a variation of themselves on screen, and Steve fit into that mold.

Our last, memorable showcase together was a performance of *Truckline Café* in which we both gave excellent performances. Afterwards, he put his arm around my shoulder and said, "Al, you and I are going to be stars." That statement always stuck with me because he was so sure of himself even in those early days.

Years later, I was driving down Sunset Boulevard past the famous movie house called The Oriental Theater, and the double feature on the marquee made me do a double take. It read: Steve McQueen - *The Blob* and Al Hedison - *The Fly*.

I laughed out loud, remembering Steve's words from just a few years before: "Al, you and I are going to be stars."

David Hedison started his career in 1955 and continues to work in theater, television and film. He resides in Los Angeles, California.

An acting head shot from the fifties.

It's doubtful McQueen knew how to play the sax for he was tone deaf. However, he is quite convincing in this fifties-era photo.

Too Cool for School
Edward Morehouse

Steve McQueen and I were fellow students at the Herbert Berghof Studio in 1952. I'm still amazed that he became a big star.

One day after class when I was running late for an appointment, Steve offered me a ride uptown. To be blunt, he frightened me to death, weaving in and out of traffic, and going at dangerous speeds. I couldn't tell you how fast he was going. He was a hell-raiser, a wild kid.

When it came to class, he wasn't that serious. He was lazy and poorly disciplined, but he didn't sit around boasting about how

fabulous he was either, as many actors do. He talked about subjects such as politics. We discussed fame one day outside class. Out of the blue, Steve said, "I'll have to work my ass off if I'm going to make it."

After Steve left school, I didn't see or hear from him for years. Then I saw him in *The Thomas Crown Affair* and said to myself, "By God, he's made it."

All the exercises we were taught to do did not seem to interest him. We were told to work on certain activities, and we did, but Steve did not. Yet in spite of this, he was the

one who became successful, the actor working more than anyone else.

He matured and his personality developed. I thought he was phenomenal because I knew him as someone who was rather street-wise. He had really done a lot of work on himself.

Edward Morehouse studied with Herbert Berghof and Uta Hagen. He has been a member of HB Studio since 1952 and a faculty member since 1957.

Preparing for the play, *Peg O' My Heart*, 1952.

Attention to Detail
Wynn Handman

It seems bizarre that Steve McQueen was once in a Noel Coward play, and a bad one at that. As Sanford Meisner's former assistant at the Neighborhood Playhouse, I directed hundreds of plays. One year I picked Coward's *Still Life*, which was later became a movie called *Brief Encounter*. The play was perhaps the worst I have ever directed, but Steve McQueen was terrific.

Steve came to the Neighborhood Playhouse in late 1951. He was a ball of clay, but with the help of Meisner, Louis Horst, Martha Graham, Carol Veazie and myself, we turned him into a granite bust with many good features. Meisner preferred what he called "untutored" students so that he could train them from the start to avoid bad habits. Steve didn't have any that I recall, but it did take some effort to reach him on a personal level.

Steve had a hard-knock upbringing and had been in the Marines. He was a tough street kid. I wouldn't say he didn't take his studies seriously, but he could be difficult and non-conforming. Over time, he became a part of the Neighborhood Playhouse family.

When I say family, I'm not kidding. My wife, Bobby and I lived one door away from the Neighborhood Playhouse on 340 E. 54th Street. When our daughter, Laura, was born, she was known as the "Neighborhood Playhouse Baby" because many of the students took turns babysitting for us. Actress Joanne Woodward helped out quite

a bit, and so did Steve McQueen occasionally. I understand he became a good parent when he had children. I'm glad to have given him the experience!

Steve showed promise when he started acting. He was good-looking and had attractive qualities as an actor and could readily involve himself in a role. His focus was amazingly intense.

Steve's sex appeal wasn't just with women—men seemed to like him, too. He came to visit me and Bobby in 1960 at our Fire Island home in the Fair Harbor community. *Wanted: Dead or Alive* was on TV at that time, and he was a big star. He wore a blue zipper jacket that he had from the Marines with his name on the back, though "Mc" was faded, so it looked like it said, "Queen". One of the places we visited that day was Cherry Grove, which was largely a gay community. Well, as good looking as he was and with "Queen" blaring on the back of his jacket, he attracted a lot of attention from members of the same sex, and for the life of him he couldn't figure out why.

I always liked Steve and thought he was a good person. I was happy for his success and to have contributed to it in some small way.

Wynn Handman is the co-founder and artistic director of the American Place Theatre in New York City.

Drinking Buddies

Richard Martin

Steve McQueen won this 1948 MG TC Roadster in a high-stakes poker game. The vehicle met its demise when he drove it into an excavation hole on Sixth Avenue in Manhattan.

I met Steve McQueen in the early fifties in a Greenwich Village bar called Louis' Tavern. The bar was a well-known hangout for actors, singers, artists and the rest of us trying to find a niche in life. Steve and I clicked as buddies as soon as we met. We both lacked direction but had an affinity for chasing the ladies.

Steve and I spent most of our time trying to get laid and little time on anything else. We both knew some actors at Louis' and decided to try that. When asked what we did for a living, we answered that we were actors. It was a good excuse for not having to work a 9-to-5 job, which, in our minds, was not an option.

We met almost every day at Café Figaro on Bleecker Street, an espresso bar and restaurant. We would talk and smoke some grass, before moving on to Midtown Manhattan for a juice at the Salad Bowl, a health food restaurant that just so happened to be a good place to meet women. From there, we walked to the NBC building on 6th Avenue and rode the elevator to the third floor where actors took a breather to compare notes after making the casting rounds.

Our next stop was the Actors Service on West 58th Street, a telephone switchboard service where actors could pick up their messages for a casting call, or a job, or just relax in the lounge. Actors we knew would give us tips on who was casting what and where in town. We played poker in the lounge for small stakes. Later we would head back to our night hangout, Louis' Tavern.

Surprisingly, during auditions, the casting directors were fascinated with Steve, but not very interested in me. Perhaps the Marlon Brando-types were in and the leading men-types were temporarily out of vogue. At the time, I mistakenly thought that Steve had no real chance of being a movie star.

My MG was much admired by Steve and on occasions, I would let him drive. Later on, after starting a car collection, Steve helped me pick the cars out. We once drove together from New York to California, stopping briefly in Slater, Missouri, before taking a detour to New Orleans. We met a couple of gals there, spent a few days at their place then headed off to L.A.

In Hollywood, we hung out at the Chateau Marmont Hotel with some New York actor friends who were working in L.A., and staying at the hotel. We spent most of our time at the pool area. One night we were skinny dipping with some ladies when the night manager spotted us and asked us to leave. It was a little embarrassing for our friends the next day when they had to explain our behavior to the general manager. Later in New York, the incident became the buzz of the month at Louis' Tavern.

On our round trip from New York to Los Angeles, we shared the driving. One of us drove while the other slept in the back seat. We were stopped several times by the police and received a few warnings, and were even hauled in a couple of times to the local jail for speeding. I had to telephone my parents to wire money via Western Union to pay the traffic fine. We had been warned before we left New York about the cross-country speed traps, but we wouldn't listen. Overall, the trip was a great experience. It was expensive, but lots of fun and well worth it.

Back in New York, Steve started to work a little and began to take acting seriously, enrolling in an acting school. When he landed the role as replacement for Ben Gazzara, the star of *A Hatful of Rain*, I was proud that my friend had finally found his calling in life as a "Broadway actor". Wrong again. After *A Hatful of Rain*, Steve left Broadway and snared starring roles in two low budget films: *The Blob* and *The St Louis Bank Robbery*. After seeing the two films, I was a little sceptical about the future of his film career.

Steve moved to Hollywood and I left for Europe. He married his New York girl friend, Neile Adams, and secured a television series named *Wanted: Dead or Alive*. I credit this as being the learning curve for Steve's film career; he had the luxury of seeing himself in each segment and could fine-tune his persona for future acting roles.

Each time I came back from Europe, we would meet, usually for lunch, and talk about what was happening with our careers and our friends in New York.

This 1954 memo from MGM producer Pandro S. Berman to director Richard Brooks indicates that Steve McQueen tested for the classic *Blackboard Jungle*. McQueen ultimately lost out to actor Vic Morrow.

INTER-OFFICE COMMUNICATION

To Richard Brooks

Subject THE BLACKBOARD JUNGLE

From Pandro S. Berman Date 8-4-54

METRO-GOLDWYN-MAYER PICTURES
CULVER CITY CALIFORNIA

The following boys are the ones who are lined up for tests:

Peter Allenbe – Puerto Rican, 17 years old. Good type, no experience.

Armand Alzamara – 22 years old, 5'10", 160 lbs. Good interpretation, good actor.

Ralph Campos – Puerto Rican, 5'6". Very cute boy. Accent good – a bit thick possibly. Fair experience.

Danny Dennis – Jewish. Could play part of Italian. 5'2". Good experience with Uta Hagen show. Recommended as actor.

The above boys are ones I interviewed and thought worth showing to you. In addition to them there is a boy named Steve McQueen whom Altman is anxious to test for the part of West. He is blonde, 5'11", 170 lbs. about 24, has been playing boys in the 18-22 year old range. Seems by all odds to be the best actor that has been discovered for the part according to Altman, having been a professional actor for four years.

I am attaching Altman's wire and I do believe, based on hearing readings in New York from the book, that if you wish to get tests that will satisfy you as to the ability of these boys, you should provide him with a couple of scenes from the script or select something from the book that you are sure will give you the range of their capabilities as Altman has no such material himself in mind.

Incidentally, Sidney Poitier, whom we signed, was described to us by Altman prior to testing as about 26 years old in actuality, although Altman felt he could look the part for us as far as age is concerned.

PSB

Encl. (1)

When Steve was tired of *Wanted: Dead or Alive*, he was able to break his contract and become a free agent. He had the inspiration to go for the gold, to become a movie star, and his film career started taking off. It was not until I saw *Love with the Proper Stranger* that Steve made a believer out of me. The rest is history.

The last time I saw Steve was at the Cock 'n Bull on the Sunset Strip. We bumped into each other, went to the back room, and talked for hours about the old days in Louis' Tavern, catching up on what happened to the people we knew, and comparing our expensive toys, such as motorcycles and planes, like a couple of kids. We also talked about doing a film together.

Steve's health problem was news to me when I read about it in the tabloids while in Europe. Just after arriving back in the States, I heard a television report announcing that he had died, leaving me speechless. A sad and premature ending for someone who had made the impossible dream come true.

He was a good friend and a great movie star. I will always remember him.

Richard Martin is the producer and director of the documentary, Steve McQueen: An American Rebel. He divides his time between Los Angeles and Palm Springs.

Driving Lessons Included
Nancy Malone

Actor Barry Truex is about to deck a cocksure McQueen while actress Nancy Malone looks on. She said McQueen watched over her like a protective brother during a national road production of *Time Out for Ginger.*

McQueen found comedy a difficult balancing act, as Melvyn Douglas and Edith Atwater look on in *Time Out for Ginger.* Douglas eventually requested McQueen be removed from the production.

Plunking down $2500 cash for my first MG was a triumph for a young, unlicensed driver. Steve McQueen thought it was a hoot.

I wanted an MG just like the car Steve had won in a high stakes poker game. He took me by the hand to a garage in Chicago owned by S.H. Arnolt, who imported MG and other British Motor Corp. vehicles, and without much knowledge on the subject, I bought my car. I didn't have a checking account, so I paid with cash, and said, "Now, do I get driving lessons with it?" Steve, of course, doubled over with laughter and said he would teach me to drive. He was very proud of me. Many years later, I brought my 1953 MG out to California. While driving along the freeway, Steve pulled up alongside in his MG. After all that time, we were still devoted to our cars.

I first met Steve in 1952 while taking Broadway's *Time Out for Ginger* on the road, my first foray away from home. It was lonely and scary. Steve joined us on our first stop, which was New Haven, Connecticut. Conrad Janis had played the part in New York, but he had other obligations and could not tour, so Steve was re-cast in the role of the love interest of my older sister in the play. I was the youngest member of the cast, around fifteen at the time, and Steve, in many instances, acted like an older brother, checking up on me, particularly when it was time to go from the theater to the hotel at night. He was very sweet and I became fond of him.

Melvyn Douglas, who was starring in the play, did not care so much for Steve. I was not aware of Steve's credits prior to *Time Out for Ginger,* but Mel found him difficult to work with. Steve would not necessarily do the same reading and blocking every night, which often meant that Mel didn't get his laughs. In a sense he was stepping on Mel's toes, and it did not go over well. Timing is everything in comedy, after all. Steve didn't know enough about performing in the genre at the time. Comedy has a certain beat and rhythm with time

for the laugh. I think whatever hit Steve at that moment would compel him to walk over to a different place or change the way he said a line. I don't believe he was behaving out of spite, he just performed how he felt with little regard to the form or the other actors. In any event, Steve left the play at the midpoint of the tour when it reached the Harris Theater in Chicago.

Naturally, Steve's acting evolved through the years, becoming more disciplined as he grew serious about his work. He was a tough guy, and everything he portrayed was the real Steve McQueen. When you saw him, it wasn't as if you were watching Laurence Olivier with a fake nose or a hunch back. There was always a bit of Steve in his parts, and an appealing hint of danger, which was a big attraction to an audience.

Peter Witt, who was mine and Steve's agent, knew Steve would be a star. When I returned to New York and was preparing for another play, I asked Peter about Steve, interested in what would become of him. He said, "Don't worry about Steve. He's going to do great things. He will be a major personality in this business." I was thrilled and very hopeful.

I'm really sorry Steve's gone. I would love to meet with him again to catch up and thank him for taking care of me on the road. I have such happy memories of when I bought that MG, and I thought of Steve whenever I drove it. Underneath all the tough-guy bravado, he was very kind and considerate. Unfortunately, many young, leading men don't understand they can be both sensitive and masculine.

Actress Nancy Malone began acting and modeling at seven-years old, making the cover of Life by the age of ten. Today she is a revered acting teacher in Los Angeles.

Intuition

Jack Garfein

Left: An original 1955 *Two Fingers of Pride* program from the Ogunquit Playhouse in Maine.

Right: Steve McQueen's bio in the play program.

> * * *
>
> STEVE MC QUEEN (Nino) was born in Indianapolis, Indiana; grew up in California and the lower East Side in New York. A Marine for three years, he went into acting upon his release, at the Neighboorhood Playhouse. Steve toured with the Broadway company of "Time Out For Ginger" with Melvyn Douglas; with Ethel Waters in "The Member of the Wedding," and opposite Margaret O'Brien in "Peg of My Heart." His only hobby is a cream colored competition TC MG which he races in sports car races.
>
> * * *

It may not be much of a stretch picturing Steve McQueen as a longshoreman working on the docks, and that's where I sent him to prepare for the role of Nino in a play that I was casting at the time called *Two Fingers of Pride.*

I always took chances on young, undiscovered talent and when the Neighborhood Playhouse sent over Steve to audition, I immediately sensed that he was right for the part. Playwright Jim Longhi, who had connections with the waterfront, and I arranged for Steve to work there for a few weeks to give him an idea of what it was like to be a dockworker.

After three days, he called, scared to death and said, "Jack, sometimes these guys don't realize I'm just an actor and they're working me pretty hard. Please, make sure I'm okay." "Don't worry, Steve," I reassured him. "You'll be taken care of." Later, he told me that he considered the waterfront gig one of the most important experiences in his life—to take on a character and learn how he talks and interacts with others.

After the play, Steve often called me for advice when he was offered a job. He was concerned about doing television, but I reminded him that he was still an unknown actor, and the exposure would help him. Once he became a star, I didn't hear from him. Then, in December 1963, I was in the Russian Tea Room in New York, when in walked Steve with Natalie Wood, followed by about ten photographers. They had just come from the première of *Love with the Proper Stranger.* He saw me, stopped suddenly, and embraced and kissed me saying "Pardon me for being corny. I owe this man a lot."

Sometime later, after I had moved to Los Angeles, I fell on hard times and was out of work. One day I happened to see Steve on his motorbike and after he had pulled over, he asked me what was happening. "Steve, I really need a job. I've written a good screenplay and I can't persuade anyone to read it." He agreed to take a look and I sent it along. It was returned with a note from Steve's manager thanking me for the submission, but—no thank you. I was deeply hurt that Steve didn't bother to tell me personally, and I was never in touch with him again.

Even so, I was devastated when he passed away. Then something remarkable happened. I was sitting at a restaurant and a young woman approached me. "Someone told me that you're Jack Garfein. Do you mind if I tell you when I first heard your name? I was in a bar in Big Sur where I was filming a movie and met a heavily bearded man who looked like a truck driver. We started talking and I found him to be charming. He took me to his cabin and we made love. Afterward, I was shocked when he said he was Steve McQueen. During the night he became deeply upset and mentioned your name. He talked about your life, what happened to you in the war, and how the two of you practically grew up together in the business. He said he felt awful about losing contact with you."

I was deeply moved. It was disappointing that we never worked together in Hollywood, but, we had so much in common in those early days—we were both alone in this world. I miss him terribly.

Jack Garfein is a Holocaust survivor and founded the Actors and Directors Lab in both Los Angeles and New York as well as The Actors Studio West in Los Angeles.

Opposite: McQueen's first paid acting gig was as a sailor in a short industrial film by Bell System Western Electric, 1952.

Above left: Acting headshot from 1956.

Above right: On stage with Vivian Blaine in *A Hatful of Rain*, 1956.

Class of '55
Robert Loggia

Steve McQueen and I had many things in common. We were born the same year, served in the military, landed our first acting gigs in the same play and ended up in the same acting class at the Actors Studio. We did, however, take diverging paths when it came to stardom.

I first took notice of Steve back in the mid-fifties. We were both cast in a live television play starring Lee Remick. They needed three guys—one each from the Army, the Navy and the Air Force—to stand on the podium in uniform. Steve and I played two of these three parts but I don't recall the third person.

The class of 1955 was a virtual *Who's Who* of Hollywood. In addition to McQueen and me, there was Paul Newman, Ben Gazzara, Tony Franciosa, Martin Landau, George Peppard, Rip Torn, Kim Stanley, Maureen Stapleton, Geraldine Page and Shirley Knight.

The electricity at the Actors Studio in those days was palpable. The actors worked together to develop their skills in an experimental environment where they could take risks as performers without the pressure of commercial roles. Students performed weird acts to find themselves. They would urinate or vomit on the floor or scream at the top of their lungs. Some women even simulated inserting a diaphragm. It was all to show that anything was fair game on the stage or in a movie. Those were the days of Stanislavsky, and I imagine they don't train like that anymore. However, McQueen didn't put himself out there emotionally. He was shy and diffident, and his style was more about sitting back and taking it all in.

Lee Strasberg, who was the head of the Actor's Studio, was a taskmaster whose critiques could cut you to the bone, but it was done to make you a better actor. However, he treated Steve differently because he knew he was sensitive. Steve did not project well in a scene under the scrutiny of fellow actors, directors and playwrights. You couldn't hear him in that small environment with perhaps fifty people in the audience. I think Steve fell under the behavior and acting style of Jimmy Dean and Marlon Brando. Their acting was more internal and quietly deliberate. Sometimes Strasberg encouraged those with strong personalities like McQueen and Al Pacino to play themselves first and let the material come second.

Steve was courageous and overcame odds that would seem insurmountable to others. I liked everything about his acting because he lived those parts and his imprint is on everything he did. He was terrific.

Robert Loggia is a veteran actor with more than 100 films to his credit. He lives in Los Angeles, California.

Dancing Queen

Janet Conway

Steve McQueen danced his way into my life and then three months later waltzed right out.

I met Steve at Viola Essen's dance studio, which was located on the eighth floor of Carnegie Hall. I was a seventeen-year-old student at the American Academy of Dramatic Arts and Steve was a struggling actor who had been hired by Viola to teach drama classes.

Viola, who was famous in her own right, liked having young men around. Marlon Brando came to many of our classes and played the conga drum while we did our routines. After class, he and Viola usually headed to her office where they locked the door behind them. We never knew for sure what went on, but we had our suspicions.

I had been on the road in a musical called *The Amazing Adale*. The show had opened in Philadelphia and a few weeks later closed in Boston. Suddenly Steve was a fixture on the New York acting scene. He was intense, attractive and kind of mumbled when speaking. His affectations were charming and he had the most gorgeous blue eyes I had ever seen. I don't know how or when, but we became an item.

Steve and his motorcycle were like a couple: you rarely saw one without the other. Most of our dates were in Greenwich Village. We'd usually go to dinner, with me often picking up the tab, or meet with friends who were fellow artists. One time, Steve took a detour and drove on a street that wasn't paved. All of the sewer lids were exposed and Steve's front wheel sank into one of the holes, causing my head to hit his. I was cut above my left eye and we ended up going to a nearby emergency room. At the time, Steve didn't have a license, so we told the doctor that I had fallen. He sewed up my wound and gave me an eye patch to wear, and I had an artist friend draw an eyeball for me. It was lovely.

Part of my attraction for Steve was that he was dead broke, but absolutely driven. Acting jobs were few and far between back then. He lived in a small, rundown, cold-water flat, and had a bus stop sign with a cement post that he used as a barbell. One job he did land was in *Somebody Up There Likes Me* starring Paul Newman. It was a small role, but he took it seriously. He had a prop on the dresser—a knife—and I remember he was working hard to become comfortable with it to make the scene look real. He had talent and nothing was going to stop him.

Our breakup wasn't a big deal or a knockdown, drag out fight. We were both preparing to leave Carnegie Hall when I saw another actor who was pretty cute. Steve must have picked up on my change of heart and told me that he was heading to the Village and for me to hop on the bike. I told him that I was going to pass.

Above: Using a bus stop sign as a barbell in his New York City apartment with Neile Adams in the background.

Opposite: Steve McQueen and Paul Newman share a laugh on a New York City rooftop in this rarely seen photo from *Somebody Up There Likes Me*, 1956. McQueen was a $19 a day extra.

Opposite inset: Dancer Janet Conway briefly dated Steve McQueen in the mid-fifties.

"Either come now or forget it," Steve said, quick to issue an ultimatum.

"Then forget it," I replied. Steve kick-started the bike and zoomed away.

A few months later, I bumped into him when he was doing *A Hatful of Rain* on Broadway. He was standing outside the stage door and invited me into his dressing room, where he proceeded to act out the play for me. I waved my hand and said, "Steve, I didn't come here to see the play. I just wanted to say hello and congratulations."

Shortly after that, he met and married dancer Neile Adams. I was happy for Steve because it seemed as if he had finally found the woman he had been looking for his whole life.

Janet Conway is a retired actress and dancer. She lives in Lafayette, Colorado.

Don't Talk To Me Till After Breakfast
Neile Adams McQueen

My first date with Steve was indicative of our lives together ever since.

We'd met at Downey's, a poor man's Sardi's, while he appeared in *A Hatful of Rain* and I did *The Pajama Game* on Broadway. He was eating spaghetti when I walked in wearing my tight-fitting sweater. Half the spaghetti on his fork dropped on the tablecloth.

I was pleased with his reaction.

My friend and I stopped to say "hello" and he asked us to join him. Before we left, he'd promised to stop by the theater. When he did, we made a date for the following Sunday.

Before he arrived, I got all prettied up in my daintiest, frilliest dress, certain he'd take me for a walk though Central Park or maybe to a movie. When he arrived in blue jeans and a black leather jacket, I should have been prepared for a different kind of afternoon, but it wasn't till we walked out of the house to where he parked his motorcycle that I realized what was in store.

"Hop on," he ordered.

"Hop on—in a dress?"

"You can ride side-saddle. Nothing to it."

He got on first, then I climbed on behind him, side-saddle as he suggested.

"Ready?" he asked.

I choked a bit. "Ready as I'll ever be!"

We took off as if we were going into orbit, flying past houses, pedestrians, trucks, cars, cops, bicycles, up one avenue, down another, while I hung on with one arm and held down my full crinoline skirt with the other.

Half an hour later we were back at the house. "Had fun?" he grinned.

"Do you always race around like that?" I gasped.

"Not always. Sometimes I'm going somewhere. How about coming on a picnic with me next Sunday?"

"I wouldn't think of it!", I cried out.

But I went. We've been racing through life together ever since!

We were married less than four months later, on November 2, 1956, at San Clemente, California.

I'll never forget the first morning in our own home, when I expected him to be pleased, and kind, and romantic. Instead when I asked him something, he snapped, "Don't talk to me until after breakfast!"

I didn't know whether to be hurt or whether I should laugh. I was somewhere in between both emotions when he finished his cup of tea—he doesn't like coffee—and turned to me to apologize. "Sorry I hurt your feelings, Neile, but that's the way I am. Just no good till after I've had a cup of tea."

Neile Adams McQueen is a dancer, entertainer and actress. She was married to Steve McQueen from 1956 to 1972. They had two children—Terry Leslie and Chadwick Steven McQueen. This excerpt originally appeared in the February 1960 issue of TV Picture Life.

Opposite top: The two lovebirds, Steve and Neile McQueen cozying up to each other in New York.

Opposite bottom: Together in Bavaria, 1962, where he was filming *The Great Escape*.

Above: The McQueens use their cars and the California sunshine as props to pose for a publicity photo.

Above: Actors Studio instructor Lee Strasberg and Steve McQueen having a colorful conversation, 1957.

Left: Publicity photo for *Never Love a Stranger*, McQueen's second movie.

Opposite: From *A Hatful of Rain*, featuring from left to right: Stefan Gierasch, Steven McQueen, Steve Gravers and Michael Tolan.

Dean and McQueen
Martin Landau

Of the 2,000 performers that auditioned for instructor Lee Strasberg's Actor's Studio in 1955, only two were accepted: myself and Steve McQueen. I eventually won an Academy Award and Steve became a legend.

Before our admission, another pupil, James Dean, was setting the pace that allowed us to enter the fray. At first, Jimmy barely found his way as he wasn't as remarkable as people thought. He was basically shy and insecure just like most actors, which is why he invited me to his dress rehearsals and live television appearances. He wanted me there because he wasn't so sure of his acting choices.

One day Lee Strasberg devastated Jimmy in one of his critiques, and he never came back to perform scenes, although he still attended class. I think Strasberg learned from that, deciding that there were some people who could take it and others who couldn't. He often criticized me, which I always felt made me stronger; but he was overly gentle with Steve, who took advantage of the fact. Steve tested Lee, too.

Jimmy and Steve were alike in many ways—they were both from the Midwest, basically shy and didn't get close to that many people. They were both complicated characters. Steve's complex personality emerged from a difficult childhood. Much rises to the surface when you come from nothing and become a movie star. To build a life, you start with your childhood, and if there's a lot of stuff put on top of that foundation, it's going to feel like a great weight. That same applied to Jimmy.

I was present when the two met in New York. Keep in mind that Jimmy had no idea who McQueen was, but Steve sure knew who Jimmy was—he was given all the parts that Steve wanted. Jimmy was giving me a ride on his motorcycle when it started sputtering. He pulled over to the nearest garage where McQueen happened to be working on a bike. I could tell by his demeanor that he knew it was Dean. He examined the bike with a laser-like focus and paid no attention to me. A few years later on the set of *Wanted: Dead or Alive*, I recalled that incident to Steve.

"Do you remember the first time we met?" I asked. Steve thought it might have been on the sixth floor of NBC when he returned from touring in *Time Out for Ginger*. I smiled and told him it was before that.

"You didn't notice me, but I was on the back of Jimmy Dean's bike when it was misfiring," I said. "You were focusing on Jimmy and his bike because he was taking roles away from you."

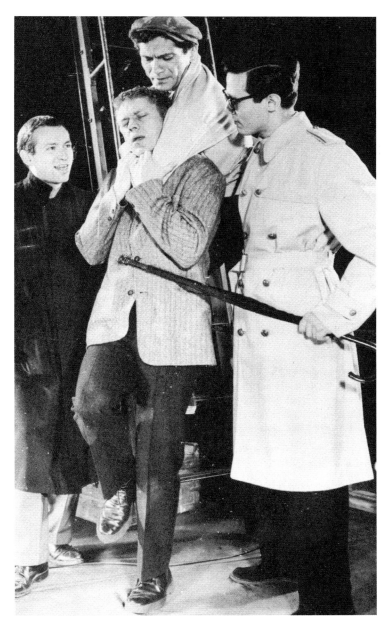

"That was you?" McQueen said.

"That was me."

Life is strange and takes many odd turns and twists: Dean and McQueen found fame and work relatively easily while I endured a long, uphill battle. I was skinny and dark, and difficult to cast. And yet of the three, I am the only one with an Oscar.

Martin Landau is a veteran actor who won an Academy Award for 1994's Ed Wood. He lives in Los Angeles, California.

The Art of Nothing

William Shatner

1957 - The Defender

I worked with Steve McQueen in a classic legal drama titled *The Defender* on Studio One in 1956. Ralph Bellamy and I played father-and-son lawyers defending McQueen on murder charges. At the conclusion I used a courtroom trick, fooling the only eyewitness by planting a McQueen look-alike in the spectator section, to get him off—at the cost of my father's respect.

I remember watching McQueen work and thinking, wow, he doesn't do anything. He was inarticulate, he mumbled, and only later did I understand how beautifully he did nothing. It was so internalized that the camera picked it up as would a pair of inquisitive eyes. Out of seemingly nothing he was creating a unique form of reality.

William Shatner is an actor, musician, producer, director and celebrity pitchman. This excerpt originally appeared in his 2008 autobiography Up Until Now courtesy of St. Martin's Press.

Above: Steve McQueen (several), Ralph Bellamy (top center), William Shatner (bottom center). Vivian Nathan is seen from the back in a photo montage by Donna Redden.

Right: Letter from CBS executive Herbert Brodkin praising McQueen for his role in the two-part series, *The Defender*, which aired in March 1957.

CBS TELEVISION

A Division of Columbia Broadcasting System, Inc.

485 MADISON AVENUE, NEW YORK 22, NEW YORK · PLAZA 1-2345

March 5, 1957

Mr. Steven McQueen
69 West 55th Street
New York, New York

Dear Steve:

Just a line to thank you for the work you did in "The Defender." We have already had many fine reports, both within the industry and without, and they convince me that, despite the skepticism of some of our reviewers, the show was a hit and had an enthusiastic audience.

And, incidentally, it would appear you've quite an audience of your own -- we've had a couple of calls from "fans of Steven McQueen."

All best wishes and again, my thanks.

Sincerely yours,

Herbert Brodkin
Producer
STUDIO ONE

Little Big Man

Richard Bright

I first met Steve McQueen on the set of *Never Love A Stranger,* his second picture. I didn't understand how Steve had been given the role in the first place. His whole demeanor was wimpy. He didn't seem to be a knock-around kind of guy. I guess that ruggedness came later with the bikes. I didn't see any spark at all.

Fourteen years later we worked together again and I was taken by the dramatic change in him. He had developed a strong acting technique and found a formula that worked so successfully it knocked me out of a big part in *The Getaway.* Director Sam Peckinpah had wanted me to play Rudy Butler, the main heavy, eventually played by Al Lettieri. However, Steve didn't feel I was large enough. He liked me as an actor but didn't think that the character he ran from throughout the picture should be someone smaller than himself. He thought it would appear cowardly and give the wrong impression.

Sam gave me the smaller part of a con man who stole a suitcase full of cash from McQueen, but later he caught up with my character on the train, sat down next to me and threw several vicious blows to my head. Steve didn't hold anything back but was in perfect control. Many of the new actors try to be more realistic, but they don't have control. Steve had mastered his power and knew how to use it. It was wonderful working with him.

Richard Bright started his career in 1957 and is best known for his role as Al Neri in The Godfather trilogy. He died in February 2006.

Top: Playing against type, Steve McQueen as Martin Cabell, a wimpy Jewish lawyer in *Never Love a Stranger.*

Bottom: McQueen throwing a vicious blow to Richard Bright in *The Getaway.*

Above: Two riders compete in the Sidcup Motorcycle Club's annual 160-yard hill climb in Knatts Valley, Farningham Kent, 1957.

Running Amok in Kent

Max Poultney

We all knew him as an American film actor who was mad about motorcycle racing; however, this was in the fifties, long before Steve McQueen became a household name.

It was at a Brands Hatch grass track event in England where I first met him. In those days, the venues for motorcycle sport were many and varied, from scrambling at Bagshot Heath, to grass tracking at Brands Hatch, before the present International Grand Prix Circuit was built.

While working as an apprentice in a Thames shipyard in 1952, I acquired my first bike, a Francis Barnett with a 197cc Villiers and joined the Kenton and Kingsbury Motorcycle Club so I could take part in Trials. A few years later I was working on Cunard's RMS *Queen Elizabeth* as an engineer and was able to afford a bit more, so I traded in my old bike and ordered a 500cc Triumph Trophy from

Comerford's—the same motorcycle shop in Thames Ditton that Steve frequented over the years, most notably, in 1964. He and the U.S. Vase Team took full advantage of its workshop and facilities, readying their bikes for the International Six-Day Trials in East Germany.

The Sidcup Motorcycle Club held its annual Hill Climb in Knatts Valley at Farningham, Kent, early in the summer of 1957. As luck would have it, I was paired in one run up the hill against a twenty-seven-year-old Steve McQueen.

My brother-in-law, Peter Steele, and I, rode our bikes to the event as we couldn't afford trucks or trailers then. Peter entered with his much-modified DOT powered by methanol, while I rode up on my Triumph Trophy. We gathered in the paddock with about forty to fifty other competitors preparing their machines for racing. To our amazement, Steve turned up on an old rigid-framed, late 1920s relic that had been modified to run like a bat out of hell. As we were waiting for the start, I asked him what he was riding.

"I think it's a Douglas factory racer that won a Tourist Trophy race in

the Isle of Man before World War II and we're running it on dope," Steve said, "dope" being a slang term for methanol. At the start, Steve revved the Douglas' engine flat out, and as the flag went down, he dropped the clutch. All I saw was the dust from his rear wheel as he flew up the hill. When I eventually reached the top, I complimented him on his prowess.

"Blimey, Steve, you flew up that hill," I said in amazement.

"Yes," he replied, "I had to because as I dropped the clutch, I came out of the saddle and then landed down so hard, I had to race to the top and finish to relieve the pain!"

I didn't win against Steve McQueen that day—it would take British Grass Track and Speedway champion Alf Hagon, to beat the actor, relegating him into second place in the 500cc class.

Max Poultney is a retired Public Health Officer who lives in England. He has been around the world twice, visiting more than 50 countries, and sailed the Cutty Sark.

Strolling through Comerford's in Thames Ditton, England, in 1964.

Outside the Windermere apartment complex on Manhattan's West side, where Steve amd Neile McQueen lived in the early part of their marriage.

Opposite, top: Billed as "Steven McQueen," the fresh faced 27-year old played the role of a teenager in *The Blob*.

Opposite, middle and bottom: McQueen and actress Aneta Corseaut briefly dated almost a year before the cameras rolled on *The Blob*.

27 going on 18

Russell Doughten

Steve McQueen was on no one's radar screen and certainly wasn't the actor we had in mind when casting *The Blob*. I consider it divine intervention when we bumped into him near Central Park while he was walking his dog.

McQueen didn't do *The Blob* for a movie credit or because he needed some quick cash. He chased down the part with gusto.

I met McQueen about six months before we started shooting the picture. The intense young man left an indelible impression on me. I was standing on the steps of the administration building of Good News Productions in Chester Springs, Pennsylvania, when I heard this strange sound out in the boondocks—it was the revving of an engine. I listened to it for about five minutes before Steve McQueen pulled up in a tiny MG. After he turned off the ignition, he jumped out of the car to ask if an actress he was dating was around. I said she was in a studio across the street. He had come from New York City, which was about a two-hour drive to see this young lady. He wasn't much on conversation but had plenty of charisma.

Good News Productions made Christian films for missionaries and organizations, recruiting films for the Salvation Army and dramatic motion pictures with a specific message. However, the company needed cash to fund those projects and formed Valley Forge Films to do commercial work. *The Blob* was our foray into "the biz". Irvin "Shorty" Yeaworth was our trusty director while I was tapped as the film's producer.

Shorty and I came to New York City to cast the picture. McQueen recognized us and asked what we were doing in the Big Apple. When we told him we were there to find actors for our movie, he became a little friendlier.

"Oh yeah? Is there a part in it for me?" he asked. We told him all of the main parts were for older teenagers. McQueen, who had turned twenty-seven that year, promised us he could act much younger if we just gave him a chance. He offered us an opportunity to kick up our heels in his apartment in between appointments while he looked over the manuscript.

We met his wife, Neile, a successful Broadway dancer, and spent a few minutes chatting with her while Steve pored over the script. He interrupted our conversation with his lovely better half to announce that he could play the part.

"Let me try a line or two and tell me what you think," Steve said. We liked it, and that was it. Steve was nothing short of magnificent. Shorty and I looked at each other and we knew we had our man, er, teenager.

Russell Doughten was the associate producer on The Blob and is the president of RD Films. He lives in Iowa.

Burn, Baby, Burn
Howard Fishlove

Steve McQueen literally started his employment on *The Blob* with a bang as he tossed firecrackers at the cast and crew.

This New York actor had a heavy-duty reputation before he reported to the set—he rode his motorcycle like a madman, cussed like a sailor. No one could quite figure him out.

The movie was filmed in August 1957 in and around Chester Springs, Pennsylvania. We were all thrown together to film a class-B movie that no one thought they'd be talking about after that summer. Turns out, the movie will outlive us all.

I met Steve a few weeks before the filming started. He was the lead in *A Hatful of Rain* and I went to see him backstage at Playhouse-in-the-Park in Philadelphia. He wasn't happy with what he had to do in the production.

"I can't wait to get out of here,"Steve said."I'm yelling and screaming and I can't stand it anymore."I told him to take it easy; he'd be out of there in just a few days to start filming *The Blob*.

The Blob was McQueen's first starring role and as embarrassing as the film was, he gave it all he had. We were working almost fifteen hours a day, every day—including weekends. I remember the night we were waiting behind Jerry's Supermarket during a break while the lights were being set up. He came down to sit with us. McQueen started off the conversation with,"I served time."I said,"You what?" He repeated,"I served time.""Do you mean that you were in jail?" He said,"That's right." He was in the Boys Republic for a few years and he seemed proud that he was there and survived it. Later on, I read that he gave a lot of money to the place. Steve turned out to be a regular guy and the crew grew to like him.

Almost twenty-two years later, I was an extra in his last movie, *The Hunter*. During a break in the shoot, I reintroduced myself to Steve and told him that I had an hour-long outtake reel from *The Blob*. Would he be interested in a copy?

"Burn it,"he said under his breath. I objected on the grounds it was hilarious and he might find it an amusing trip down memory lane.

"Burn it,"he said again. Steve went on to explain that he had had a successful career and mentioned some of his classic films—*The Magnificent Seven*, *The Great Escape*, *The Sand Pebbles*, *The Thomas Crown Affair* and *Bullitt*. He didn't have to tell me about his cinematic accomplishments—you had to live in a cave not to know of his incredible résumé of films. I was proud of him.

But damned if *The Blob* isn't one of the most enduring and loved films of all time. It's a legacy he should have been proud of.

Howard Fishlove is a retired actor and lives in Glenview, Illinois.

Troublemaker in Checkout

Jack Harris

Top: Aneta Corseaut, Steven Chase, Olin Howlin and Steve, all in a scene from *The Blob*.

Bottom: John Benson, Steve, Aneta Corseaut, Elinor Hammer and Earl Rowe in *The Blob*.

Steve McQueen's reputation as a troublemaker took on new life on the set of my movie, *The Blob*. Demanding as they come, he insisted on a bigger dressing room, upstaged his female lead, raced his sports car in between takes, and brought his black German Shepherd named Thor to the set with him. Whenever Steve left his chair to act, the dog wanted to go with him and that required a little restraint. Steve was hard to deal with throughout my little $130,000 production.

Director Irvin S. Yeaworth, would call me and say, "Well, your star is acting up again." I'd run to the set, sit down with Steve, and try to figure out what was wrong. Steve's mantra "I'm going to call my agent, I'm going to call my manager, I'm going to call my lawyer" eventually ran out of steam. In the end, we came to terms. He wanted approval. What he was looking for was somebody to be daddy and say, "You're a good guy and I like you."

And I truly liked Steve, because in the end, he delivered the goods. *The Blob* made a net profit of $6 million for the studio in 1958, and several more millions over the years. I made a lot of money on that movie and always tip my hat to Steve for that. Contrary to popular belief, Steve was never offered $2,500 cash or 10 percent of the profits. When the picture started grossing tremendous amounts of money, he called me. "You know, I should have held out for a piece of the action." I laughed. "Well, Steve, you wouldn't have gotten it."

I saw Steve occasionally after we made *The Blob*, and he was always kind and gracious. One of the last times I ran into him was in line at the Hughes Market in Beverly Hills. He was a few people ahead of me and didn't see me, but the cashier noticed him. "Mr. McQueen, it's so good to see you. I just love all your movies. Which one was your favorite?"

"Well, I'm partial to *Soldier in the Rain*," he said cordially. The movie had just been released.

"What about *The Blob*, Steve?" I piped up rather loudly. He turned around, noticed it was his old friend, Jack Harris, and true to form, didn't change expression.

"Well, now, it certainly wasn't *Othello*," Steve deadpanned.

No, it wasn't. But, it is a huge slice of Americana and pop culture history.

Producer Jack Harris is the daddy of The Blob and lives in Los Angeles, California.

Street Smarts
Robert Fields

There's no other way to put it. Steve McQueen's street smarts and finesse in tense situations still impresses me after all these years. His combination of unlimited talent and life experience gave him quite the edge over just about everybody on the film set of *The Blob*.

Steve was a good decade older than me when we worked together on the movie. I had just started my tenure at the Neighborhood Playhouse in New York City that summer. Steve had attended in earlier years, but we were both fortunate to have been taught by the remarkable Sanford Meisner. Steve took me under his wing driving me on 100 mph jaunts to Philadelphia in his sports car for hunting excursions in the woods. He also protected me on the set.

Seventeen and just graduated from high school, I was excited to have landed the role of "Tony" in my first movie, *The Blob*. During one scene, I just couldn't satisfy the director, Irvin Yeaworth. After several takes, Shorty told me I wasn't giving him what he needed. Steve held up his hand.

"Wait a minute, Shorty," Steve said. "Bob and I worked at the Neighborhood Playhouse together and we both speak the same language. I think I know what you're asking him to do. Let's take a break and I can tell him what you need."

Shorty said, "Sure Steve, good idea."

Steve and I walked away from the set. As soon as we were out of earshot, he spoke with an intensity I'd never seen before.

"Fuck 'em! Keep doing what you're doing, Bob," Steve said. With that, Steve and I walked back to the set and took our places.

"I think we've got it now," he said with a smile. We shot the scene in one take.

It goes without saying that Steve knew how to handle people. He figured out how to handle the director, fix the moment and resolve an impasse. And for that, I loved Steve.

Did I say street smarts and finesse?

Robert Fields is a veteran actor who resides in Los Angeles.

Top and middle: Actor Robert Fields (dark hair, blue shirt) was impressed not only by McQueen's acting ability but his street smarts.

Bottom: The McQueen persona of the defiant hero who acted alone, started on *The Blob*.

A Lil' Blob'll Do Ya

Dave Lentz

Above: The Colonial Theatre in Phoenixville, Pennsylvania, where hundreds gather every year for "BlobFest."

Top: In his only monster movie, McQueen plays Steve Andrews, a teenager who is searching for clues to the origin of the "Blob".

Bottom: The gelatinous ball of goo is the real star of *The Blob*.

We gather every July at the Colonial Theatre in Phoenixville, Pennsylvania, to celebrate *The Blob*. Produced in the summer of 1957 by a small local crew, *The Blob* was made to support the work of a religious film group called Good News Productions, which was headed by its leader and visionary, Irvin S. "Shorty" Yeaworth. Who could have known that this little movie would have such a lasting hold on film audiences and fans around the world half a century later? If its star were alive today, Steve McQueen would be smiling a half-cocked smile. It is one of my favorite films.

We all relate to *The Blob* in our own way. Some of us take it seriously and want to know every detail. Others just like to watch it. It's not another monster-in-a-rubber-suit flick from the fifties. It made viewers use their imagination to create their own terror, (in the best Hitchcock style), guided only by a mere scattering of visuals of the creature.

Although using the ubiquitous "teen theme", *The Blob* did not make them the obligatory threat to society, but the hope. It also featured twenty-seven-year-old McQueen in his first starring role. One can literally watch him creating his style here, crafting that unique brand of "cool". And in color, too. I would also be remiss not to mention that the movie included character actor Olin "Howlin" Howland's last appearance, when he played the old man who discovered the meteor containing the "Blob". A veteran of hundreds of movies,

including *Gone With the Wind* and many silent films, Howland handed over the reins to McQueen.

McQueen wisely chose not to play down to the age of his character. In doing so, he infused the performance with his own lifelong, youthful energy and sense of purpose that fitted the character perfectly, molding his rapidly developing talents around the role. What is most evident in his performance in *The Blob* is the evolution of the various acting styles that would serve him so well for the rest of his career. A wide range of emotions are sometimes played a little larger than life to fit the material, appropriate for this little Sci-Fi "B" movie that he (and almost everyone involved with it) was sure would quickly rocket into obscurity. By following the "less is more" path in future films, he showed us all how cool you appear when you don't overuse your expressions and body language while totally maintaining intensity and control. This is particularly noticeable in *Bullitt*, *The Sand Pebbles*, and *The Great Escape*.

We "locals" treasure the filming locations, which are still around, and have changed little. It's as if we have our own time machine— returning to a long-gone era simply by driving around town or sitting in the Colonial Theatre balcony.

Dave Lentz is a businessman, a Blob historian and one of the founders of BlobFest. He resides in Pennsylvania.

Left: Steve McQueen as George Fowler, a former star athlete turned getaway driver in the semi-documentary *The Great St. Louis Bank Robbery*.

Opposite: Steve McQueen on the set of *The Great St. Louis Bank Robbery*.

All the Difference

Bob Griffin

I never met Steve McQueen, but I can safely say I owe him a debt of gratitude.

I attended graduate school for theater at the University of Nebraska, but moved to St. Louis in the summer of 1957 in pursuit of a girl I was dating. Of course, when I arrived, she dumped me. I was in a strange place without a job, no girlfriend and no money in my pocket.

As I pondered my future, I was walking down the street and saw piles of huge electrical cables coming out of a building. Being the curious lad I was, I thought I would check it out. Recognizing that it had something to do with the theater, and there might be an opportunity for me, I went inside and discovered a movie was being made.

I introduced myself to a few people, who, impressed with my qualifications, hired me on the spot as a production assistant for a movie called *The Great St. Louis Bank Robbery*. They gave me an advance to pay the rent on my new apartment and I was happy that I was going to have a roof over my head.

Shortly thereafter, I received a phone call from a director in New York, who had wanted me for a role that I had originated in Arkansas.

I was told that they weren't happy with the lead actor and they wanted me for the part. When I presented my dilemma to the producers of the movie, they didn't let go so easily.

"You want to be an actor, right? Well, acting is knowing the right people," I was told. "In this movie is a young man named Steve McQueen who's not well-known now, but he's going to be a big star, and when he becomes famous, you can go to California and use his name."

The pitch fell on deaf ears and I replied, "I don't care who Steve McQueen is because I've never heard of him. I'm going to New York."

Well, the good Lord places you where you should be. In 1961, I was hired as a sports anchor for a television station in Louisiana where I continue to work on a semi-retired basis. I couldn't have asked for a better employer.

I credit Steve McQueen for my career and saving the world from another failed actor.

Bob Griffin is a semi-retired sports anchor for KSLA News 12, and has a daily radio column on 710 KEEL FM, both in Shreveport, Louisiana.

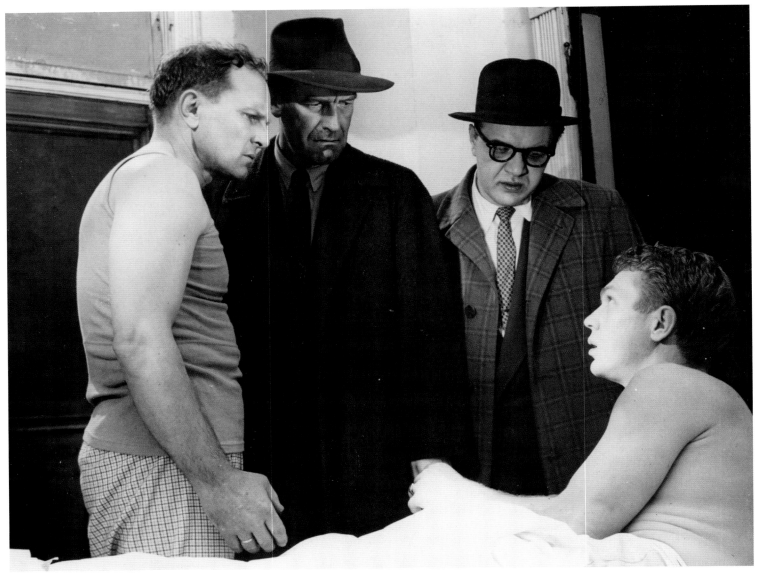

The Great St. Louis Conversationalist
Melburn Stein

I played a small role in the 1959 heist film *The Great St. Louis Bank Robbery*, but I played a much bigger role in the real life robbery.

I worked as an officer for the St. Louis Police Department and was on duty the day four bandits from Chicago tried to rob the Southwest Bank of about $140,000 on April 24, 1953. The gang cased the bank for a week in advance. However, they didn't count on me and my partner, Corporal Robert Heitz, being so close. We had pulled up to a restaurant in the vicinity when the call came through at 10:10 a.m. that a bank robbery was in progress. That's when the hair goes up on the back of your neck.

Corporal Heitz ran to the side door while I made my way to the front. Shooting broke out and bank employees and customers cowered inside. Heitz shot one robber in the buttocks but he returned fire and caught my partner in the neck. I fired twice through the door then ducked behind a metal newspaper stand on the street. It was a good thing because two bullets whizzed about four inches over my head. My days as a Marine Corps drill instructor served me well. They taught me to make myself a small target and take cover.

Pandemonium erupted as the robbery went awry. Dozens of police cars had arrived and police tear-gassed the building. The driver of the getaway car fled while another robber, Frank Vito, shot and killed himself because he feared a return behind bars.

Fred Bowerman, who was the gang leader and on the FBI's "Ten Most Wanted" list, held a shotgun to a woman's back and marched her outside. Crouching to the left of the front door of the bank, I steadied my gun. When the hostage passed and Bowerman walked in my line of sight, I squeezed off a round. The bullet pierced Bowerman's spine and went through his kidney. He died a week later in the hospital. Miraculously, none of the bank staff or customers was injured in what later became one of the nation's most famous bank robberies.

After a trial of the two surviving thieves, I put the robbery behind me until five years later when director Charles Guggenheim, a four-time Oscar-winning documentary filmmaker, decided he wanted to immortalize the robbery for the silver screen.

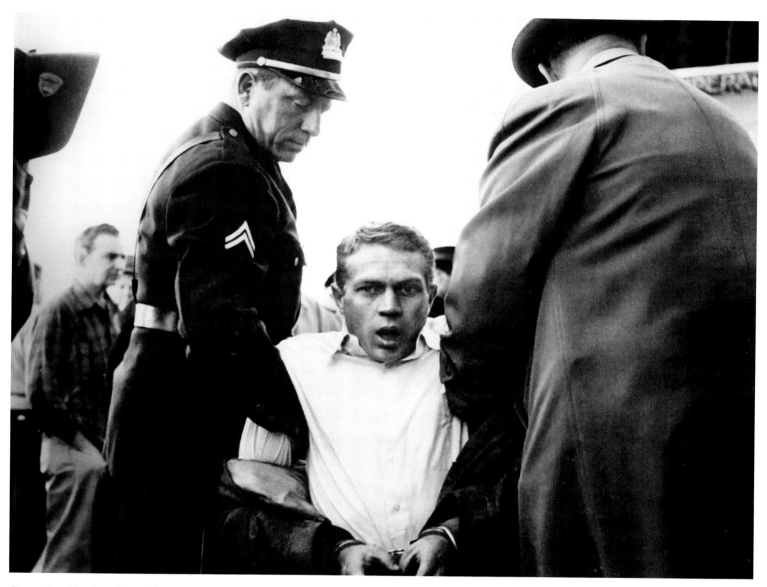

Opposite: Plotting the robbery of the
Southwest Bank in St. Louis, Missouri.

Above: At the end of the botched heist,
Fowler is dragged away by St. Louis police.

Only the last quarter of the picture is based on the true incident, and Guggenheim, who was shooting it as a semi-documentary, wanted me to play myself. I had no problem with that and neither did my superiors, who felt the movie would reflect positively on the police department. For the record, I wasn't paid one cent by the movie production company for my participation.

When we discussed shooting the scene, I suggested to Guggenheim that it should be filmed exactly the way it happened, and he readily agreed. It was completed in one take, although I had no acting experience, unlike my "co-star," Steve McQueen, who portrayed George Fowler, a college dropout hired to be the getaway driver.

The laconic actor may have been able to convey a lot on the silver screen by not saying much but I quickly discovered he didn't have much to say off-camera either. I don't know if McQueen was nervous because this was his first above-the-title billing in a movie or if he was indifferent. Let's just say that he wasn't much of a conversationalist. I've discovered over the years many people have a hard time being friendly with an officer in uniform. Given McQueen's

reform school background and his history with the police, it's easy to see why he kept his distance.

To give McQueen his due, it was a confusing shoot. There was a lot of movement with the cameras with many people in the scene and a large crowd watching. We didn't stand in place for long. Today, you would call this shooting technique "guerrilla-style".

I can't say I was pleased with the picture when it came out because it contained too many historical inaccuracies. But there isn't a day that goes by where somebody asks me about the robbery or Steve McQueen.

Melburn Stein is a retired marine who was awarded the Medal of Honor for his military service. He retired from the St. Louis Police Department in 1973 as a Corporal. At 95, he walks two miles a day. He and his wife, Mavis, reside in Creve Coeur, Missouri.

Steve McQueen Slept Here
Steve Ferry

The McQueens had been New York residents when they first came out to Los Angeles looking for television work. Since we were the only people they knew, it made sense for them to stay with us. Steve slept on our floor for nearly a month while Neile was in Las Vegas working.

Steve and I found a mutual interest in cars. At the time he was driving a beat-up Jaguar and I owned a Porsche. Steve asked me if he could take my car for a spin. Coming over the hills of Laurel Canyon, I managed to hang on for dear life. Steve realized that he could go around corners much faster in a Porsche, so he sold his Jaguar and bought one.

Steve could not sit still for long, and he had to stay busy doing something every minute. It was as though he had a surplus of energy and didn't need to sit and rest and was troubled by inactivity.

Another McQueen trait that caught my attention was that he never carried any money, often leaving me stuck with the bill. It was a quirk that I never fully understood and certainly one that became irritating. If he had any money in his pocket, he scored it from a producer or agent or me or any of his friends. He was just as quick to pay it back in strange ways. He would arrange a weekend that didn't cost you anything. It all came out in the wash.

Steve Ferry is a former actor and property master.

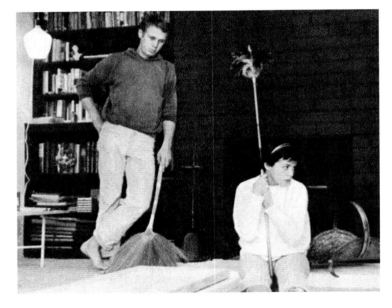

Steve and Neile McQueen at work and play in their first home.

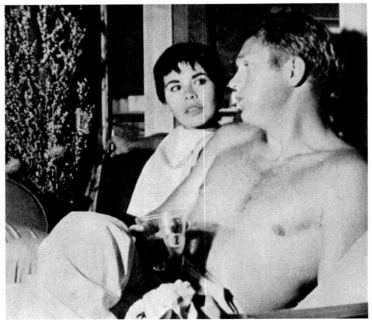

Trial by McQueen

Richard Donner

McQueen as a gunfighter in *Tales of Wells Fargo*, December 1957.

Wanted: Dead or Alive was my first foray into television, but Steve McQueen did not make my transition from New York to Hollywood an easy one.

The opportunity to move to California and venture into the world of film was extraordinarily exciting for me. Desilu Studios asked me to come over and work with them exclusively making commercials.

One day, I was shooting a Westinghouse commercial with Lucille Ball, Desi Arnez, Bill Frawley, Vivian Vance and Betty Furness. Bottles of vodka had been emptied well before noon, making the Desilu actors a tremendous handful to work with. A man, who was visiting our sales manager, came over to me and said, "Boy, if you can work with that crowd, would you work with Steve McQueen?"

"Hell yeah."

Not as easy as it sounded. I knew Steve when we were actors together in New York, but that association wasn't enough to seal the deal. The producer wanted me. Steve didn't.

"He's an actor, not a director," he told the producer.

The producer insisted—because he was producing, not Steve. Still Steve gave me a horrible time. I finally sat down with him and said, "Look, I'm going to quit because obviously you're not happy with me." He became very upset and said, "Nobody quits my show!" So I said, "Well, Steve, you will have to give me a hand." He turned his attitude around and was tremendous. We did that show, and I ended up directing about seven of them. That was my start.

Richard Donner is a veteran TV and film director.

A Face I Could Look At Forever

Donna Redden

I was five-years old when *Wanted: Dead or Alive* went into its first season. For the next three years, Josh Randall, along with Richard Boone's Paladin, left an indelible impression on me. Westerns may have ruled the airwaves but—the Cartwrights? Phooey. The Rifleman? Ho-hum. Randall and Paladin were all that counted in my childhood thoughts.

But I grew up, and over the years I managed to see Steve in only three films, *The Magnificent Seven* and *The Great Escape* on TV, and *Tom Horn* in the theater. When "Vin" scrambled to the back of a running horse or "Hilts" gunned the engine in a futile attempt to jump that barbed-wire fence, "Josh Randall" was always in the back of my mind. In the mid-eighties when the episodes were colorized, I saved the announcements from the papers, wishing I could see the series again. I still had those clippings in 2002 when the Canadian western cable channel, Lonestar, started airing *Wanted: Dead or Alive* where I could receive it. I was on the phone to subscribe so fast it made the dishes rattle in the cupboard. I made sure to be in my armchair every day, for every episode, VCR running. It aired three times a day Monday through Friday, and it was not unusual for me to catch at least two of the airings, even though I'd already had it on tape by then. I was not disappointed—my childhood memories of my hero were uncannily accurate.

Randall was the blueprint for what a man should possess: integrity, a sense of ethics, a moral compass that runs deep and true, a sense of fun, a romantic nature, but tough and always trustworthy. He was the man to get the job done. Steve lived this role for three years and made it so thoroughly his own that I can't think it was only the writers' words in action—"Randall" truly had to be the basic Steve, without all the insecurities, the kind of man Steve was in his gut, with children and with those few he trusted, and when he wasn't side-tracked by the pitfalls of fame and drugs and the headiness of success.

My curiosity now fully aroused, I started looking for information on Steve's life. First, I read all the biographies, and there was some information that shocked me, but for every flawed side of him, there was something wonderful. I started scrolling through Ebay listings, bidding on and winning a satisfactory number of times. I bought all his films, watched them avidly and saw how brilliant he was in *The Sand Pebbles, Papillon,* and *The Reivers,* among others, but I didn't stop there. I went all the way back to *The Defender* and *The Blob* and multi-generation fuzzy copies of early TV work and even the Bell Telephone industrial film from 1952 when he played a lovesick sailor boy.

I was mesmerized by his face. I still get a kick out of reading early magazine articles that spoke of his potential for stardom, knowing how rarely those journalistic premonitions come true as new stars rise quickly and fade faster. Steve was the exception that blew everyone else out of the water! And of course, I had to read up on everything even remotely related to Steve: B-17s used in *The War Lover,* the defensive Siegfried Line used for the setting of *Hell is for Heroes,* poker played in *The Cincinnati Kid,* motorcycles, the racing world, and rodeos in *Junior Bonner*—what an education for me!

To cap it off, I've come into contact with other fans worldwide, some of whom have become good friends. It is a joy to share the information, photos and footage I've collected with both long-term fans and new ones discovering the "King of Cool" for the first time. Indeed, that may be the best thing yet as all of us, with love and respect in our hearts, keep Steve's memory alive.

Donna Redden is a Canadian fan with one of the most extensive Steve McQueen collections in the world. She has a Fine Arts degree with a major in photography, has worked as a truck driver, a deburrer on aircraft engine parts, at a number of bookstores and is a backshift security guard. She lives with a gazillion books and a cat.

Baker Man

Fred Krone

Left: "The Monster" was one of the most popular *Wanted: Dead or Alive* episodes because it featured a five-ton circus elephant that terrorized a small town.

Right: McQueen with actress Linda Wong, who co-starred in the *Wanted: Dead or Alive* episode, "The Long Search."

Like most big movie stars, Steve McQueen had a healthy ego. He could be moody and a pain in the ass, and had to be put in check every now and then.

I worked as a stuntman on *Wanted: Dead or Alive* in 1960 and 1961. Four Star Studios, who produced the show, pushed Steve an awful lot and sometimes the pressure became too much. He worked many hours—and all the production cared about was getting the film in the can, developed and on to the next. It was a grind.

Our days usually started at 6 a.m. and we frequently worked until the sun went down. However, one time, McQueen was running about five hours late. Needless to say, production was not happy because the cast and crew were all on the clock doing nothing. A call was placed to Dick Powell, who ran Four Star Studios. He was one of the most powerful men in Hollywood at the time.

When McQueen casually strolled in, he calmly sat in his chair and the makeup artist began powdering his face. A few minutes later, Powell appeared and asked to have a chat. The two men walked outside. Powell basically told McQueen to shape up or ship out.

"We are a bakery and you are the product," Powell said. "We tell you how you're wrapped, presented and sold, and that's how the cookie crumbles."

McQueen was humbled and Powell never had a problem with him again.

Fred Krone retired as a stuntman in 1974 and resides in Fillmore, California.

No Favors
While in Second
Hal Needham

Relieving tension on a Triumph dirt bike in the California desert.

Steve McQueen was a great actor, a good friend, a graceful athlete and a fierce competitor.

As a stuntman on *Wanted: Dead or Alive,* I first met Steve in the late fifties. Steve was a physical person with a bundle of energy. Much like John Wayne, Jimmy Stewart, Burt Reynolds, and Dean Martin, he truly respected stunt men and the profession. He enjoyed our company and loved the way we made him look good on screen.

But it was in the desert on a motorcycle where I came to know Steve well. The two of us raced competitively almost every weekend. One time during the middle of a race, his motorcycle broke down and he could not start it because of a bad spark plug. I drove past him and stopped. I had a wrench and a spare spark plug and in less than a minute, he was back in the race. About five races later, the opposite situation occurred. My bike had conked out and I saw McQueen coming around the bend. I expected him to stop and give me a hand but he zoomed right past me. When the race was over, I mentioned how he had snubbed me.

"Thanks a lot, Steve, for helping out your good buddy," I said. "I'll remember that next time your bike breaks down."

"I'm sorry, Hal, but I was running second and I just couldn't afford to stop," Steve said with a twinkle in his eye. I understood where he was coming from and returned his smile. I admired his competitive spirit.

Hal Needham is a retired stuntman, stunt coordinator, writer and director. He lives in Southern California.

STIRLING MOSS LTD

46 SHEPHERD STREET LONDON W.I.

DIRECTORS:
ALFRED E. MOSS
STIRLING MOSS, O.B.E., F.I.E.
KENNETH A. GREGORY

GROSVENOR 3272 - 7967
CABLES ESSEMM LONDON W I

28th June, 1962.

Mr. S. McQueen,
C/- Mirisch-Alpha Production,
Munchen-Geiselgasteig,
Bavariafilmplatz 7,
MUNCHEN.

My dear Steve,

Thanks very much for your letter which was most welcome.

Unfortunately I am not sure that Neile will still love me because I am a bit broken up, I also happen to have a little bit of a scar down the left hand side of my face which I am glad to be able to report does not really show that much. However, please tell her that I still love her.

The new film sounds as though it could be good. It has a jolly good name and if it has the same director as "The Magnificent Seven", and if you behave yourself he may not make a mess of it!

Thanks very much for your kind offer of a room. This is most appreciated but unfortunately I shouldn't think I shall be able to take you up as much as I would like to, the reason being that I hope to get off to Nassau soon and back to racing in the not too distant future. If I don't get back to racing I guess I'll be selling matches on the street corner!

In closing I send both of you my very best wishes, and one of you my love.

Yours sincerely,

Stirling Moss

A Stirling Friendship
Sir Stirling Moss

Opposite top: Formula One driver Sir Stirling Moss enjoyed an enduring friendship with Steve McQueen that started in the late fifties.

Opposite bottom left: Legendary racer Moss and Steve McQueen shake hands at the 12 Hours of Sebring, circa March 1962.

Left: McQueen was visiting Montana in the late seventies when he had his last telephone chat with Moss.

Steve McQueen was a one-off; a good race-driver and eternally cool.

I met Steve back in 1959 in California. He was keen on racing bikes and cars and he heard that I was going to be at a particular race. Steve found out that I was staying in Beverly Hills and invited me to stay with him and his wife, Neile. At the time I'd never heard of Steve but he was so friendly and persuasive, it was hard to say no. The McQueens were living at the time in an extraordinary little house tucked away at the back of Hollywood.

When I next met Steve, he had hit the high spots. If you become successful in Hollywood, life changes almost overnight, and the McQueens had moved from their little home into a palatial estate in Brentwood with a panoramic view of the ocean. His garage was parked with great automobiles.

Steve was also generous. Learning that I was a bachelor, he set me up on a date with a lady named Dorothea. I went to pick her up at her lovely home, which also had an attractive garden. I remember knocking, and, bugger me, if The Lone Ranger didn't open the door. "Oh my," I thought, "what have I let myself in for?" He was so tall I would have been knocking on his chest. Dorothea asked me to take no notice of him, he was just a friend.

While Steve was making *The War Lover* in England, he rang me up and we met. Our conversation was fairly simple: girls and cars. Yes, in that order. I also taught Steve some advanced skills in motor car racing. He was keen to learn, interested to listen to advice and take it—which I consider very intelligent.

Some of the film stars who raced back then weren't very fast, but Steve was quick. There wasn't much difference in some of our times—only a second or two. If Steve had buckled down and given up acting, he would have become a very competent driver.

I encouraged Steve to race at the Brands Hatch circuit in Kent, about fifteen miles from London. He raced the same Mini Cooper that Sir John Whitmore had just won the British Saloon car championship in, although he didn't fare as well. He did, however, take third place honors behind Vic Elford and Christabel Carlisle.

Steve parlayed his passion for racing in *Le Mans*, which I found to be a ghastly film. I know many race car fans think it is the definitive film on racing, but that's because most of the other sport films were no good or worse than *Le Mans*. There's much more relationship between the driver and his mechanic than was shown on the screen.

I didn't see Steve much in the seventies, because he became a bit more reclusive in the end. He called me one time out of the blue from Montana. He said he was up there watching the grizzly bears and was taken aback by the natural beauty of the state. With Steve one didn't have normal conversations. He also had a great sense of humor.

His life made such an impression on me because of his character and that he was clearly his own man.

Sir Stirling Moss is a retired racing driver from London, England. Moss, who raced from 1948 to 1962, won 212 of the 529 races he entered, including sixteen Formula One Grand Prix races.

Hand Prints in The Cement
David and Dalton Ross

A star arrives: Steve McQueen immortalizing his hands and feet in cement at Grauman's Chinese Theatre in Hollywood, March 21, 1967. First wife Neile is seen in the bottom right image opposite.

When I was seven-years old, we lived in Santa Fe, New Mexico. My dad would take me to the Albuquerque Hilton where, with white towels draped over our shoulders, we'd pretend to be guests so we could use the indoor swimming pool. One such Saturday, the pool area was empty, except for me and another kid my age playing and splashing in the shallow end. Dad was treading water at the opposite side of the pool keeping an eye on us.

A scruffy-bearded man in a plaid shirt and faded jeans hunkered down at the edge of the pool and leaned over dad's shoulder to call to the kid I was playing with, "Hey, Josh, it's time to go!"

The voice echoed. I'll never forget the look on dad's face when he turned and realized it belonged to Steve McQueen.

Later as we dried off and were dressing, dad explained how he had first met McQueen back in 1959 on the *Wanted: Dead or Alive* set. Dad was a student at the Art Center School in L.A., and he was visiting the set with actor-buddy David Hanigan who'd been cast as a soldier in the episode, "The Tyrant" where Josh Randall was to be executed by firing squad for a murder he didn't commit. "Some day when you're old enough I'll tell you the whole story," dad promised.

That had been almost twenty years earlier, and McQueen had a beard because he had just finished filming *An Enemy of the People,* starring as the portly Dr. Thomas Stockmann.

McQueen was in Albuquerque with his wife at the time, Ali MacGraw, who was starring in Sam Peckinpah's *Convoy* with Kris Kristofferson. McQueen was baby-sitting Ali's seven-year-old son, Josh Evans, the 'other kid' in the swimming pool.

As we headed for the parking lot, dad spotted McQueen at a patio table chatting with *An Enemy of the People* director, George Schaefer. Dad gave me a nudge and steered me to McQueen's table. "Steve, I'd like you to meet Dalton." Steve looked at me with a big grin, reached out and shook my hand. "Hello, son!"

That night, dad and I watched *The Great Escape* on TV. Dad paused the VHS player at the scene where McQueen was surrounded by Nazi soldiers. Untangling himself from the barbed wire and his busted motorcycle, he turned to face the enemy with one arm crippled, his other raised cockily above his head, and the same grin I'd seen pool-side spread across his face.

"He's paying homage to James Cagney," dad said in a hushed tone. "It's Cagney's stance of defiance from *White Heat.*

I was hooked, a confirmed McQueen fan. Sixteen years later, I made a pencil rubbing of the same hand that had shaken mine. I had joined dad in L.A. for a Robert McKee seminar in screenwriting. We visited Grauman's Chinese Theatre in Hollywood between lectures to check out movie stars' footprints embedded in the cement out front. Lo and behold there were Steve McQueen's hand prints!

Afterward, dad and I popped into a nearby watering hole for a beer to toast McQueen, and now that I was old enough, dad told me the rest of the *Wanted: Dead or Alive* story.

It was 1959, and dad, the art student, was sketching madly away on the *Wanted* set as the crew prepared for a complicated scene involving three cameras and almost a hundred extras. A badly beaten McQueen (without his trademark "Mare's Laig," a stubby, but lethal sawed-off Winchester that Von Dutch had designed), was to be dragged through the town square past curious village folk and lined up against an adobe wall facing a military firing squad made up of a dozen soldiers. Dad's actor friend, Hanigan, was one of them.

Central casting had trucked in fifty beautifully costumed "extras" as townspeople. The cameras were ready to cover the scene in one long continuous take. The segment director, Donald McDougall, who filmed more than twenty episodes of *Wanted*, climbed onto a Chapman crane that hovered twenty feet in the air with camera "A". Cameras "B" and "C" dollied alongside on the ground picking up angles and close-ups. The scene had been rehearsed a dozen times

and the crew was ready for the star. The actor arrived on set pedaling his bicycle, wearing a black leather, ankle-length duster coat and sipping a chocolate milkshake. Three makeup artists rushed in for a quick touch up on McQueen's bruises and blood. The actor took his place and nodded to McDougall that he was ready.

A sudden silence fell over the scene. The director called "Action!" and McQueen turned magically into a dazed and dying prisoner. It was an awe-inspiring piece of method acting. No one was breathing. The squad of soldiers dragged McQueen through the square, past the gawking bearded men and sobbing frontier women. McQueen's knees buckled, his boots dragging in the fuller's earth that Special Effects has laid down for its billowing dust-effect. McDougall leaned forward. The soldiers slammed McQueen viciously up against the adobe wall in front of the firing squad.

"Lock and load!" commanded Captain Young, played by veteran actor, William Forester, who began the traditional countdown to the final "Fire!"

Screenwriter Tom Gries (*I Spy* and *Mission Impossible*) called for a last minute reprieve at count four; but on count three, in front of everyone, Josh Randall suddenly came out of his dazed stupor and stood erect with a typical McQueen grin spread across his face and did a broadly animated masturbation gesture into the camera.

You could hear a pin drop as a sudden hush fell over the crowd which lasted all of thirty seconds before the actors, crew, and yes, even the director, broke into gales of laughter! That episode aired on Halloween in 1959.

Dalton Ross is a psychiatric clinician at the Denver VA Medical Center where he treats combat veterans diagnosed with PTSD. He lives in Denver, Colorado. His father, David Ross, continues to live in Santa Fe where he works as an artist and screenwriter.

Above: Behind the wheel of a 1958 Porsche Speedster, McQueen's first factory-owned sports car.

Left: Steve McQueen's first racing trophy was a silver engraved pewter tankard awarded to him by the Sports Car Club of America. He won the event in Santa Barbara, California in May 1959.

Road Tested and Approved
Bob Bondurant

Steve McQueen preferred being on a race track more than acting in front of a movie camera.

That was quite evident when I first met him in May 1959 at the Santa Barbara Raceway. This was his first official motor car race and as I recall, he was driving a 1600 Super Porsche. It was a strange race for its day—it was held at the airport and had a mix of big and small cars. McQueen did a fantastic job and finished in first place. He was hooked on racing after that.

I had enjoyed watching him in *Wanted: Dead or Alive,* and when we met that day, he was quite congenial and much more interesting in person. We talked about cars and Indian motorcycles, which were also my first passion. I believe his handling of motorcycles helped him as a race car driver because the handlebars of a bike are close, just like the steering wheel of a car. Not all actors know how to race, but he most certainly did.

I also believe that Steve made the definitive race car movie. I trained James Garner for *Grand Prix,* Paul Newman for *Winning,* and Tom Cruise in *Days of Thunder,* but for my money, *Le Mans* is the best racing picture because it is "pure". Sure, it was panned when it first came out. I believe the critics tried to compare it to *Grand Prix* and *Winning,* both of which had a storyline. *Le Mans* did not. But if you ask anyone what is the greatest racing movie of all time, almost 90 percent of people in the know will tell you *Le Mans.* It was fantastic and stands the test of time.

As for McQueen, he stands the test of time as well. He was an original.

Bob Bondurant is an internationally recognized authority on advanced driver training, and has been at the forefront of professional driving instruction since 1968. The Bob Bondurant School of Performance Driving is located in Phoenix, Arizona, where Bondurant resides.

The Vinton Dogwood Festival held in Vinton, Virginia, scored a major coup when Steve McQueen accepted the town's invitation to be parade marshal in 1959. McQueen was the star of the highly popular television series *Wanted: Dead or Alive*, but festival organizers nearly had to put a bounty on the actor's head after he arrived in town.

The festival began in 1955 as fundraiser to purchase new uniforms for the William Byrd High School band and has become a rite of spring that celebrates the beautiful dogwood flowers of the area.

As parade marshal, McQueen was required to ride a horse through Vinton, but he darted in and out of the activities all day with a buddy. He wasn't terribly cooperative, frequently AWOL, and it was apparent he wanted to have a good time.

The festival is a big draw for flesh-pressing, backslapping politicians. I think McQueen, like his character Josh Randall, preferred the company of common folk and a quiet place to whet his whistle.

I can't honestly say that Steve McQueen was our greatest parade marshal, but the rascal sure made a lasting impression.

Wallace Cundiff was a retired pharmacist in Vinton, Virginia. He died in August 2009.

A Rascal in Dogwood

Wallace Cundiff

These poster images show that some things require no translation—McQueen is the "King of Cool".

Konichiwa Forever Steve McQueen!

Ryuken Tokuda

Konichiwa means hello in Japanese. Japan has never said farewell to the quintessential charisma of Steve McQueen. Even now, he reigns as an influential figure in terms of fashion and lifestyle beyond the normal boundaries of a movie star.

Why? We identified with him.

Think about it. World War II decimated the country for a time, and then an influx of American products and culture permeated the Japanese scene. Consequently, not only the economy improved, but attitudes about our own daily activities changed as well. For instance, the mainstay of the Japanese diet was rice and fish, but we began to turn to foods such as meats and dairy products, basics of the American diet.

Of course, there was also television. Those who watched American TV dramas were attracted by the affluent lifestyles that were portrayed. The star that Japanese men grew to love and admire the most during this period was Steve McQueen.

Many felt an affinity with his slight physical frame but it was the spirit displayed on screen, easily recognized by the Japanese people, which was the reason for his popularity.

Japan, with few natural resources, made progress during the period of postwar reconstruction by importing raw materials and manufactured goods from abroad, thoroughly researching them, and then making excellent, affordable copies for exporting all over the world. Such tenacity takes spiritual strength and energy. Steve McQueen's on screen personas epitomized what we were going through—facing challenges and never giving up even when failure seems certain. McQueen loved cars and motorcycles, the manufacture of which later became important industries that sustained Japan.

McQueen's movies were enormously influential. He was gaining attention due to the remake of Akira Kurosawa's *Seven Samurai*, and caught the eye of Kurosawa himself upon the release of *The Great Escape*. Kurosawa told his son that he wanted to make a movie about a blond-haired, blue-eyed Samurai who made quite a name for himself during the Age of Civil Wars and wrote a script called *Ogre*. It would have been a spectacular Samurai movie had it been made.

Bullitt was a special movie for Japanese people. Frank Bullitt's silent pause when he killed the villain at the airport, and the way he held his gun without moving were popular for their similarity with Japan's Bushido or "the way of the Samurai". It's the minute gestures coupled with the use of props, such as the gun, that count. Bullitt is silent, fair, has a sense of justice, and even shows mercy to evil. It is the same with the Bushido that the Japanese and Kurosawa loved.

A key difference between the Japanese and Americans lies in the question of who can understand *Le Mans*. McQueen put his heart and soul into the movie, and although it bombed at the U.S. box office it was a hit in Japan. Boring, not enough dialogue and too many racing scenes are what is said to have killed it in the United States. That's what made it a smash to the Japanese. "Silence is beauty" and "action without words" are adages of the Japanese culture that cherishes such behavior as being honorable and wise. Few words, few gestures. That is why we Japanese are moved by the sense of reality and excitement that is portrayed in *Le Mans*. Steve McQueen's character, Michael Delaney, who had about a dozen lines in the movie, said all that needed to be said.

His reactions and gestures cannot be learned at acting schools. They are born from real life experiences and a strong spirit like that of a Samurai. Additionally, McQueen's understanding of the mentality of martial arts from Bruce Lee probably enhanced this quality.

According to Eastern astrology, Steve McQueen, was born under a star that lives in the world of the soul. He was a hard-headed idealist with a strong sense of justice, had many likes and dislikes, saying whatever crossed his mind. This star caused him to display an originality that could not be imitated and made him an isolated person who looks at the world from above.

Akio Miyabe's voice-over in the television series of *Wanted: Dead or Alive* is another reason why McQueen is so popular in Japan. It was a voice so cool that it even filled McQueen with envy.

McQueen's characters had the aesthetics of the ultimate man. He was the American actor with the Bushido spirit, portraying American culture as cool as it could be, and he demonstrated the qualities that the Japanese look for in an actor. So konichiwa always, Mr. McQueen. Thank you for bringing, even today, a sense of tradition that connects Japan with its past.

Ryuken Tokuda is a resident of Tokyo, Japan.

Above: Seen with actor Jim Hutton in *The Honeymoon Machine*, it was McQueen's first stab at comedy.

Left: Steve and Neile in Alaska on a Christmas USO Tour with Bob Hope between them, 1959. Jayne Mansfield is on the bottom right.

Below: Singing the National Anthem for the troops on the Bob Hope USO Tour in Alaska.

Opposite: Steve McQueen in "Alfred Hitchcock Presents" *Man From the South* and as Josh Randall in *Wanted: Dead or Alive*.

Mutiny on the Bounty Hunter
Hilly Elkins

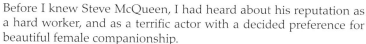

Before I knew Steve McQueen, I had heard about his reputation as a hard worker, and as a terrific actor with a decided preference for beautiful female companionship.

At that time, I was managing Neile Adams—a talented and pretty singer and dancer starring in *The Pajama Game*. She informed me that she had met and been quite taken with Mr. McQueen. I warned her that he was known as a "chaser," and to be careful—he was probably after her money and I was concerned.

About a week later, I happened to see several minutes of Steve in *The Defender* which just blew me away. He was terrific, his eyes came through the screen, and it was an extraordinary performance. I called Neile and told her that whatever warning I'd given her, it had nothing to do with his talent. I definitely wanted to represent him, and shortly after, we became client and manager. Eventually, I found him a role on a series called *Trackdown* that starred another client and friend, Robert Culp. The pilot was fascinating to both Steve and me because he played a bounty hunter, a character that had not yet been seen on television.

Wanted: Dead or Alive, as the series came to be known, was an immediate success and it generated considerable interest on the film side. There was one call in particular that we just could not ignore from producer Walter Mirisch asking about Steve's interest and availability for *The Magnificent Seven*. We explained that there was an overlap in shows, but based on the relationship we had with Dick Powell of Four Star, the producing company of *Wanted: Dead or Alive*, it was likely that any scheduling conflicts could be resolved.

I went to Mr. Powell who advised me that he no longer dealt with that part of the operation and recommended that I should have a word with Tom McDermott, a knowledgeable and tough executive

in the television business whom I knew from New York. I explained the situation and he said "Don't start that Mafia approach with me, kid. He's got a deal, he's got a contract, and that's what he's going to be doing."

I said, "Mr. McDermott, I think you might want to give this a bit of thought. It's a matter of moving or delaying a couple of shows, and this could be the kind of film that breaks him out as an amazing star and will help the show as well."

He said, "Hey, listen, kid. When we need help, we'll call ya." That was my dismissal. I called McQueen, who was on holiday with Neile in Boston, and I explained the situation and said, "I think you'd better have 'an accident'."

I felt comfortable advising Steve on that level because of his racing and driving skills, and I knew he'd be careful but convincing.

Steve proceeded to drive his rented Cadillac into the side of the Bank of Boston, narrowly missing a police officer, and came out with a neck brace. McDermott called and advised that he wasn't buying any of it, and I said, "Hey, look. It was an accident, he has a neck injury and he can't do the show, he can't do the movie. We have a problem." Eventually, McDermott called asking me to meet him in his office. He said, "Okay, look. This isn't what we like to do, but you win this round. We'll let him out early to do the picture." I said, "Thank you Mr. McDermott. That was then, this is now—there's another requirement, and that is you double the salary."

They did and the rest, of course, is history.

Hillard "Hilly" Elkins was Steve McQueen's first manager and eventually became a producer. He lives in Los Angeles, California.

So Long, Architect
Jim Harper

Opposite: On location with *The Great Escape* director John Sturges.

Above: Director John Sturges was Steve McQueen's film mentor and gave the actor several big breaks.

Director John Sturges was my client for almost thirty years. He possessed an incredible mind. Like an architect, he was precise. He planned his movies in great detail, which is why they turned out so well.

A star is like the foundation of any building, and Steve McQueen was the basis for some of John's best work.

John was from the old school and wholeheartedly believed in the star system. The star was given whatever he wanted; the co-star had almost everything he wanted, and so on down the line. On *Never So Few,* Frank Sinatra was the 800-pound gorilla, and he wanted Sammy Davis Jr. off his epic World War II picture for a negative remark he made about "Sir Francis" on the radio. Sammy wasn't the only one singing the blues. John had to fill that spot with a piece of inspired bit of casting; and he did, thanks to his wife, Dorothy. She spotted Steve on *Wanted: Dead or Alive* and mentioned to her husband that a charismatic young man on television just might serve the picture well.

Steve and Sinatra got on famously and Frank, who was secure in his stardom, directed Sturges to "give the kid all the close-ups." John obliged and suddenly a star was in our midst.

John moved Steve up on the roster to the No. 2 man for his next picture, *The Magnificent Seven.* Even though Steve had only seven lines, he managed to steal the movie from underneath Yul Brynner. John could sense Steve was ready to breakout, and gave him a plum role in *The Great Escape.* However, Steve didn't necessarily think so after he read the script.

The Great Escape was an ensemble film and Steve McQueen wanted the spotlight. His instincts were correct, but his actions were not.

He refused to step in front of the cameras until his part was beefed up. John shot around Steve for six weeks until he told his star that his part was about to be eliminated. Within twenty-four hours, Abe Lastfogel, head of the William Morris Agency and Stan Kamen, Steve's agent, arrived in Munich, Germany to save Steve from getting fired. They told him that he'd better listen to John or that he was out of the picture for good. Thankfully, he listened. *The Great Escape* was a smash and the film made Steve a *bona fide* movie star.

Le Mans was a different story. Steve was by now a superstar and let it rule his head. On *Never So Few, The Magnificent Seven* and *The Great Escape,* John was the man with the megaphone. On *Le Mans,* he was a hired hand. The two had switched roles and Steve's ego wouldn't allow him to be second guessed. Sturges felt the picture lacked a story; Steve wanted to make a "pure" film that resembled a documentary about the sport.

The movie was in such disarray that the studio finally stepped in. They told Steve to shoot a script and finish the picture, and production was shut down for two weeks to give John and Steve time to work on the script. Steve agreed to work with John on the rewrite, but then left for Morocco the next day. John walked away from the movie, something he had never done before. That ended their relationship.

To Steve's credit, he called John just before *Le Mans* was released and admitted he was wrong. John was never one to hold a grudge, and accepted his apology. The two, unfortunately, never worked together again.

Jim Harper was John Sturges' business manager from 1946 up to the director's death in August 1992. He resides in Glendale, California.

The Magnificent McQueen
Robert Vaughn

After Jimmy Dean died, most of the actors in town strove to adopt a persona that reminded people of him. I think Steve McQueen certainly fitted into that category although he eventually developed his own screen personality.

When I first saw Steve, he seemed surly and complicated, but after I came to know him on the set of *The Magnificent Seven*, I found that he was quite different. I'd say the outstanding quality Steve had, which directly influenced his success, was paranoia.

Steve was paranoid about Yul Brynner, who was the star of the picture. One time he said to me, "Did you see how big Brynner's horse is?" I said, "No, as a matter of fact, they're calling my horse 'Elefante.' I think my horse is bigger than his." He said, "No, no, Brynner's horse is a lot bigger!" He was angry about this. Shortly after that, he came to me to talk about Brynner having a white handled gun or something, which he hadn't noticed. He thought it might take attention away from him. He plotted every day to better Yul Brynner, who was given the star treatment.

Yul and his wife stayed at a private home while the rest of us bunked in a place called Posadas Jacarandas, which was basically a motel. I had a room that was connected to Charlie Bronson on one side and to Steve McQueen on the other side, and we got to know each other. We played poker every night, drank glasses of margaritas and saw a lot of the local ladies. Steve didn't talk much about international affairs or politics, so we mainly kept it light: women and cars. I knew nothing about cars. We used to drive around on sunny afternoons and stop in at the Whisky-a-Go-Go, make small talk and watch the girls.

Sometime later, I accompanied Steve to a car race, which we followed for a couple of hours. He talked with a few of his friends and then we drove back on the freeway in his convertible two-seat Jaguar. And, of course, it began to rain. We stayed dry because he was driving so fast! It seemed that he had so much emotion bottled up

The Magnificent Seven from top left to bottom right: James Coburn, Brad Dexter, Robert Vaughn, Charles Bronson, Horst Buchholz, Steve McQueen and Yul Brynner.

inside from being at the race and not being able to participate. When we arrived back at his house, his wife Neile asked if I wanted a drink. That was a no-brainer. The ride had been quite harrowing. It took four fingers of scotch to calm me down. I'm sure Steve got a kick out of that.

For some reason, Steve was friendly towards me. He cast me in *Bullitt*. It was his first movie under a multi-picture deal with Warner Brothers. He wanted me and no one else. I remember telling him that I

didn't like the script and didn't think the picture was going to be any good, and asked him why he was going to do it.

Well, I was wrong and he was right. The picture became a huge success and gave my career a welcome push.

I liked Steve. We spent a lot of time together and shared many a laugh.

Robert Vaughn is a veteran actor who resides in Los Angeles, California.

Reaction to Action

Eli Wallach

The cast of *The Magnificent Seven* was extraordinary. The seven were Yul Brynner, Steve McQueen, James Coburn, Charles Bronson, Robert Vaughn, Horst Bucholz, and Brad Dexter.

Once director John Sturges asked me to stand beside the camera and watch a scene being shot in which the seven gunmen rode across a river. Brynner was the head man, and sometimes he would resent the tricks that McQueen used to draw attention to himself. Brynner led the seven across the river, riding high with a determined look on his face. McQueen took off his hat and dipped it in the water. In another scene, as they were taking a hearse to the cemetery, Brynner was fixing his holster and lighting a cigar by striking a match on his boot while McQueen pretended to test a shotgun cartridge by shaking it next to his ear before loading it into his gun. Yul's eyes darted toward McQueen with a look of "What are you doing there?" It was a wonderful competitive moment. Sturges loved the competition and never chastised his actors for it.

McQueen and I had trained together at the Neighborhood Playhouse and the Actors Studio. Even then McQueen had the raw skill. His chief talent lay in being observant. He could always find in an earlier scene what had led logically to his actions later. In *The Magnificent Seven*, he once asked Sturges to cut some of his dialogue.

"Please," he said, "movie acting is reacting. Silence is golden on the screen."

Nobody quite grasped the poetry in the flow of the film like he did. What McQueen had learned to do was what separates the true artist from the ham—to watch and, above all, to listen. McQueen was the best reactor of his generation.

Eli Wallach is a veteran theater and film actor. This excerpt is from "My Brief Atonement" in The Good, The Bad, and Me, copyright © 2005 by Eli Wallach, reprinted by permission of Houghton Mifflin Harcourt Publishing Company.

Expert Handling
Tim Thomerson

To come off like a pro takes talent whether you are cocking a shotgun or a facial expression, and Steve McQueen pulled it off effortlessly.

I have a clear memory of the Robert Culp series *Trackdown* where the Josh Randall character was introduced back in 1958 and which later became *Wanted: Dead or Alive.* My father, who first made me aware of Steve McQueen, was an aviation ordnance man in the Navy, an expert pistol shot and a world class skeet shooter, so consequently, we watched all westerns.

"Look how this kid handles his weapon, that sawed-off .44-40 (Mare's Laig)," my father said with an eye to the familiar. He noted that McQueen must have had military training because no one could handle a weapon so expertly unless they had done military service.

Fast forward to the early sixties and McQueen's portrayal of Reese in *Hell is for Heroes.* Reese was one of the most fleshed out characters McQueen ever played. The war torn intensity, the vacant-eyed, thousand-yard stare and once again, expert handling of weapons, along with one of the best death scenes ever as he charged the German pill box, were remarkable to this first generation TV watcher and baby boomer.

I admit I'm an avid Steve McQueen fan. He was a true actor with a unique style, and his clipped, terse, reactions in scenes were well rehearsed and worked out. There isn't a single film of his that I haven't enjoyed. There are the obvious choices of favorites that I could mention, *The Great Escape, The Thomas Crown Affair, Love with the Proper Stranger, The Sand Pebbles, Papillon* and *Bullitt.* But I'm going out on a limb to say that even though the Tony Randall/Doris Day type comedies of the sixties were not typical Steve McQueen films, the comedy timing he delivered in *The Honeymoon Machine* (a military caper where Naval officers try to break the bank in Venice) is as good as it gets. Aside from the silliness of this film, the double takes, the asides, the physicality of his performance—all the beats were spot on. And that stuff is hard to do. To make that work is a testament to his ability as an actor.

Tim Thomerson is a former stand-up comedian and veteran actor with more than three hundred credits to his name. He lives in Southern California.

This sequence of photos demonstrates Steve McQueen's quick draw. He often challenged Hollywood luminaries, including Clint Eastwood and Sammy Davis, Jr., to mock gunfights to see who was the fastest gun in the west.

Above: Handwritten note from Steve McQueen to Elisabeth Osborn.
Middle: McQueen with Columbia executives in London preparing for the filming of *The War Lover*.

Right: A pair of nickel-plated spurs by Mexican silversmith Edward H. Bohlin presented by Steve McQueen to Basil Heath, who was Elisabeth Osborn's father and a big fan of the Western movie genre.

A Cache of Personal Assistance
Elisabeth Osborn

In the late summer of 1961, I was contacted by Columbia Pictures in London to work on a film version of John Hersey's book, *The War Lover*. The timing was perfect and I readily accepted the position of production secretary on the movie that was to star Steve McQueen and co-star Robert Wagner. I was truly thrilled.

I was asked to locate possible rental homes for Steve to visit upon his arrival, so that he could choose one for his wife and children to stay in when they came a few weeks later. This was the family's first visit to London—and the only English-based movie Steve made. He decided on a beautiful house on a Belgravia square, 200 yards from my own residence, so it was very convenient.

During the course of a couple of afternoons reviewing houses, Steve asked me about my family as we rode along in a taxi. I told him the story of my father, who had been so ill when he was eleven that he was in bed for a year. His first outing after his long recovery was to a performance of the Wild West Show, starring William "Buffalo Bill" Cody and Annie Oakley. It also starred Wild Bill Hickok and Chief Sitting Bull, and after the performance he had the pleasure of speaking with both of them. As I was growing up, the history and peoples of the American West were always top subjects in our house, and during the World War II bombings of London, my father used to devise quizzes on the subject to keep us entertained. His favorite question? It was asking us to name Native American tribes beginning with every letter of the alphabet. I tried doing this the other day and still couldn't think of V and X! His favorite film cowboys were William S. Hart and Gary Cooper, and after *The Magnificent Seven*, Steve immediately became number three.

Steve enjoyed hearing about my father. When Neile McQueen arrived with three-year-old Terry (who called me "Diz" and shared hot chocolate with me three mornings a week) and eleven-month-old Chad, she brought with her a pair of spurs made by Steve's silversmith in Mexico inscribed: "For Bill from Steve McQueen." My father was simply thrilled. Just one of the kind deeds Steve did for so many people during his short life.

Rehearsals, locations, schedules and more proceeded for *The War Lover* with one rather long delay. Columbia Pictures was having three World War II Boeing B17 bombers flown from Texas to our location airfield outside London where a large chunk of the movie was set. The intrepid expedition leader was Captain John Crewdson, and they had to land the three bombers on every island en route in the Atlantic in order to make repairs.

While John was trying to reach England, I was summoned by the head of Columbia Pictures in the UK, and shown a telegram that had been signed in my name. It was addressed to their studio in Los Angeles requesting, from the wardrobe department, the US Air Force uniforms that Steve had tried on before coming to England. Since London had insisted that the uniforms should be made in the UK and they had already been ordered, this confused

the issue no end. I was fired the same day despite denying any knowledge of the telegram.

I ended up in tears at the foot of the staircase in Steve's home crying about how cruel it was and that I would miss working on his film. He stood at the top in true movie fashion and seemed surprised by what had happened. The next morning, a messenger delivered a red rose with a note from Steve written in red ink saying "I'm writing in Blood so that you will know I'm sincere. A man once said, 'it's the little things that count'." Shortly afterwards, Hillard Elkins, Steve's manager told me that Steve would like me to be his personal assistant for the duration of the film. I was overwhelmed by Steve's generosity.

During filming we were on location at a muddy airfield, and when he had a free moment, Steve would often get out one of his scramble bikes and do wheelies. Once he said to me: "This one's for you, Liz!" as he sprayed mud in the direction of the crew member who had taken "my" telegram to the head of Columbia. Steve didn't forget that.

Sir John Whitmore, the British Saloon Car Champion and the first driver to go down the Cresta Run, the famous winter sledding course in St. Moritz, Switzerland, in a Ford motor car, stopped by the location. He and Steve became fast friends, and John helped him buy a Mini Cooper, arranging it with John Cooper himself.

Steve called me at 5 a.m. one morning to say that he had been robbed of his umbrella and bowler hat. I asked him where he had left them. "In the car," he said. "So where's the car?" "The car? Oh, that's been stolen, too." I think of Steve every time I see a Mini Cooper these days!

At Christmas time, Steve and Neile wanted to give a special party for American actors and actresses who were unable to be at home with their own families. It was a star-studded cast, with Robert Wagner teaching us the Watusi, Johnny Dankworth and Cleo Laine providing the music, famous race car drivers, including world champion Graham Hill, and Lionel and Joyce Bart who danced for everyone. Actor Van Johnson couldn't come at the last moment because he had an injured thumb! Many of the supporting cast came by, including Al Waxman who was to be Lt. Samuels in *Cagney & Lacey* and Michael Crawford, the singer now known for his appearances in *Hello, Dolly!, Phantom of the Opera* and many more. It was more than a memorable evening.

Finally, it was time to say goodbyes. It was with sadness that I couldn't fly to Los Angeles with Steve and Neile. They invited me, but didn't realize that there was a major problem—I couldn't drive and Los Angeles didn't have buses!

Elisabeth Osborn (then Liz Charles-Williams) was Steve McQueen's personal secretary during the shooting of The War Lover in England. She is semi-retired and has lived in Norwich, Vermont since 1975.

Opposite: Going over the script for *The War Lover*.
Elisabeth Osborn, who served as McQueen's personal
assistant, is seated and wearing shades.

Steve and Neile McQueen, late 1961.

STEVE McQUEEN

80 Chester Square,
London S.W.1.

5th December, 1961.

Dear Hedda,

Just a note to let you know I am
still alive. Neile is fine and the kids are
growing like weeds.

We are working very hard on the
film and if the rushes are any indication of
us having a good movie, the census of opinion
from the Cutters, Assistant Directors and our
Producer, it looks as though we might have
something kind of interesting.

England's fun, Hedda, but I miss
California very much. I am an American and I
never realised how deep rooted this was until I
was a foreigner in someone elses land. We have
a great country there and you don't realise how
great it really is until you are away from it
for a while. This might sound a little hokey,
but it is exactly the way I feel.

It pretty well rains all the time
now and yesterday, last night, I got caught for
three hours in a fog coming back from Shepperton
Studios, the traffic piled up for three miles and
I was getting hungry, but having my Land Rover I
put it in four-wheel drive and cut across a
Farmer's ploughed up field and made it on to the
next Highway. I told Neile that Land Rover would
come in handy one time.

Sometimes when I get home from work
if I have got a few hours to spare, Neile and I go
down to the market along the Thames and have fish
and chips. In the evening, if it's not raining,
it's kind of pretty sitting there watching ships
going down the Thames. I should be back home about
the middle of January and I'm going to make a bee-
line for Palm Springs and do nothing as hard as I
can until I go into The Great Escape for John
Sturges.

If you get time, Slim, drop me a
line as we are yearning for news of home.
Love,

Damn the Torpedoes
Mike Frankovich, Jr.

Above: Steve McQueen and actress Shirley Anne Field in *The War Lover.* The two didn't get along either on or off-screen.

Opposite and right: As bomber pilot Captain Buzz Rickson in the same film.

Opposite inset: A letter from a homesick Steve McQueen to famed gossip columnist Hedda Hopper when he was shooting *The War Lover* in England.

Steve McQueen was friendly enough, but he was hell on wheels.

At the time I knew him, my father, Mike Frankovich, Sr. was the head of Columbia Pictures, which was producing *The War Lover* starring Steve McQueen and Robert Wagner. My father placed me in charge of publicity. I had arranged a *Life* magazine cover story, which was a stroke of luck on McQueen's part, considering that this could launch him as a movie star.

Life writer George Barris and I were supposed to meet McQueen at the Carlton Towers Hotel in London at a specified time. When he did not appear, I had to apologize

to Barris and the cover story was scrapped. I don't think he understood the value of publicity then. Later on, most of the press he received was for his "bad boy" behavior, which contributed to his success.

McQueen was also ill-mannered on the set. He treated English co-star Shirley Anne Field in such a rude and brash manner that she developed an intense dislike for him.

"Americans are real actors," Steve would goad Field. "Here, you don't know the first thing about acting for movies."

He could turn his character on and off. At certain moments, he became the little boy

with that side grin of his—then, boom, he was back in the driver's seat as an actor, completely immersed in the role once the cameras were rolling. If I were to make a judgment, I think he was having a little fun at people's expense. He was expected to be the consummate Method actor in the mold of Marlon Brando, but he fooled a lot of people, he had his own Method.

He lived life as if there was no tomorrow. Damn the torpedoes, full speed ahead.

Mike Frankovich was a publicist, screenwriter and assistant director in Hollywood. He died in December 2007.

Steve and Bob Hope performing a comedy skit for the Bob Hope 1960 Buick Show filmed in Colorado Springs.

His Toys

James Coburn

According to many McQueen intimates, he was a big kid trapped in a man's body.

Steve was very individualistic in his methods and his ideas. And he never really grew up—he always had the machines, from the motorcycles to the airplanes, to play with—and as he became more affluent, the bigger and the more valuable were the toys.

He frequently tested the producer, the studio and the limits of how much he could get away with. During filming of *The Cincinnati Kid*, he went to wardrobe and ordered four dozen pairs of Levi's. The wardrobe guy said, "We don't even wear Levi's in the movie." Steve said, "I wear them to and from."

We'd go out to lunch and he'd say, "Oh, geez, I didn't bring any money. Can you take care of it?" I don't know if it was calculated or if Neile wouldn't give him any money. He did grow up very poor, of course. Whatever he had in those days he would have to beg, borrow, or steal.

He did have personality, and I think that's what he thrived on. Once, when we were driving to the *Hell is for Heroes* shoot together, he complained about the way something was written - "Why can't they do a story about one guy? Me." I said, "Oh, that's pretty egotistical." But he tried to do it. I don't know if it was a script or just an idea for a script. It was about a pilot who, flying a jet during the war, had crashed in the desert. The story was all about him surviving in a hostile environment. He thought that would be perfect—he wouldn't have to share this dream with anybody.

James Coburn co-starred with Steve McQueen in The Magnificent Seven, Hell is for Heroes and The Great Escape. He died in 2005. This passage originally appeared in the March 1999 issue of Interview.

When Legends Collide

Sonny West

Tight, coiled and combustible, McQueen's role as Reese in *Hell is for Heroes* garnered high praise from director Stanley Kubrick who said, "It is the best portrayal of a solitary soldier I have ever seen."

When I first worked with Steve McQueen, he wasn't yet the international superstar that he was destined to become, but it didn't take a genius to figure out he was going places.

In 1960, I worked for Elvis Presley as his personal bodyguard, but we parted ways because my real ambition was to be in the movie industry. I found a steady job as a $22 a day extra on the Western TV series *Outlaws*, which starred Barton MacLane, Don Collier, Bruce Yarnell and Slim Pickens.

When the show went on summer hiatus, and I was getting down to my last dollars, I bumped into director Don Siegel on the Paramount lot. I had worked for Don on *Flaming Star*, a picture he directed that starred Elvis Presley. We made small talk for a while until I worked up the nerve to pitch him for employment. My timing couldn't have been better. Siegel was about to shoot interiors for *Hell is for Heroes*, a World War II ensemble piece starring Steve McQueen, Bobby Darrin, Fess Parker, James Coburn and Bob Newhart.

McQueen was definitive in his approach to acting, which made it interesting to watch him work. He was intense, a loner, and gave off a vibe that made it obvious that unless he expressly invited you to speak to him, you shouldn't. When McQueen wasn't shooting a scene, he pumped weights, often joined by James Coburn, with the grim intensity of someone trying to work off a lot of pent-up tension.

A few years later I was in a limousine with Elvis on Beverly Glen in Los Angeles as we made our way to MGM Studios when McQueen rolled up alongside us at a stoplight in an expensive sports car.

"Elvis, is that you?" McQueen said, squinting into the back of the limo. Elvis rolled down the window and said, "Hey, Steve. Whatcha doin'?" McQueen said he was working at 20th Century Fox on *The Sand Pebbles*. The conversation didn't go much further because the light turned green.

Elvis respected McQueen's work on his TV series, *Wanted: Dead or Alive*, and especially in the movie *The Great Escape*, which he screened many times at the Memphian Theatre. I always thought that Elvis was a little professionally jealous of McQueen. Steve landed many of the plum dramatic roles in the sixties that appealed to Elvis, including *Baby, the Rain Must Fall*.

Later, the two men competed for the affections of a beautiful starlet named Barbara Leigh, who was Steve's co-star in *Junior Bonner*. Barbara once told me that Elvis would always ask, "How's that motorcycle hick?" while Steve asked, "How's that guitar hick?" Both men came from humble beginnings, but it was funny they called each other hicks.

Sonny West was Elvis Presley's bodyguard and close personal friend for sixteen years. He resides in the Nashville, Tennessee area.

The Soul of a Racer

Joanna Chapman

Those baby blues melted a lot of hearts.

Steve McQueen didn't like to lose—especially to members of the opposite sex.

Steve and I both loved fast cars. We lived near each other in the early sixties, so I only knew him, literally, as a passing acquaintance.

I drove a 1964 E-type Jaguar and Steve owned a black Ferrari which he'd often roar out of the canyon at the same time as I left for work in the morning. Occasionally, we'd sit at the stop light at the Beverly Hills Hotel going the same way on Sunset Boulevard. We'd look over at each other, gun the engine, and when the light turned green, it was off to the races. It was a curvy mile-stretch involving numerous gear shifts and pin turns. Whoever took first place waved goodbye in the rearview mirror. We never stopped to talk or chat because it was all a game.

We had these encounters about a dozen times a year, with Steve taking the checkered flag every time except once. I think he let me win because he had the car, the experience and the soul of a racer. When I waved and looked back in the rearview mirror, Steve had a big grin on his face—his way of letting me know that he didn't lose the race; he just let me win.

Joanna Chapman is a resident of Carmel, California, where she owns and operates The Chapman Gallery.

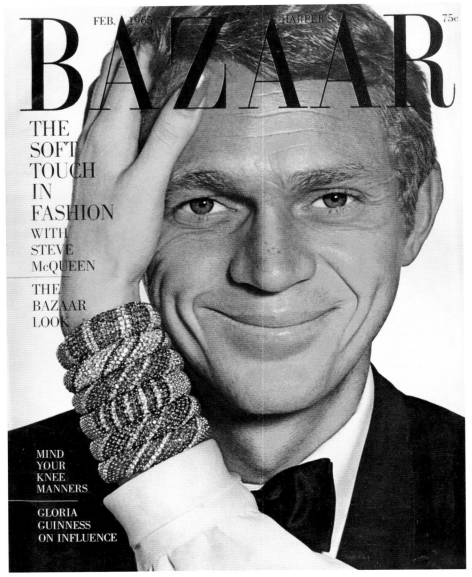

A Girl's Guide to a Bad Boy

Gina Gershon

This cover of the February 1965 issue of *Harper's Bazaar* solidified McQueen's status as a sex symbol.

Tough. Defiant. Dangerous. Sexy. Steve McQueen was a juvenile delinquent, a Marine, a movie star. He worked the oil fields, raced cars with Mario Andretti, and rode motorcycles before it was hip. He demanded and received his price in Hollywood before it was status quo. Men wanted to hang out with him; women simply wanted him.

McQueen's personal style mirrored his acting style: understated simplicity. He would cut dialogue from his characters' speeches in order to evoke the same feelings with a look or movement. This stripped-down quality could also be found in the clothes he wore: T-shirts and jeans (Levis, to be exact). He knew who he was, felt comfortable in his own skin, and made confidence his style. "I believe in me," he said. "I'm a little screwed-up, but I'm beautiful." No wonder why he scored the hottest chicks around— women are suckers for vulnerable, blue-eyed boys with a seductive, cocksure swagger.

Sure, he appeared on the cover of *Harper's Bazaar* in 1965, but his sexiness came from within. Take another look at *The Getaway*,

Bullitt, The Thomas Crown Affair, and *Papillon*—it was McQueen's raw self-reliance and genuine sense of danger, as well as his disdain for bullshit, that made him so compelling. People respond to those who walk their own path.

McQueen was an ad man's wet dream. It's no accident that when he sported the Heuer Monaco wristwatch in *Le Mans*, it became so popular that it was re-released in the '90s. Rolex named their Explorer watch after him. If he were alive today, there's no doubt in my mind that he'd be offered serious bread to have his image, dressed in jeans or khakis, splashed across the side of some building. And I'm just as certain that Hollywood's quintessential bad boy, the king of cool, would decline.

Gina Gershon is a television and film actress and has appeared in Bound, Showgirls, Face/Off, Curb Your Enthusiasm, Just Shoot Me! and Rescue Me. This passage originally appeared in the October 2003 issue of Premiere.

Viva la Cool!

Patrice Hennebert

Left: Steve and Neile attend the Paris première of *Love with the Proper Stranger* with Natalie Wood.

Right: McQueen donated a "Mare's Laig" used on *Wanted: Dead or Alive* for auction to raise money at the Ritz Hotel in Paris, France, for a charity benefiting orphans. The gun was purchased by French singer and composer Gilbert Bécaud.

The French have always held "cool" on a pedestal and it doesn't get higher than with Steve McQueen.

France discovered Steve McQueen in 1963 when *Wanted: Dead or Alive* was first aired. The TV show was a huge success and Steve McQueen as Josh Randall was perceived as a flawed hero in an American tradition that was readily understood. The program was broadcast repeatedly over the years, always attracting new generations, mine included. Josh Randall's popularity in France was such that the episodes of this serial were issued on DVD there even before they were released in the United States.

Most of the films starring McQueen such as *The Magnificent Seven* and *The Great Escape* were highly appreciated by the French audience. Steve's face was everywhere in the sixties—on the covers of magazines, on TV and the silver screen, and could hardly be ignored. His good looks earned him the admiration of legions of French women. He was often compared to Paul Newman, but Steve was considered more accessible. McQueen's dubbed-over voice in French sounded manly and coupled with a certain twinkle in his eye, he made the opposite sex weak at the knees.

McQueen's visits to France cemented the love of the French audience, first by attending the première of *Love with the Proper Stranger* in Paris with Natalie Wood. Steve also came to France to sell a Josh Randall Winchester at a charity auction—it was bought by a famous French singer. *Le Mans* required many non-professional actors for the crowd scenes, and the ones I've met described

McQueen as down-to-earth and easy to approach. This particular movie spread Steve's popularity among the racing crowd too, forever linking his name to the *Le Mans* competition. Steve's character became so popular that a widely known comic strip creator, Jean Graton, who met McQueen on the set of *Le Mans* honored Steve by introducing him in one of his books.

Another French link was Steve's portrayal of Henri Charrière, the famous prisoner of Cayennes, in the classic epic, *Papillon*. This movie is adapted from the controversial best-seller written by Charrière himself. A few years later, *An Enemy of the People* was well-received at a worldwide première at an American movie festival in Deauville, France, although Steve didn't attend. French composer Michel Legrand created three McQueen soundtracks, most notably "Windmills of Your Mind" from *The Thomas Crown Affair*.

Even though I never met him, I felt the best way to pay back the pleasure of watching McQueen's movies was to display some of the items I have collected on Steve's life in a temporary exhibition which was held in 2004. I happily shared my memories and feelings with visitors, because no matter what your personality, there has to be at least one of Steve's characters with which you could identify. That was my small way of paying homage to both the man and his muses.

Patrice Hennebert, a French businessman, is the owner of an impressive collection of memorabilia on Steve McQueen and The Beatles. He lives in Paris with his wife and twin daughters.

The Great Escape
Bud Ekins

Opposite: It was Bud Ekins, McQueen's close friend and stuntman, who performed the dangerous jump over a barbed wire fence in *The Great Escape*.

Above: Bud and Betty Ekins and Steve and Neile McQueen enjoy a night out in Las Vegas.

When Steve McQueen died, he played the biggest joke of all on me: every interview I give invariably ends up about Steve.

I first met Steve at my motorcycle shop in Sherman Oaks. I recognized him from *Wanted: Dead or Alive,* but I had worked with movie industry types and certainly didn't look at them through rose-colored glasses. Steve wasn't magical or special, he was just a fellow human being. In fact, he was a bit of a nuisance, and invariably picky, even with technical matters he did not understand. I think he liked that I didn't give him preferential treatment.

Our friendship developed because he knew he could learn from me. He wanted my motorcycle knowledge. He was an excellent rider and he once confessed to me that he didn't care for acting.

"You know something, Bud? I don't like being an actor. It's the publicity. If anything, I'd rather drive a truck," Steve said. "However, acting opens a lot of doors."

Steve opened a door for me when he was getting ready to go to Germany to film *The Great Escape*. "Gonna make a movie in Germany with a motorcycle chase in it. Wanna come and double me?" I thought, *"Bullshit. It will never happen."* A week later, I received a phone call from Steve, who asked me to put on a suit and tie so that he could introduce me to director John Sturges, and in a few weeks, I was in Germany.

I was there to jump over the barbed-wire fence on a souped-up Triumph. When I was successful, the crew applauded and Steve walked over and stuck out his hand. "That was bitchin'" he said with a smile, shaking my hand.

Five years later I doubled for Steve in *Bullitt,* but he was annoyed as hell at me. He had been given a late call to the set one day only to find me with my hair spray-painted blond, driving recklessly around the streets of San Francisco.

"You did it to me again!" Steve said. "Now I'm going to have to go back on Johnny Carson and explain to the world I didn't do that stunt."

Steve was competitive with everyone, including me. We collected antique motorcycles and often we'd trade barbs. "Bud, you won't believe what I just picked up today," Steve would brag over the phone, and then he'd tell me what bike he'd just purchased. It took me twenty-five years to collect one hundred and thirty antique bikes. It took Steve two years. It's called money.

I can't say that I miss Steve because I talk about him every day. I know he's up there in the sky laughing his head off because I'm stuck here having to answer for him.

Bud Ekins was one of Steve McQueen's best friends and one of the foremost stuntmen of his generation. He died in October 2007.

DRIVER'S INTERNATIONAL LICENCE
LICENCE INTERNATIONALE DE CONDUIRE

FEDERATION INTERNATIONALE MOTOCYCLISTE

STAMPS
TIMBRES

Z 6285

Full Licence/Licence Normale
Restricted Licence/ Licence Limitée
See over/Voir au verso

La présente licence pour être valable, doit être revêtue de la vignette de l'année en cours et de la signature du titulaire, qui en la signant, déclare connaître le Code Sportif de la F.I.M. en vigueur et s'engage à le respecter.

This licence is not valid unless bearing a current stamp and signed by the holder who thereby accepts the provisions of the current Sporting Code of the F.I.M. and acknowledges it.

Signature / Signé

This licence remains the property of the F.I.M. and must be returned to the F.M.N. when it expires
Cette Licence demeure la propriété de la F.M.N. et est à lui être restituée à l'expiration.

Sec. Gen.
7 Rue Carteret,
Geneva

Délivrée par
Granted by   MICUS   (F.M.N.)
To Mr.
à M.   McQUEEN
First name Prénom   STEVE
pseudonyme autorisé
authorised assumed name _____
né le
born the   24 MARCH 1930
nationalité
nationality   AMERICAN
domicilié
permanent address   1411 S. BEVERLY Dr.
LOS ANGELES, CALIF, USA.
Certificat de la F.M.N. Certificate of the F.M.N.
La licence est valable pour. This licence is valid for:—

	DATE/DATÉ
TRIALS & SCRAMBLES	1964

U. S. MOTORCYCLE CLUB
33 N. Fullerton Avenue
Montclair, New Jersey

Signature of the Secretary of the F.M.N. Signé par
le Secrétaire de la F.M.N.

Printed in England by Howard & Longman Ltd., Totton, Southampton

Six-Day Trials and Tribulations

Dave Ekins

Top left: McQueen holding an American flag during the 1964 International Six-Day Trials in East Germany.

Top middle: The Six-Day Trials roster included Dave Ekins, Bud Ekins, Steve McQueen and Cliff Coleman. John Steen, who is not pictured, served as an alternate.

Top right: McQueen did well in the Six-Day Trials until he was sideswiped by a spectator who suddenly rode his motorcycle out on the track.

Bottom: McQueen's International Driver's License.

Steve McQueen had such incredible power and charisma that he could have ruled a communist country, and darn near did.

Let me begin my story with a bit of background. Movie stars have always been a big part of my life. My brother was Bud Ekins, and he owned a motorcycle shop in the San Fernando Valley where the stars migrated when they wanted to buy a bike or talk shop. Robert Wagner, Keenan Wynn, Warren Beatty, Lee Marvin were all fixtures. I was in the back working on a couple of Hondas when Steve McQueen sauntered into Bud's motorcycle shop one day in 1960.

Bud was born James Ekins, on Mother's Day, May 11, 1930. And boy, what a mother's day gift he was! Steve was born the same year and they lived parallel lives: early delinquents graduating into reform school and later, self-made men who liked their booze and their talk straight. Of course, they loved their machinery and the freedom of the road. I believe they were destined to find each other.

Bud became a Triumph motorcycle dealer while Steve was still doing the *Wanted: Dead or Alive* series. He searched out Bud to buy a Triumph 650cc and to ask him to "show him a thing or two about dirt riding." Steve had done his homework. Bud was one of the most accomplished riders in the world and knew every fire road, sand wash, and mountain dirt trail in the area. He was the old "Desert Fox" taking the likable and willing Steve out to learn the young-man skills necessary for competitive off-road racing.

Perhaps the closest I observed Steve was during the September 1964 International Six-Day Trials in East Germany, when I caught a glimpse of real power. The day before the race, all the teams were required to attend a dinner hosted at the Erfurt University gym. Each table had a flag in the middle representing the respective country, which indicated our seating assignment. Even though this was an Olympic event, all the teams were served cold cuts surrounded in eel. As this fish eye stared at us from the table, Bud said, "Well guys, it's the same for everybody so let's eat up." Something smelled fishy to Mr. McQueen, who stood up and waved the waiter over.

"Where does the jury eat?" Steve asked. He was told they were huddled in the dining room of the Erfurt Hof Hotel just down the street. With that, Steve stood up and told the U.S. Silver Vase 'A' Team to follow his lead. Our British and Swedish counterparts, who had watched the scene unfold, marched out as well and followed us to the Erfurt Hof Hotel for a grand dinner. The rest, including the U.S. Silver 'B' Team, remained guests of our East German hosts. Maybe they liked cold cuts and boiled eel for dinner. The rest of our meals were Western-style and the communists were forced to shape up their act.

The U.S. Silver Vase 'A' team consisted of Bud, Steve, Cliff Coleman, and myself. Competing as an alternate, John Steen also earned a Silver Medal. Our team was in the lead on the third and toughest day of the race, when Steve, hurtling along a narrow ravine on his 650 Triumph was sideswiped by a spectator who suddenly rode his motorbike out onto the track. Steve was sent airborne and landed brutally, his face smashing against a rock, and the skin was torn from his kneecaps. That same day, Bud broke his ankle.

I've often been asked how well Steve rode a motorcycle and I have always answered it this way: During the final chase sequence of *The Great Escape*, Steve is expertly using throttle brakes and balance power sliding around a grassy knoll, feet up. Try it.

Dave Ekins is a two-time gold medalist and is considered a pioneering off-road racer who helped usher in the era of lightweight, smaller-displacement off-road motorcycles. He was inducted in the Motorcycle Hall of Fame in 2001 and lives in Southern California.

McQueenmania

David Foster

Steve McQueen's visit to Paris, France in September 1964.

In the late fifties I was a publicist for Jim Mahoney & Associates and was assigned to work with Dick Powell at Four Star Studios Television, which owned *Wanted: Dead or Alive.* Steve McQueen and I had grown up together in the entertainment business. He had a rebel image but we had much in common. We were the same age and our wives and kids were the same age. Our kids would go to each other's birthday parties.

We got along well, even though he was a difficult, moody person to know. A psychologist would have a field day trying to figure him out. One day he would be your best friend and the next day, your enemy.

He would fire me three times a year. I would fire him a couple of times, and then our wives would always get us back together again. This went on throughout our relationship. It was definitely a love/hate thing.

My happiest memory of Steve was in Paris, France, when he was at the height of his popularity. The French department store, Le Printemps, was having a big promotion for "Le Ranch Steve McQueen". The store wanted to turn its second floor into Steve McQueen's ranch, a western-themed promotion with boots, hats, Levis, and all-American gear.

Since his name was being used, the store agreed to pay McQueen a percentage of the sales, so the four of us, my wife and I, and Steve and Neile went to France for a week. We drank wine, went to discos, and had

great meals. The only part of the trip that was disconcerting was that Steve was trapped in the hotel for two days. He was the single biggest movie star in France, and every time he walked out, hundreds of kids would mob him. It was worse than The Beatles. He couldn't go anywhere. We just roared with laughter.

He kept saying, "I can't believe this is happening to a kid out of reform school. Can you believe this, Foster?" It was a happy time.

David Foster is a publicist-turned producer and resides in Los Angeles, California.

Mechanically Inclined

Manuel Ramirez

McQueen is smiling in this photo for good reason—he was the world's biggest box-office star in the sixties.

Sitting at the wheel of one of his many sports cars.

In 1963, my buddy, Jim Horton, and I worked at a popular Union 76 gas station at Oak Street and Thompson Boulevard off Ventura Highway. We were both studying auto mechanics at Ventura College and kept our British sports cars in the back. They were our babies and we showered them with love.

We were both at the gas pumps when an expensive sports car pulled in and immediately attracted our attention. When the driver jumped out (the car had no doors), I knew instantly it was McQueen because I was a big fan of his movies, especially *The Great Escape*.

McQueen wasn't as tall as I thought he'd be, but was wiry and handsome. He also seemed friendly and approachable. He told me he was on his way to the Santa Barbara Airport races and was fueling up. While I filled his tank, I asked him if he had a few minutes to talk. We were ecstatic when he agreed.

We knew McQueen was a car buff so Jim and I showed off our cars. Mine was a 1959 Austin-Healey 106 and Jim's was a 104. "Wow, you guys keep them in good shape," McQueen said, and his eyes lit up when we took off the covers.

Taking the time to talk to two young men about their cars was a small gesture of kindness indicative of the man's character that made the brief encounter so memorable.

Manuel Ramirez is a retired mechanic who lives in Ventura, California.

Forever in Blue Jeans

Jack Dieterich

Whenever I think of Steve McQueen, I'm reminded of a gentleman in blue jeans.

I met Steve in 1963, when I was 26-years-old and ran a factory operation for International Harvester Company in Van Nuys, California. Our company produced scouts, pickup trucks, Travelalls and Travellettes. One of my duties was working with the movie studios because I had connections to the film industry. I was constantly trying to place our product in front of the public through films.

My work brought me one day to Columbia Studios to visit Dick Miller, who held a senior position there. After our business was finished, Dick walked me to my car, which was an International Travelall and spotted Steve McQueen on the lot. Dick asked me if I'd like to meet him.

"Well, there's two ways we can do this," said Dick. "One is to simply introduce the two of you or you could raise the hood of your car and pretend something is wrong. I guarantee he'll be over in five minutes." So that's exactly what I did, and almost as if on cue, McQueen came over to lend a hand. After going through the motions of seeing if the car would start, Dick walked up to McQueen, lightly slapped him on the back and laughed heartily. McQueen made the comment that we were "jerking his chain".

My first impression of Steve was that he was a good man who was overwhelmed with what was happening to him. *The Great Escape* had just come out and propelled him to stardom. He seemed to be fiercely protective of his privacy.

A few months after that first meeting, he called me at the factory and said that he wanted a beige three-quarter ton pickup to haul his motorcycles when he raced on weekends. I agreed to deliver it to his house.

We arrived around breakfast time. Steve took us outside on the patio where we had coffee and smoked cigarettes. His two children, Terry and Chad, were in the living room watching television. Neile came out last, and I was impressed when Steve stood up and gave her a big kiss.

After breakfast, Steve checked out the truck and said everything was fine. I presented him an invoice for $5,000, a tidy sum at the time, and asked him for a check. Then he nearly gave me a heart attack.

"Send the bill to your friend Dick Miller," Steve said. "He owes me. I read a script for him." I thought I was either going to lose my job or end up buying a pickup truck for Steve McQueen. He could afford it and I couldn't. As it turned out, Dick did pay for the truck.

I saw Steve a few more times at Bud Ekins' motorcycle shop and at Columbia. We had lunch once at a five-star restaurant near the studio with a strict dress code. I never saw Steve in anything but blue jeans and a T-shirt and thought there was no way we were going to get in, but because he was Steve McQueen, we succeeded.

Steve reminded me of that famous saying, "Never judge a book by its cover." He may have dressed working class, but he was first class all the way.

Jack Dieterich is retired and divides his time between Southern California and Palm Springs.

Top left: McQueen cooling off after riding his motorcycle through the California hills.

Top right: Photo taken in Wharton, Texas in 1963 for *Baby, the Rain Must Fall.*

Bottom: In the driveway of "The Castle", admiring his new toy—a 1963 International Travelall.

Just One of the Guys
Tim Gilligan

Steve McQueen sure didn't act like a movie star. He was a pure racer at heart. I have no doubt that he would have raced professionally, but just couldn't turn down those big pay checks from his day job.

I was fifteen when I started working for Bud Ekins at his motorcycle shop in the mid-sixties. Located at the intersection of Ventura and Van Nuys Boulevards, the shop was the hub of the motorcycling world at the time and there I met several Hollywood legends, including Steve McQueen. So I didn't mind washing motorcycles, sweeping floors and emptying trash!

A couple of times a week McQueen would drop by Bud's shop around 7 p.m. That's when Bud shut the doors so that McQueen and other racing buddies could talk shop, and "wrench their bikes" for a few hours. Steve owned a Rickman Metisse Triumph in British Racing Green, and lavished the 650cc bike with attention. On those nights, Bud usually fished out a ten spot, instructing me to pick up a bottle of the hard stuff at a liquor store down the street. It didn't matter that I was a teenager; the owner knew it was for Bud and gang. On Saturday nights, we'd venture off into the desert, and Bud raced on Sunday mornings. Our lives revolved around our motorcycles and we loved the sport. It was a magical time.

After graduating from high school in 1972, I caught up with Steve at the Indian Dunes racetrack in Valencia, California. The two of us sat on a bale of hay while motocross racer Mike Runyard rode a few laps around the track. He was poetry in motion. I told Steve I was contemplating becoming a fireman for the Santa Monica Fire Department. He smiled and said he was excited for me.

"Man, that's great. I have the greatest respect for the profession." Steve told me about a fire that had broken out at the Paramount lot in 1966 during the première of *Nevada Smith*, and that he had pitched in to help battle the blaze. He said firefighting might have been something he would have done if acting hadn't come his way. Almost a year after that conversation, Steve accepted the role of a battalion chief in *The Towering Inferno*. His portrayal of a fire fighter was not only heroic, but right on the money. He brought an authenticity to the role that no other actor of his time could.

Steve's life eventually drifted away from everyone at the shop and we lost contact. But I'll never forget him or the fact that he had been "one of the guys" to us.

Tim Gilligan retired from the Santa Monica Fire Department in 2007 after 34 years of service. He lives in Santa Paula, California.

Opposite: McQueen did the majority of his dirt bike riding in the sixties on a Rickman Metisse Triumph.

Above: One of McQueen's prized possessions—a Von Dutch wrench.

Broken Chains

Adrienne McQueen

In his breakout role as Captain Virgil Hilts
in *The Great Escape*.

He died before I was born, but mention Steve McQueen and my knees and stomach get a little weak.

I first watched *The Great Escape* as a young girl of twelve. Immediately, I was drawn to this blond-haired, blue-eyed man with the crooked smile. Not understanding quite why, I loved this movie and the American actor who starred in it. Still do. So much so, I traveled to the Bavarian studios where the film was shot, and visited the site of the prison camp built by United Artists. Being from Germany and young to boot, I didn't appreciate the significance of the era or the reasons that Steve McQueen was so important to his generation. My parents helped me to understand the movie and the counter-culture that drove the likes of McQueen into the realm of legends.

After World War II, Germans still had a narrow mind-set. "Be quiet and never, ever speak up" was the older generation's advice to their offspring. Obey, and God forbid, don't even think of rebellion. Germany broke free of this, largely due to the counter-culture movement of the sixties in which movies played a big part. Film rebels such as James Dean, Marlon Brando, Dennis Hopper, Peter Fonda and Steve McQueen began questioning authority through their words and actions on film.

When people watched movies like *The Great Escape*, they forgot their own weaknesses and fears of daily life. They were suddenly reminded of the bravery of youth and admired those not afraid to speak up for themselves. I have always been impressed by the dialogue between McQueen's character, Captain Hilts, and Lt. von Luger at the beginning of the movie:

Lt. von Luger: Are all American officers so ill-mannered?

Hilts: About ninety-nine percent.

Lt. von Luger: Then perhaps when you are with us, you'll have a chance to learn something. Ten days isolation, Hilts.

Hilts: Captain Hilts.

Lt. von Luger: Twenty days.

Hilts: Right. Oh, uh, you'll still be here when I get out?

Lt. von Luger: Cooler!

And then McQueen grins.

This exchange explains why *The Great Escape* was a huge hit in Germany, especially after the war. People in our country longed for the genuine camaraderie that the British and the Americans showed in the film. It was released in Germany under the title *Gesprengte Ketten*, which translates to English as "broken chains". This fits the picture perfectly.

People were inspired, not only by new screen heroes like Steve McQueen, but also by the American way of life they so perfectly conveyed. McQueen seemed approachable, a friend, someone who was authentic and honest. No matter what film it was, he appeared fearless, self-confident, nonchalant, and charming. He oozed sex appeal, but had vulnerability behind the blue eyes that made him an international heartthrob.

Steve McQueen had the most striking personality of all the "film rebels". He conveyed many messages through his actions on and off screen—"You, too, can be tough!" "Don't obey, be sovereign!" "Don't care what others think." "Be yourself." Today we are missing people who are rough around the edges, who stand their ground and "don't answer to anybody", as McQueen once famously boasted.

His charisma grabbed me right off the screen. A director friend once said, "Film acting is what's going on in the eyes, and with the real good ones, it's pain." As an actress, I cherish this quote and believe this divides the good from the exceptional. He had so much depth without even trying and he could touch you deep inside through the screen.

I should know. Steve McQueen reached out and touched me, and I have never been the same.

German-born Adrienne McQueen is an actress, singer and producer. She lives in Hollywood, California.

Non Action Hero
James Garner

About a month or so into the filming of *The Great Escape*, we had an hour-and-a-half of dailies and they said, "Anyone in the cast who wants to come see them, is welcome." After seeing them, he left so angry that he was going to quit the picture. He wanted to re-shoot everything. And we were hurting for money and time. So a couple of days later, John Sturges came to me and said, "Jim, you're the star of the picture. Steve is out."

I took Steve and the other co-star, Jim Coburn, to my house in Munich and we went through the script, discussing several scenes, and I said, "What's your problem, Steve?"

"Well, I don't like this. I don't like that."

I said, "This is silly. You don't like anything." We finally figured out that Steve wanted to be the hero, but didn't want to do anything physically heroic. He didn't like the part where the little Irishman climbed the wall and was shot, and he then had to pull him down.

So they changed the script to make him the hero by the way he escaped and was captured, but when he came back, he had information about the area. Oh boy, what a hero, and he didn't have to do much at all! John Sturges called me one day when he was putting the film together and he said, "Jim, I have to tell you, the two best acting scenes in the film with you and Donald Pleasence are on the cutting room floor. I have to stay with McQueen and the bike."

Hey, it made the picture. Sturges was absolutely correct, but as far as acting went, it was out the window.

James Garner is the renowned TV and movie star, and was Steve McQueen's friend and co-star in The Great Escape.

Above: First Daughter Luci Baines Johnson dancing the Watusi with McQueen at the Young Citizens for Johnson barbeque on August 22, 1964. The fundraiser was on behalf of her father, President Lyndon Johnson, and made headlines around the nation.

Right: A letter from President Johnson thanking Steve McQueen for co-hosting the Beverly Hills fundraiser in support of his campaign.

THE WHITE HOUSE
WASHINGTON

November 19, 1964

Dear Mr. McQueen:

Mrs. Johnson joins me in thanking you for your valuable participation in the campaign. A great deal of the success we achieved on November 3 was due to the time and talents that responsible citizens such as you gave to the effort.

The unity of the American people, demonstrated in this election, is both a great trust and great opportunity for us all. I pray that we may work together, as we have voted together, to keep our country safe, strong and successful as we continue our responsible efforts to assure freedom's victory in a world of peace.

With warmest best wishes,

Sincerely,

Mr. Steve McQueen
27 Oakmont
Los Angeles 49, California

McQueen as an actor was fabulous: One of the guys who came from the school of mumbling who kept their feelings to themselves.

There's that fantastic scene in *The Great Escape* where he throws a baseball up against the wall while in solitary confinement. Of course in real life, the Nazis would never have allowed a prisoner to take a ball and glove into jail to give him something to while away the hours . . . but that's Hollywood. And, my God, if I was sent to jail, I'd want Steve McQueen as my roommate.

Gene Simmons is the co-founder of Kiss. This passage originally appeared in the March 1999 issue of Interview.

Kiss This
Gene Simmons

McQueen was a world-class car collector and motoring enthusiast.

Making Tracks
Steve Rubin

It was the summer of 1963 and I had recently seen *The Great Escape* at the Fox Wilshire in Beverly Hills. For an eleven-year old, it was the most exciting movie, featuring the coolest actor on the planet— Steve McQueen. I vividly remember riding my Schwinn Stingray bicycle with the high handlebars, elongated seat and "sissy bar", while pretending I had stolen a German motorcycle and was headed for the Swiss border.

One Saturday afternoon, I was on my bike, headed for the local slot car track to race my miniature car. I had stopped at the northeast corner of Palms Boulevard and Motor Avenue (about a mile north of MGM Studios) when I heard a voice behind me.

"Could you tell me where MGM Studios is?" I turned my head and there, sitting in a Ferrari convertible was Steve McQueen, aka Captain Virgil Hilts, "The Cooler King". I would love to have a portrait of the look on my face. I pointed south towards the main studio on Washington, mumbling something, and then Steve asked me where I was headed. I told him that I was going to race my slot car at the *Le Mans* track on Sepulveda.

Now, you forget much over the years, but I will always remember that Steve found this interesting and mentioned that he had heard there were even slot motorcyclists racing the tracks. I agreed I had heard that too, even though I was aware of no such thing. If he had told me that green men from Mars were about to land on our roof at home, I would have undoubtedly believed him.

With that, he said goodbye and drove off, turning south on Motor Avenue, heading for the lot. Wistfully, I gazed at that Ferrari, probably hearing Elmer Bernstein's soundtrack from *The Great Escape* in my head. Certainly a star encounter of the first magnitude that would stay with me forever.

Steven Jay Rubin is a producer, film historian and author who resides in Los Angeles, California.

Lord Richard Attenborough and Steve McQueen on the set of *The Great Escape*, where the two commenced their lifelong friendship.

Fear at Full Throttle
Lord Richard Attenborough

Just as I was finally starting to film *Gandhi* in 1980, I received the news I'd been dreading—at the age of 50, Steve McQueen was dead.

We first met in the summer of 1962 in Bavaria on the set of *The Great Escape*. This was my big international acting breakthrough. Just three members of the all-male cast were billed above the title: Steve as the Cooler King, Jim Garner as the Scrounger and me as Big X.

Right from the outset, both on screen and off, there was intense macho rivalry between the Brits and the Yanks. It came to a head when the two separate groups were lounging around in the sun during a break from shooting. As always, when time hung heavy, Steve was riding his 500cc Triumph, zooming off between the POW camp huts and returning to skid around us Brits in ever decreasing dusty circles.

Finally, those piercing blue eyes hidden behind dark glasses came to a halt beside me and sat there, twisting the throttle provocatively.

'Wanna ride?' I hesitated. It was thirty years since I'd ridden pillion and having ended up in hospital as a result, had sworn I'd never do it again.

But national honour was at stake and I knew I couldn't refuse the challenge. 'You bet,' I said heartily.

The next fifteen minutes were the most terrifying I can remember as I clung on for dear life, but they cemented a deep friendship.

Steve was a speed freak. He was devastated when the insurers ruled against him performing the most famous motorbike stunt in movie history—but never took the credit for it, always careful to point out

it was performed by his double, Bud Ekins. He had to settle for playing the part of a German chasing Bud in that scene.

There's a belief that screenwriters disliked Steve because he was always angling to make his parts bigger. That, in my experience, was untrue. He was forever fighting to cut lines because he knew, better than anyone, that one telling look is worth any amount of dialogue.

I last saw him a few months before he died. I was on a flying visit to Hollywood and we arranged to meet at his favourite restaurant. Because I'd been delayed, it seemed strange not to see him when I arrived. About to sit down, I caught sight of a ravaged old man beckoning from one of the bar stools. A shiver ran through me: the old man was Steve.

How do you say farewell to one of your closest friends? What do you talk about that last time? I'll tell you.

We ribbed each other about the day he scared the shit out of me on his motorbike. He reminded me about the time I dragged him to a football match at Stamford Bridge.

He didn't mention that he had cancer and had only six months to live. When we hugged outside, neither of us said goodbye. I valued his friendship profoundly and miss him more than I can say.

He was one of the best screen actors of all time.

This excerpt is from Lord Richard Attenborough's autobiography, Entirely Up to You, Darling, which was published by Hutchinson and reprinted by permission of The Random House Group Ltd.

Here's Hollywood...
and Germany Jack Linkletter

I lived only a few blocks from Steve McQueen. Though I seldom saw him, on occasion we would visit and share our enthusiasm for motorcycles.

I flew to Munich during my *Here's Hollywood* show to interview Steve and the cast while they were making *The Great Escape*. On a free night, Steve found three Harleys for himself, Jim Garner and me, to go to Obermensing for a folk fest. Neither Garner nor I had many cycle hours. The narrow streets, humped in the middle and made of cobble stones, would have been scary enough, but to have cars flying by within inches made us think it was our last trip anywhere.

We arrived at the folk fest with lots of carny offerings, bumper cars, etc. From a big tent we heard classical oompah music. Inside, we found picnic tables, the locals, many in leather pants, the band and lots of beer. Steve and Jim were recognized immediately and room was made at a table with a policeman, a dairyman and others. While we didn't understand German, we were soon singing along as if we knew the words, and Steve was standing on the table—everyone loved it.

Going home in a light rain was horrible.

Jack Linkletter was the son of famed broadcasting personality Art Linkletter and the former host of seven television shows, including Here's Hollywood, America Live and Hootenanny. He died in December, 2007.

Above: Doubling as a Nazi on *The Great Escape* in Germany.

Opposite: A McQueen letter to columnist Hedda Hopper, August 1962. He wrote from Germany where he was filming *The Great Escape*. McQueen failed to mention that he walked off the picture until director John Sturges beefed up his part. The movie made him an international superstar.

MIRISCH-ALPHA PRODUCTION

MÜNCHEN-GEISELGASTEIG BAVARIAFILMPLATZ 7
c/o BAVARIA ATELIERGES. M. B. H.   TELEFON 4 76 91

Munich, August 8th, 62

Dear Hedda,

Just came back from location for a few days. Then back to the Alps
and more locations with the motor-cycle.

Neile and I are off to Paris, I promised Neile a new wardrobe for
her anniversery, so we will be sitting at all those fashion shows.
I promised Neile I would wear a tie, so all is well.

I am going to export some German driving gloves for all the sports-
car minded people in the U.S. under the Steve Mc Queen banner. So it
looks like I am going to be in the glove business.

see attached wire

Terry, my daughter, speaks German and I must say it is a little embarrassing when she has to interpret for me. She has picked it up
plain with the children in the village and I have asked her please
not to talk German at the dinner-table, as I don't know what she is
saying.

Other than that, old girl, I have just been plain working and hope
to be back in the U.S. in about three weeks. Then four months off,
a vacation in Palm Springs, a camping trip with my family and back
to work preparing SOLDIER IN THE RAIN with Blake Edwards and Marty
Jorrow, as this is the project that Mr. Edward's company and mine are
doing together.

Neile sends her love, and the children, and I would give half of my
domain for one hot, juicy Califonian Hamburger with raw onions. Vie-
ner Schnitzel is starting to come out of my ears.

SMcQ : CvL

CABLE ADDRESS: MIRALPHA, MUNICH

Opposite top: Revving up the Triumph TR650 motorcycle.

Opposite bottom left: "The Cooler King" getting ready to serve another stint in isolation.

Opposite bottom right: Taking a smoke break on *The Great Escape*.

Above: Drinking and distributing moonshine during a Fourth of July celebration in the enemy camp.

Reckless Abandon
Michael Manning

The question for me is an existential one. What is it about this Beech Grove, Indiana, kid who was abandoned by his alcoholic mother and good-for-nothing father that forever annealed within him an emotional pain so jagged that it would wreak havoc with the world he was forced to navigate alone for fifty years? In spite of such a cruel fate, McQueen's very being manages to inextricably weave—for lack of a better description—a primordial imprinting within so many of us who are drawn to his searing intensity on screen. At its core is a search for truth. Much has been written about his anti-hero persona, his troubled relationships (personally and professionally), his promiscuous nature and macho tactics with motorcycles and cars. He was a tortured soul whose life was lacking stability. But in the end, he found the peace with God that had eluded him until the last three and a half years of his life, and true love with model Barbara Minty. What emerges for me is a dichotomy.

Like Steve, I came from the Midwest in what has become today a hardscrabble environment. At the age of nine, I first saw Steve in his breakthrough movie role as Virgil Hilts, "The Cooler King" in *The Great Escape*. Later, into my teen years, I was privileged to have attended first-run theater releases of *Bullitt, On Any Sunday, The Thomas Crown Affair, Junior Bonner, The Getaway* and *The Towering Inferno*.

Steve McQueen, the actor, was visceral and transcendent with his on screen persona. But underneath that image lived an insecure man who, in spite of his riches and fame, rose above the crowd as the finest example of what a "man among men" meant for me. As the publicity for Steve's favorite film (and mine) *Junior Bonner* states, he is "The last of his kind."

What I identify with in this loner who trusted few, and who endured enormous loneliness and personal anguish, is the fact that Steve had come full-circle in his quest to begin living again. Devoted to his own children, Steve was also a philanthropist to others less fortunate, particularly at the Boys Republic in Chino, California, where he spent part of his childhood. He visited with the boys there throughout his career, sharing of himself and the lessons that served him well. His authenticity came from vulnerability, bringing the complexity of his conflicted life to every screen role, and articulated with keen instincts borne of the streets. He laid bare a humanity that I have grown to embrace and celebrate as the inspiration in my own life to overcome far lesser obstacles. I choose to honor Steve's memory as a man who at the end of his life embraced the love of a devoted wife, and the forgiving peace he discovered within his faith that paved the way for his journey from tragedy to reaching up and touching the face of Almighty God. This is the Steve McQueen who lives within me, and always will.

Michael Manning's career as a broadcast journalist for twenty years has included appearances in over 6,000 radio & TV commercials. His website, www.michaelmanning.tv, hosts The Annual Steve McQueen Film Festival as a blog page feature during the week of Steve's birthday on March 24th. He lives in Scottsdale, Arizona.

Steve McQueen with *Soldier in the Rain* director Ralph Nelson. This 1963 film was the first project McQueen chose after *The Great Escape*.

The 170-Pound Gorilla
Tony Bill

Soldier in the Rain was my second movie and Steve McQueen's next picture after *The Great Escape*. I just treated him like a normal person and we got along well. I can't say the same for him and co-star Jackie Gleason.

Ralph Nelson, the director, was a gentle, kind man, but it was clear that he was not in charge of decision making on the set. It became obvious that was Steve McQueen's call. He also pushed the limits with "The Great One".

McQueen, whose company was producing the picture, had star billing and, caught up in that heady feeling of stardom, was prone to arriving late on the set. He decided he should appear after Gleason, and so his co-star found himself in the awkward position of waiting on the arrival of young Mr. McQueen. Gleason, being a consummate professional and experienced performer, became annoyed with this. Shortly after we started filming, he let it be known that he would no longer show up at the set before McQueen. Steve caught wind of this and there was a short-lived stalemate—neither of them would arrive before the other—that was worked out as the movie progressed.

Tony Bill is a former actor turned producer turned director. He won an Academy Award for The Sting in 1973.

Top: Co-star Tony Bill shared a lot of laughs and good times with McQueen in 1963's *Soldier in the Rain.*

Above: McQueen and Jackie Gleason appeared as buddies on screen but often bumped heads on their only film collaboration.

Compliments Will Get You Everywhere
Chris Noel

Opposite top: McQueen lounging in a sand trap with co-stars Tuesday Weld, Jackie Gleason and Chris Noel.

Opposite bottom: *Soldier in the Rain* was one of Chris Noel's first starring roles. She learned that the right compliment could get you far in Hollywood.

Right: His role as Sgt. Eustis Clay set McQueen back a few notches after the success of *The Great Escape*.

I took the standard route that most young ladies do when trying to crash Hollywood—cheerleader, model, beauty pageant winner and finally actress. Steve McQueen played a big part in my success as an actress when he agreed to cast me in my first film, *Soldier in the Rain*.

It was 1963 and McQueen was about to become the next big thing in Hollywood. His movie, *The Great Escape*, hadn't been released to the general public but there was buzz surrounding his performance at the première in New York. When I did my first screen test with him, I complimented him on the picture. He did a double take because the movie had only been screened once publicly, which I had just happened to catch.

"How did you see it?" he asked. I told him someone within the industry had escorted me to the première and judging by the audience's reaction, he was going to be a major star. That certainly got his attention.

"You're hired!" Steve said. His company, Solar Productions, was producing the picture and he had the final word on everything. I later discovered that the film also featured Jackie Gleason and Tuesday Weld, and I was going to be part of a talented group.

Steve was a fantastic actor and thoroughly professional. I wouldn't call him a Method actor but during filming he took on a certain accent and intensity—his character was a Southern bumpkin'— and he had a completely different persona.

He was also approachable on a personal level. You could talk to Steve about anything. Often I would walk by his trailer, where I usually found him parked outside nursing a Corona beer with plenty more in an ice chest at his feet. Many times we'd just shoot the breeze discussing everyday events or how we could improve a scene. I was flattered that he took the time to pay attention to me on my first big picture.

Steve was an exciting person to be around, and there were few that were as stimulating. He was always moving ahead in a way that many others never managed.

Chris Noel is a former actress and was the host of "A Date with Chris", which was on the Armed Forces Network from 1967 to 1971. She is a veterans' advocate and is the founder of Vetsville Cease Fire House in Boynton Beach, Florida.

Above left: McQueen's love of driving fast cars often gave him an acquaintance with local authorities on the streets of Hollywood. Many a police officer was sent to the movie star's home, who told him "to slow it down".

Above right: Steve McQueen's 1957 Jaguar XK-SS. Today it is housed in the Petersen Automotive Museum in Los Angeles.

Opposite: McQueen at a black-tie affair around 1966.

Bait and Switch
Fred Romero

Steve McQueen's racing exploits in the Hollywood Hills gave morning roll call and water cooler chats plenty of fodder within the Los Angeles Police Department, where I worked as a young officer in the early seventies.

McQueen, known for baiting cops into chases, was putting his dark green Porsche through its paces on Mulholland Drive, a winding and twisting ridgeline road. McQueen smiled and gave a quick wave as he drove past me, well above the posted speed limit. My turn at the barrel.

This chase, however, was a little more serious than the average citizen going a few miles over the speed limit. I remember looking at my speedometer, hovering at times between 85 and 90 mph. It took all I had to keep up. McQueen's car was much more powerful than my old "black and white".

I eventually lost McQueen in a cloud of dust, but my superiors knew he lived in an expensive spread in Brentwood. About ten minutes later, my partner and I pulled up at his home, spotting the Porsche in the driveway. The smell of engine and hot rubber brake pads permeated the air as we exchanged knowing smiles.

When we knocked on the door, McQueen answered. He was the perfect host, asking us to come inside. We discussed Mr. McQueen's extracurricular racing activities until I decided to mess with his head. I told him how much I liked him in *McClintock*. McQueen, who was polite and low key up to that point became animated, ranting that *McClintock* was a picture that starred John Wayne. My sly smile let McQueen know that I was baiting him just as he had baited me on Mulholland Drive. He gave me a look that said, "Touché."

I didn't give McQueen a ticket but we came away with a mutual understanding that I wouldn't be talking movie trivia with him again if I caught him racing that Porsche on anything other than a track. We shook hands and left, thinking that was the end of that. However, the next week at roll call, the sergeant notified all the black and whites that McQueen was back to baiting police cars up on Mulholland.

Fred Romero is retired from the Los Angeles Police Department and is an insurance fraud investigator in the Simi Valley.

A Man and his Castle
Edd Byrnes

It's been said that Steve McQueen was competitive with fellow actors. I can sincerely say that wasn't the case with me.

Steve was one of the few actors who showed support during my contract dispute with Warner Brothers when I wanted a raise after three years on *77 Sunset Strip.* At the time, I was making $500 a week and would regularly receive $250,000 movie offers from various studios. Today, that would be the equivalent of a $10 million film offer. I had to turn them all down because of my obligation to the TV series.

This was not the first time a contract dispute had arisen at Warner Brothers. James Garner refused to go to work on *Maverick,* as did Clint Walker on *Cheyenne.* James Cagney, whose name appeared above the title in *The Public Enemy,* was under contract for $350 a week. Warner Brother's policy was always the same: "Not a penny more."

Surprisingly, I didn't get much sympathy from the acting community. Lucille Ball, whom I had not met before, read me the riot act one night at a party. Steve, who was having the same problem with Four Star Studios regarding *Wanted: Dead or Alive,* sent me a telegram saying that he respected me and to "hold my ground." I always appreciated his vote of confidence.

Later on, Steve and I bumped into each other a couple of times. When he first bought his house in Brentwood, known to everyone as "The Castle," he confided to me, "I have no idea how I'm ever going to pay for this place. You'd better believe I'm not going to be late for work one single day."

By the time Steve was married to Ali MacGraw in the seventies, he had become the world's number one box-office star. However, he liked to walk around incognito. One day I ran into him outside the Cock 'n Bull while window-shopping for antiques. A voice behind me asked, "Do you own this shop, Edd?" I turned to see a man with a full-grown mustache and beard, wearing a black sailor's cap. He looked like a hairy version of the Old Spice man.

"No, I just had lunch at the Cock 'n Bull," I replied.

He was pleasant enough, and we struck up a casual conversation. Then his voice started to sound familiar.

"You son-of-a-bitch! Steve?"

It was the one and only Steve McQueen, but he looked so unlike himself. I think that Steve had reached a level of superstardom that only a few in our industry have ever occupied and he needed a little anonymity.

I liked Steve, and I can proudly say he was my friend.

Edd Byrnes is a veteran actor who has worked in television, movies and the stage. He lives in Beverly Hills, California.

A Critic's Critique
Andrew Sarris

Film critic Andrew Sarris views McQueen as "the classic fatherless child." In *Love with the Proper Stranger* with Natalie Wood, the two discuss how they will handle bringing a child into the world after a whirlwind romance.

Steve McQueen turned out to be an interesting and introspective actor. He is irreplaceable and there's no one like him today, except perhaps Russell Crowe, who has some of McQueen's quality in *L.A. Confidential.*

The interesting thing about McQueen is that he's a classic fatherless child. Truffaut, who was also something of an orphan, once said, "When a child is not happy, he's never, ever happy as an adult." McQueen could never quite overcome all the anger, sorrow and pain he had as a child, and this came out in his acting. He was an interior actor, much in the vein of the modernist school—Brando, Dean, but he had a quality of his own, a quirkiness that was original. He wasn't talky, he didn't rationalize or apologize, and he was also extremely vulnerable. He communicated just the same. Some people are so numb they're simply blocks of wood, but he was very expressive. You can feel his pain.

I think of him as an action star, though one of his most effective performances was in *Love with the Proper Stranger*, with Natalie Wood. Now, they were two basket cases, full of vulnerability and pain, but they were fantastic together. Also, he's beautiful in *Soldier in the Rain* and *Baby, the Rain Must Fall* with Lee Remick. These were his key performances. However, what made him world famous was riding a motorcycle in *The Great Escape*. He dominated that film. He knew the escape probably would not succeed, but he was going to give it a try. That's a masculine trait, and it's very attractive. You think you're going to lose, but you're willing to go down fighting. That's Steve McQueen.

Andrew Sarris was a former film critic for the Village Voice. This passage originally appeared in the March 1999 issue of Interview.

Maturation of a Movie Star

William Claxton

This photo was taken by William Claxton for a 1964 *Paris Match* article. McQueen wore the hat as if he were Josh Randall from *Wanted: Dead or Alive*, which had been syndicated in France the year before. The show proved to be wildly popular with French audiences.

Steve McQueen appeared difficult to many people, because he was embarrassed that he had little education—although he was very intelligent. His wife read his scripts to him. We were on one of our trips, and he wanted to send a postcard to somebody and could hardly spell any of the words. My wife started kidding him about it because she didn't believe it, and he was defensive and embarrassed. Also he was deaf in one ear. Those two weaknesses made him crazy. When he became a big star, the pressure was on him for many different reasons and his paranoia blossomed. He became difficult to work with.

He took great care of his car collection, and kept it spotless. But rental cars? I remember on location just outside New Orleans, Ford gave the movie company a group of cars to use for publicity. Steve had a new Ford convertible. He'd say, "Hey Clax, I have the afternoon off, let's go." We smoked some dope and then drove way out in the country. Once he saw a clear road, he just floored it until the car started heating up. I said, "Steve, I smell the car." And he said, "Yeah, I know, don't worry about it." We were probably going over 100 mph, when smoke started coming out from under the floorboards and it became hot. I said, "Steve, this motor's on fire." He slowed down and said, "OK, now get ready to jump out." He slowed down to almost a stop, and I was first out of the car, followed by Steve. It burned right down to the ground, while he just sat laughing. The headline in the local paper the next day was STEVE MCQUEEN ESCAPES DEATH AS CAR BURNS.

When stopped by state troopers, he would charm them, and they would melt and say, "OK, Mr. McQueen, don't drive so fast." He knew how far he could push his luck, and how to play it.

I think that now would be a perfect time for him, because he was an iconoclast, and interesting-looking. He doesn't have that little-boy look that is so popular now. It's going to change as soon as that cycle is over, and we'll be back to having mature movie stars.

William Claxton was one of America's premier photographers and enjoyed a worldwide audience for his work. He passed away in 2009. This passage originally appeared in the March 1999 issue of Interview.

Movie Star vs. Actor
Norman Jewison

Steve McQueen wasn't an actor, he was a movie star. He had a large Roman head and pale blue eyes that never blinked. He photographed beautifully. But his star quality came from his believability on screen. It was more apparent on camera with him than other actors with more technique.

If you put Steve on an empty stage with a chair and a soliloquy to read, he wouldn't hold an audience. That took acting—a Laurence Olivier. But if I asked Steve to walk across a room for the camera, he would be natural and immensely appealing. Olivier would act the walk of a character. Steve would simply walk. The audience would be more convinced by Steve than Olivier.

Many top Hollywood movie stars were never talented actors in the theatrical sense. Yet they had a personal charisma and magnetism in front of the camera that made them unique. It was the look, the large expressive eyes, the walk, the body language, and the charm that made some people become movie stars and others just actors. Movie stars are always the same no matter what movie they are in. We always feel comfortable when they are on the screen. John Wayne, Humphrey Bogart, Cary Grant, Jimmy Stewart, Gary Cooper, Gregory Peck—all of them were personally more important than the characters they portrayed.

Left: McQueen and Jewison on the set of *The Cincinnati Kid*, New Orleans, 1965.

Right: McQueen and director Jewison discuss how the camera will pick up a shot in the graveyard scene for *The Thomas Crown Affair*, Boston, 1967.

Norman Jewison is an Oscar-winning film director, producer, actor and founder of the Canadian Film Center. He directed Steve McQueen in The Cincinnati Kid and The Thomas Crown Affair. This passage is from his 2004 autobiography, This Terrible Business Has Been Very Good To Me and appears courtesy of Key Porter Books.

A Brief Memory of Steve McQueen

Roy Frumkes

Opposite: Two of the biggest stars of their times—Steve McQueen and Ann-Margret in *The Cincinnati Kid.*

New Orleans was so entrenched in its own identity—Jazz, Creole and Cajun culture—that it was difficult to interest the city in Hollywood intrusions onto their turf. In order to earn their keep, film publicists were quite receptive to visitation requests from the *Tulane Hullabaloo,* the University newspaper, to generate some publicity. I happened to be the rag's Entertainment Editor when *The Cincinnati Kid* came to town, and was thrilled to be invited onto the downtown locations to watch the cast and crew work.

It was 1965. At the time I was unaware that Sam Peckinpah had been fired from the shoot. This was years before he successfully directed Steve McQueen in two wildly disparate features, *Junior Bonner* and *The Getaway.* He had been replaced by Norman Jewison, a thirty-nine-year-old Canadian director whose gifts weren't yet in full bloom; he'd done some light comedy, but *In The Heat of the Night* was still a few years up the road.

I was twenty, and enraptured with Hollywood and the star system. As soon as I arrived, the publicist shifted into gear. First up was Karl Malden, outgoing and overly friendly, remarking as he spotted my old reel-to-reel tape recorder "You must be a wealthy young college student…" Edward G. Robinson was gruff and required constant attention from his handlers, being seventy-two. He strolled around the French Quarter, scoffing derisively at every piece of art on display. Ann-Margret couldn't have been friendlier, but seemed oddly devoid of anything enlightening to impart: "How did you like working with Elvis Presley?" "I loved it." "What is your experience being on this film with actors like Steve McQueen and Edward G. Robinson?" "I love it."

The next level up in terms of access to royalty was Terry Southern. Southern was the author of *Candy* and *The Magic Christian,* and was considered a 'literary catch' in the tradition of writers like Raymond Chandler and William Faulkner who, in a previous era, were lured to Hollywood, mainly for the big bucks. Southern had recently co-authored *Dr. Strangelove* to great acclaim, and was on location with *The Cincinnati Kid,* polishing the screenplay as it was being filmed. The day I visited the shoot he was out perusing New Orleans graveyards, but we had lunch together later in the week, and our extensive interview mainly concerned the Kubrick film.

Which leaves Steve McQueen.

Upon meeting him, the actor struck me as fascinatingly complex. Trim and casually dressed, his features were not as accentuated as they appeared on celluloid. Obviously, the medium loved him.

He seemed introverted, perhaps caught up in his character, and despite his reticence, he exuded a powerful aura. It seemed to dominate the space around him for a good twenty or thirty feet in every direction. I've seen few actors who were naturally able to do that.

He shook hands, smiling slightly, and I sensed his bemusement—he wasn't sure why the publicist was wasting his time with a college student. However, he was also generous enough to make an effort to be cordial. I asked if I might possibly interview him later. Someone rode by on a motorcycle and revved the engine in obvious tribute. McQueen's face lit up, and he acknowledged the cyclist with a wave. He turned back to me, and said, "We'll see", in a stand-offish yet friendly way. I then watched him work for a while. He was professional, focused, and intense. No joking around whatsoever.

The publicist, an older man who'd been doing this at MGM for ages, was quite pleased that he'd introduced me around, and it looked good for him. He made sure I posed for pictures with all the actors, though somehow we missed McQueen. And we missed that interview as well. Several months later a première event was held in New Orleans, and again I was slotted to spend a little time with him, but his mother died and he left immediately, not staying for the festivities.

It felt strange watching the finished film, and I was unable to judge it objectively after I had been hanging around during production. It was following in the shadow of *The Hustler,* which had been released four years earlier, but the fact that it was in color, immediately and smartly distanced it from direct comparison. Philip Lathrop's cinematography struck me as consistently dark, moody and reflective of the filmmakers' vision, rather than the reality of the locations. Everything I learned there I was able to put to use decades later when making my own features. Jewison's direction drew tight, compelling performances out of the terrific cast. McQueen was the centerpiece, grounded and mesmerizing, around which the other actors fell into orbit. Not surprisingly, the movie holds up well even now.

Today, Daniel Craig is tipped as the new Steve McQueen, and I can see it. We have met, and he has some of the same reticent qualities, especially those eyes. Interestingly, it has taken over a quarter of a century for someone to come within striking distance of filling McQueen's shoes.

Roy Frumkes is a producer, screenwriter, author and the editor of Films in Review and filmsinreview.com

The Cincinnati Bengal
Karl Malden

Actor Karl Malden (left) compared Steve McQueen to a tiger when working together on *The Cincinnati Kid*.

Steve McQueen realized the importance of the challenge when he made *The Cincinnati Kid*, and I felt that he achieved the big leagues with this movie.

I played the part of a professional card dealer called Shooter, dealing in favor of The Kid (McQueen) so that he would win the game. He wanted to take some time off to rest, and he asked me to accompany him. Once in his room, he confronted me with the question "Are you cheating?" McQueen sprung at me like a tiger. He had the quality of appearing so tense and high that he was ready to explode at any minute.

Karl Malden started his career in 1940, and in 1951 he won the Oscar for his performance as Mitch in A Streetcar Named Desire. He died in July 2009.

Kissing Your Sister
Suzanne Pleshette

Steve McQueen felt brotherly towards *Nevada Smith* co-star Suzanne Pleshette, whom he first met in New York in the late fifties.

I first met Steve McQueen at an actor's party in New York, sometime in the late fifties. Only fourteen years old, I was with an older man, an actor acquaintance of Steve's. Though Steve didn't know me, he thought we were an inappropriate couple, and he offered me a ride home. From that day forward, until the day he died, he always treated me like a baby sister. He was protective and loving.

Several years later, we happened to be at the same party in Hollywood, and I asked Steve if he knew who the leading lady would be in *Nevada Smith*. He replied that he didn't know, and when I announced that it was me, his reaction was unexpected.

"God, no. You have to be kidding!" Steve said, slapping his forehead. I know why his reaction was as strong as it was—the script called for a scene in which we were to kiss.

Love scenes are particularly uncomfortable for actors, but for Steve, this was like kissing his sister. It was so awkward. We didn't know where to put our lips and we were terrible at it. We had never considered each other as a love interest. I knew of his reputation as a ladies' man and later discovered that Steve bedded practically all his co-stars. To this day, I don't know whether to be flattered or annoyed. When it came down to it, Steve never thought of me as a working actress, but as a kid, although I had some outstanding credentials. He just saw me as "Suzy".

In the movie, I was the only woman on location with thirty-six men. The backwoods of the Louisiana bayou were awful conditions for a woman to work under. If you needed to go to the bathroom, you had to excuse yourself and swim upstream. I think what Steve loved about me was that I behaved well under those conditions. He was extremely kind.

Suzanne Pleshette achieved television immortality in her role as Bob Newhart's wife on the seventies classic situation-comedy The Bob Newhart Show. She died in January 2008.

Clash of the Titans

L.Q. Jones

I worked with Steve McQueen twice during his career—in *Hell is for Heroes* and *Nevada Smith*.

Don Siegel of *Hell is for Heroes,* and Henry Hathaway, who was in charge of *Nevada Smith,* had quite different directing styles.

Siegel was someone who got along well with everyone and had a clever way of demonstrating what he wanted by example and observation. He provided an outlet for Steve, letting him do whatever he felt was best for the picture and it paid off.

Henry Hathaway was a director who nailed an actor's boots to the floor. Steve McQueen knew what he could do well as a performer. He would take a scene and work it out so that he could manipulate it to his advantage. If a director was unwilling to change the dialogue to Steve's liking, he could be difficult. With a director like Hathaway, who wants to go by the letter, you know there will be problems. In most of Hathaway's pictures, he is the one who prevailed. In *Nevada Smith*, it was a stand-off between the two.

L.Q. Jones was born Justus McQueen and adopted the name of the character he portrayed in his first film, Battle Cry. He was also one of Sam Peckinpah's favorite actors.

Opposite: In *Nevada Smith*, McQueen brought a unique cool to the American cowboy. This outtake shows him in an outfit that was never used in the final cut of the movie.

Right: Taming the wild beast in *Nevada Smith*. McQueen once famously said, "When a horse learns to buy martinis, I'll learn to like horses."

The Sound of McQueen
Robert Wise

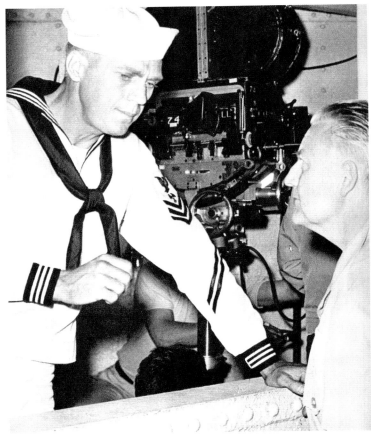

Top left: A rarely seen photo of McQueen, director Robert Wise and Candice Bergen, who are discussing an upcoming scene in *The Sand Pebbles*.

Top right: Robert Wise led McQueen to his only Oscar nomination for *The Sand Pebbles*.

In a single decade, McQueen went from being broke and hungry to living in a mansion on a hill.

In 1956, Steve was a $19 a day extra on a film I directed called *Somebody Up There Likes Me*. He came in dressed in a sport jacket, looking gangly and loose and had a little cap around the top of his head. It was his cocky manner, not fresh, but relaxed and a bit full of himself that caught my eye and I cast him in a small part. It was the part of a kid in a rooftop fight in New York.

A little later, I cast his wife, Neile, in *This Could Be The Night*. At the time, Steve was unemployed and a bit of a pest. Finally, I had to shoo him away from the set.

When I drove to his house in Brentwood, up the long winding driveway to ask him to play the lead role of Jake Holman in *The Sand Pebbles*, I couldn't help but think how times had changed.

Steve was the perfect choice for Jake. I've never seen an actor work with mechanics the way he did. He learned everything about operating that ship's engine, just as Holman did in the script. Jake Holman was a strong individual who didn't bend under pressure, and was desperately determined to maintain his own personal identity and pride, much like Steve, who was marvelous in the picture, because he had the attitude and looks to carry the dialogue. He was not only an emotional and instinctive actor, but a thinking actor.

You never quite knew what Steve's mood was going to be. Once, I was trying to line up a dolly shot. It was difficult, and then all of a sudden, I felt a tap on my shoulder and it was Steve. He said, "Now, Bob, about this wardrobe," and I blew up. I said, "Steve, for heaven's sake." I used a little stronger language than that, frankly. "Please don't bring that up now, I'm in the midst of something difficult. Let's talk about it tonight." Well, he was hurt, and he didn't speak to me for three days. There I was directing the star of the film, giving directions to him and he would listen to me, but no word came back from him.

When Steve saw the dailies and how good he looked, he decided to talk to me again. As a matter of fact, Steve never gave me a hard time again.

Robert Wise directed nine different actors in Oscar-nominated performances, and won two of his own for West Side Story and The Sound of Music.

A Most
Complicated Man
Candice Bergen

Top left: McQueen is the recipient of a kiss from co-star Candice Bergen, who says their relationship wasn't always so cheerful on *The Sand Pebbles*.

Top right: A pensive sailor on the bow of the *San Pablo*.

Above: Two shots of McQueen and Bergen.

Originally, I had no ambition to be an actress and it was lucky how it happened. Aged only nineteen, and after appearing in one movie called *The Group*, directed by Sidney Lumet, I received a call to take a screen test for Bob Wise for *The Sand Pebbles*.

Reporting for action in Taipei, I had to borrow a toothbrush from Bob because my luggage had been lost. I don't think anyone ever got to know Steve too well, and I certainly didn't, but he was understanding of my youth and how I was bored witless at the Grand Hotel, where the cast stayed. He was with his family and he included me in their activities.

Steve clearly suffered emotionally in life. He had experienced a painful and difficult childhood, and he was a textbook case of that kind of neglect. He grew up in the Boys Republic, and I think he carried the pain with him all his life. The hostility and resentment he felt caused tremendous mistrust and anger, and he was constantly testing people. He really simmered, which made him such a complicated, interesting and appealing presence on screen.

He was compelling in the role of Jake Holman because you saw him experiencing the dilemmas of the role which he communicated powerfully. He was also unpredictable and that's what was so charismatic about him on screen. He projected a tremendous sense of threat and menace. You just didn't know with him and he could turn on a dime either way. He could be unbelievably endearing and then so mistrustful. But he gave such a wonderful performance in that film.

Candice Bergen is an actress, author and photojournalist. This passage appears courtesy of 20th Century Fox.

A Real Head Scratcher
Mako

Character actor Mako said McQueen viewed him with suspicion but lightened up over time. The two were magnificent together in *The Sand Pebbles*, which garnered both actors Academy Award nominations.

I met Steve McQueen on the lot of 20th Century Fox shortly before we filmed *The Sand Pebbles*. He seemed like an unassuming type of fellow possessing a quiet confidence and charisma. He was wearing blue jeans, a blue polo shirt, sweat socks and sneakers.

Robert Wise left me to do my own acting without much direction. McQueen, however, liked to be prepared beforehand. In one scene in the engine room, I scratched my head during rehearsal and it aroused McQueen's suspicions.

"Are you going to do that again when we shoot?" McQueen asked. I responded that I didn't know. He thought I might be trying to steal the scene.

McQueen's acting impressed me. Not so much while working with him, but seeing the results afterwards. He came to know the camera so well. His technique was subtle and right on the money showing little wasted emotion. He chose to do less, and thus brought simplicity to the screen, and at the same time was the image of the American man.

Mako garnered an Academy Award nomination as Best Supporting Actor for his first film role, as the coolie Po-Han in The Sand Pebbles. He died in July 2006.

Born Ready
Richard Crenna

Steve and I had a wonderful relationship. I first met him prior to arriving in Taiwan to shoot *The Sand Pebbles*. Later, while settling into the hotel there with my wife and children, the phone rang. It was Steve.

"Hey, Dick," he said. "I'd like to come over and shuck."

I looked over at my wife and said, "What the hell is 'shuck'?" He wanted to see how we would fit together in the great scheme of things and whether the filming was going to be a collaborative effort or a competition. After talking for about ten minutes, I saw him relax, and we realized that we had quite a journey ahead of us on the film.

He was complicated in the sense that he was ambitious, but had insecurities that manifested themselves in interesting ways. He was a superlative actor, and without a doubt, *The Sand Pebbles* was my favorite Steve McQueen picture. He had never been better than he was in the film. You hear the comment "Born to play this role." He was just that.

Richard Crenna's acting career started in 1950 and continued up to his death in January 2003. His passage appears courtesy of 20th Century Fox.

All photos: Actor Richard Crenna felt that Steve McQueen was born to play the role of Jake Holman in *The Sand Pebbles*.

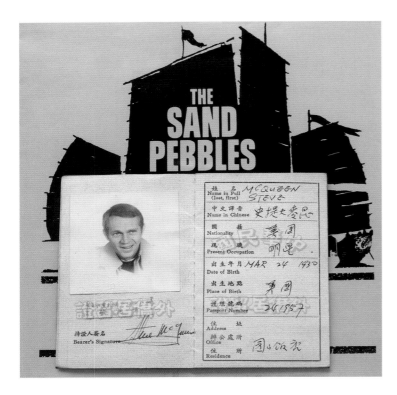

Kiss The Bride
Kaori Turner

Top left: Steve McQueen's Taiwanese passport, 1965.

Above and detailed opposite below: A contact sheet from a scene in *The Sand Pebbles*.

Millions of women would have given anything to walk down the aisle with Steve McQueen, but I had the next best thing.

I met Steve McQueen in Taiwan when he was filming *The Sand Pebbles*. The entire film crew stayed at the Ambassador Hotel in Hong Kong, where I was working as a dancer. One night, most of them came to the show to escape the daily grind of the set. Bill Turner, a makeup artist, seemed especially taken with me. A few days afterwards, Bill asked me out to dinner. Only two weeks later, he asked me to marry him. I said no at first.

The idea of moving to the United States had no appeal to me because I didn't want to live in a foreign land and spoke little English. Bill became sad and said he couldn't live without me. He decided to enlist the help of his friend, Steve McQueen, to vouch for him. At the time, I had no idea who Steve was. He seemed normal enough and I thought he was just trying to help out a friend. Steve sang Bill's praises, but it took the local police to clinch the deal.

One night, I was picked up by the local authorities for breaking Hong Kong's curfew laws. I was from Japan and not familiar with their customs. Bill and Steve came to the rescue. Steve's clout as a major movie star was a big part of why I was able to go home that night. A month-and-a-half later, Bill and I married on a ship anchored in Hong Kong. Steve stood in for my father, because I had no family at the wedding to represent me.

Bill and I were together for twenty-five years until his death in 1992. We shared a wonderful and full life together.

Many people say that Steve was a macho man, but for me, he was a regular guy—and a gentleman.

Kaori Turner is an award-winning makeup artist who was the first Japanese national to become a member of Hollywood's Makeup Artists Union. She resides in Los Angeles, California.

Coming Up For Air
Bill Bennett

Opposite and below: McQueen liked to scuba dive to relieve the tedium during the marathon shoot on *The Sand Pebbles*.

In 1966 it was my privilege to spend a day aboard the *San Pablo* while Steve McQueen was filming *The Sand Pebbles*. Needless to say, the visit was a highlight of my naval career.

My visit was arranged by Steve McQueen's makeup man, Del Acevedo. Del and I had been stationed together on a U.S. Navy ship in 1951. He had left the Navy shortly after, and years later our paths crossed again in one of the clubs at the Hilton Hotel in Hong Kong when my ship was visiting the port.

I met the film crew in front of their hotel around 6 a.m., where the bus waited to take us out to the *San Pablo*. On the way to the motor launch pier, Steve McQueen and his son Chad passed us in a small red convertible sports car.

I watched them shoot the scene where the soldiers aboard the *San Pablo* start firing at the Chinese. Because it was such an epic film, everything was done on a grand scale. The scene required hundreds of actors and during filming there were speed boats patrolling the bay to ward off any modern-day vessels that might sail within camera range. My fascination was short-lived, mostly because the pace was tedious at best.

During the lunch break, Steve and another actor went diving. Something in the water must have frightened them, because when Steve came up for air, he asked his buddy, "What was that? Did you see it?"

I was amazed at McQueen's endurance because he had to film another grueling scene when he returned from his dive. I never heard an "Okay, print" from director Robert Wise before I left, so I assume they continued until dark.

Bill Bennett is a retired sailor and resides in Washington.

A Stand-In Guy

John Norris

Top left: Taking a break from shooting
The Sand Pebbles on location in Hong Kong

Top right and bottom right: Enjoying
a spin on a Suzuki motorcycle.

Bottom left: Candid shot of McQueen taken
by John Norris during *The Sand Pebbles.*

I was a twenty-year-old army brat attending Tam College of Arts and Sciences in Taipei in 1966. I was invited by Steve to be both his stand-in and photo-double during the filming of *The Sand Pebbles* in Taiwan, before the production moved to Hong Kong and then back to the studio.

What kid could resist such an offer?

I have so many fond memories of Steve and the cast and crew while filming in Taiwan. I had a Triumph motorcycle and Steve had a cafe racer Suzuki, and we got on well. Believe it or not, Steve drove around in a Beetle when he wasn't on the bike, which was perhaps just as well, for director, Robert Wise, was not too pleased to see his big investment risking his limbs on a two-wheeler.

The scene I remember best was where Candice Bergen was trying to persuade Steve's character Jake, to go AWOL, and it included a kiss. While the lighting, sound and cameras were being attended to, Steve and Candy were off in makeup, so Mr. Wise had us go through the motions. Once the two stars arrived on set, Steve was uneasy with everyone around. Mr. Wise asked all non-essential people to leave, but Steve signaled that I should stay. Surprisingly, there seemed to be a little tension about the kiss. At the suggestion of going AWOL, his response was supposed to be something to the effect of, "Do you know what they will do when they find me?" I think there was supposed to be a pause before Steve continued the dialogue, but Candy responded, "What?" Steve never missed a beat and said, "They would cut my balls off."

Everyone howled with laughter. This broke the tension and the scene was reshot. I think Candy still had a smile on her face.

Our friendship continued, even after my draft notice arrived. I had dropped out of college to work on the film and was invited by Steve to go with the production to Hong Kong, but being somewhat of a patriotic brat, I took off for boot camp at Fort Ord instead. We corresponded for the next five years. I finished boot camp, intelligence training, and officer's candidate school before being shipped off to Vietnam for a thirteen-month stint. He sent me postcards while I was away.

After my return to the States, Steve and Neile invited my new wife, Jo Anne, and me to their Brentwood home. While the ladies worked on dinner, Steve and I test drove Neile's new pea green 911L Porsche with the "Sportamatic" transmission. It was frightening and hilarious riding in the car, which Steve had not previously driven, as it went into neutral whenever he touched the shifter.

I ran into Steve several years later in San Marcos, Texas, during the filming of *The Getaway*. It was impressive, watching both the sparks between Steve and Ali, and the relationship Steve had with director Sam Peckinpah. Suffice it to say, the two men were equally strong-headed and Sam's reaction to Steve firing off a blank behind him ended with the crew and co-star, Al Lettieri, breaking them apart as they rolled down a hill cursing each other!

I spoke to Steve by phone several times in the late seventies, but didn't know about his illness until I read about it in the papers. By then, he was unreachable, and I am not sure what I would have said had we spoken.

He was an excellent, dynamic actor. He once asked me what I thought about someone who had nothing, came from nothing and now had everything. It seemed that in private, he still had some self-doubt or insecurity, but his actions both on and off the screen belied this perception.

John Norris originally wrote this piece in 2000 for TheSandPebbles.com.

Hello Engine, I'm Jake Holman

Jim Fritz

Top left: Intensity was McQueen's trademark as an actor.

Top right: Smoking a cigarette during a break in *The Sand Pebbles.*

Middle right: With the film crew in Taiwan.

Bottom left: A shirtless McQueen working the water hose to keep the enemy at bay.

Bottom right: Giving specific instructions to the crew how to execute the scene.

In late 1965, I received a phone call from a public relations person employed by our Los Angeles Cummins Distributorship to tell me that they had recently sold a pair of C-180M Cummins marine engines to Solar Productions at 20th Century Fox. The folks at Solar had contacted the distributor to see if Cummins would be interested in a film about the use of the engines in the movie, *The Sand Pebbles.*

I told him that it could be the case, since this movie was a major production and carried an impressive list of actors. He suggested that I come out to see them at the studio as soon as possible. That spring, my wife and I drove our new Corvette from Indiana to Los Angeles where we had a meeting with the Solar folks. They wanted ten-to-fifteen thousand dollars to take all the footage already in the can and make a movie for our corporate use.

I had a better idea. Since the movie was to be shown on a "Road Show" basis, with all theater seats sold in advance like a Broadway play, I knew they wanted all the hype they could muster ahead of the opening. Cummins made marine engines for pleasure as well as work boats, and so I took a look at the schedule of shows and told them that we would be exhibiting our products in the New York Boat Show at the same time the movie was opening in New York. This was also true in Miami and Chicago. I suggested that if they would produce the film for us at no charge, I would see that it was exhibited in all our marine shows and build a special backwall that would highlight the movie as well as plug Cummins' role in it. After some discussion they agreed. When the meeting was over, they asked if we would like a tour of 20th Century Fox and since they didn't offer tours at Fox to the general public in those days, we said "yes!"

We not only had a memorable tour, but we were taken onto the set of *The Sand Pebbles,* where I stood behind Robert Wise as he directed Steve McQueen and others in the action scene where Jake came ashore to catch Frenchy and take him back to the boat, as he was AWOL. Jake was jumped by some of the locals and the scene lasted about a minute-and-a-half in the movie.

I had already met McQueen briefly in the late fifties when I was working in an imported car business in Fort Lauderdale, Florida. He came in with his wife and a new red Austin Healey 100 they had driven down to Florida from New York for a short vacation. He had just appeared in a live TV drama. His performance had impressed me, so I knew who he was when I saw him.

We didn't make contact on the set that day and I doubt that he even knew anyone else was there, apart from the crew, since this was a closed set. After the picture had opened in New York, we received an invitation to attend a première party at The Athletic Club in Indianapolis. Robert Wise, a native Hoosier, was to be the guest of honor. The head of the marketing group and I attended the event, and I was able to speak with Wise at some length.

We decided to call our short film *The Secret of the San Pablo,* as it pointed out that while steam engines were used in the original gunboats of the period, the more modern boat used in the movie had diesels. The smoke was produced by a machine they had on board. The selling point in our film was this: since shooting costs exceeded $50,000 a day, though not much by today's standards, they couldn't afford "sick" engines, so they chose Cummins. The film included footage from the movie and the studio was kind enough to give us Richard Crenna as the host. He also interviewed Robert Wise about the difficulties they had with the boat while making the film.

As I look at *The Sand Pebbles* today, I have even more respect for it than I did at the time it was made. It preaches a strong lesson about racial tolerance and learning to live with others who may be different than ourselves, which is something we still need to strive for in this country.

Jim Fritz retired from Cummins Engine Company in 1998 as the Director of Marketing Communications after thirty-six years with the organization. He originally wrote this piece in 2002 for TheSandPebbles.com.

The Essence of Cool, the Essence of Life

Albert Mora

Opposite: "High and tight" is how McQueen's character, Jake Holman, kept his hair length.

Born in 1958, I started life as a Steve McQueen fan when *Wanted: Dead or Alive* went on the air. My parents watched many an episode with me on their laps. I was a hyperkinetic toddler, but I would sit still to watch Josh Randall. When the commercial breaks started, I would cry. "Don't cry," they'd laugh, "Josh will be right back!"

It has been the same all my life. I am in perpetual motion, but when Steve McQueen is on the screen, he has all my attention, and when it's over, I miss him. He is my favorite actor and I have watched his movies many times. I love all his characters from the gunman who protected the Mexican village to the aging bounty hunter.

One day, shuffling along a crowded Chicago sidewalk, I spotted a bold yellow "McQueen" title in a bookstore window, and stopped in my tracks. Steve McQueen was dead! I bought the book asking myself, *"Why am I crying inside? What is it about Steve McQueen?"*

After reading, *Steve McQueen: Portrait of an American Rebel*, I felt the answer was the nature of life itself. We are billions of human beings in a swarm of activity driven by conscious and subconscious energy. Thinkers from all disciplines have studied these driving forces for centuries, and it always comes down to the same question. "What is the essence of a human being?" The answer is *the will to live, which* explains our behavior from the beginning of time.

In movies, we watch an actor face every test on the screen in microscopic detail. The measure of his greatness is the degree to which he projects the character's will to live. Steve McQueen succeeded convincingly. In my opinion, four elements made him the most believable action star in movie history.

First, in life he faced many significant challenges, which enabled him to perform his own version of vulnerability. He was abandoned by his father, and his mother was an intermittent and disastrous presence. He moved around often, struggled with school and grew up aimless. Steve McQueen's version of vulnerability was to understand when he was cornered. However, he was never anyone's victim. What followed vulnerability was deft action.

Second, he was obsessed with realism. Starting with his work on *Wanted: Dead or Alive* and to the end of his career, Steve never indulged in embarrassing scenes where he defeated a hundred of the enemy with a hundred bullets in him. He had the genius and conviction to change many a script and to take heroism to the brink of believability, but never beyond.

Third, Steve McQueen had exemplary physical ability. In *The Magnificent Seven* he fired his pistol with Marine-trained deftness. In *The Cincinnati Kid*, he nearly threw Karl Malden through a wall, and in *The Sand Pebbles,* he dispatched a bully with a few quick, deadly blows. He turned getting in and out of a race car into physical poetry in *Le Mans*, and risked his life riding a motorcycle through desert and mountains alongside the most accomplished motorcyclists in the world for *On Any Sunday*. Every one of these scenes and hundreds more, are unforgettable because Steve McQueen's strength, agility, and coordination, looked spectacular in motion.

Fourth, and most importantly, the giant screen revealed that Steve McQueen didn't merely act; he demonstrated the will to live. Steve McQueen lived life to its maximum and fought to the end. He died bravely.

Albert Mora is a businessman, musician and lifelong Steve McQueen fan. He resides in Crown Point, Indiana, with his wife Barbara and their three daughters.

The Roots of Growing Up Determined

Veronica Valdez

Opposite: Aboard the *San Pablo*, where McQueen shot a majority of his scenes in *The Sand Pebbles*.

Left: McQueen's "lost boy" quality was catnip to women.

You don't realize as a child, the impressions that will stick with you as an adult. Watching Steve McQueen die in *The Sand Pebbles*, hit me hard when I was about seven-years old in the early seventies. He played Jake Holman, a man with piercing blue eyes. I didn't understand much of the movie, being so young, but I remember crying when Jake was shot. I still remember his dying words, "What happened? What the hell happened?" It's a sadness I recall to this day.

Then came *Papillon*. Steve played a prisoner who studied the break of the ocean waves, in an attempt to escape the hell of the penal colony. It didn't make sense to me. All I could think was, "Why didn't he just wait and serve his time?'" Children call it as they see it. By the time I saw *The Thomas Crown Affair*, I was hooked.

I began to read about Steve's life, especially about his youth. He seemed even then, determined to live life on his own terms. I visited his childhood home of Slater, Missouri, and the Boys Republic in Chino, California. I have a better understanding of why Steve appeared to gravitate toward movies involving determination. He may not have been the world's best actor, but he seemed to choose roles that reflected a part of his life with which he could identify. Maybe it was his way of sending a message to others to create a life on their own terms.

I can only imagine the drive in him to change to the man he later became. He grew up in a dysfunctional home without a father. His young mother left the farm for a city life that must have been so exciting back in the 1920s. She never grew up. Steve's life was transient, shuttled back and forth between his mother's single girl life in the city and Uncle Claude's farm. There was no consistent formal education and one can imagine the painful, lonely existence that forced him to become self-reliant at an early age. This upheaval must have played a key role in his emotional development, but Steve didn't let his past limit his future, though it seemed to color it

somewhat, as it does for all of us. That is what I respect the most about him—taking life head-on with a determination to succeed.

It's easy to blame the world for misfortune and our lot in life. Steve became a star, and was rich financially and later, in love. He could have fallen into the narcissism of Hollywood and never looked back. But he didn't. Although he was notorious for being tight-fisted, Steve never forgot what life was like for him as a child. He gave back publicly and privately to those in need—not just materially, but of himself. He visited the Boys Republic often, speaking with the boys, sharing his life story, letting them know that someone understood because he had walked those halls. *Life* magazine documented one such visit in its July 12, 1963 issue. Steve assured the boys they also could live the school's motto of "nothing without labor" and reap the true success life gives to industrious and compassionate hearts and minds.

I grew up as one of the East Los Angeles working poor, but was blessed with loving parents, who despite being unskilled laborers, worked hard to provide for their three daughters. My early education was of low caliber, but that didn't stop me. I labored without knowing where life would take me, forging ahead, without letting anyone dictate my possibilities. I worked my way through college to a wonderful career and the opportunity to travel the world. Like Steve, I preach "nothing without labor" and give back as much as possible.

Steve impressed on me that determination would lead to where I wanted to be. He may be remembered as the "King of Cool", but to me he was the kid of humble beginnings, who took the world by storm and never forgot where he came from. More of us should aspire to such a legacy of humanity and humility.

Veronica Valdez is an International Trade Sales Analyst with Bank of America. She lives in Los Angeles, California.

"DAY OF THE CHAMPION"

POSITIVE FILM

Can 1 & 1A   Goodwood Tests

Nurburgring

For Bob Can 2		Race Day - Selected Roll
For Bob 3		Race Day - Selected Roll - Helicopter Shots
	4	Practice Day - Selected Roll
For Bob 5		Camera Tests - Selected Roll
	6	Race Day - Hold Roll
	7	Race Day - Hold Roll
	8	Race Day - Hold Roll
	9	Race Day - Hold Roll - Helicopter Shots
	10	Race Day - Hold Roll - Paddock Shots
	11	Practice Day - Hold Roll
	12	Practice Day - Hold Roll
	13	Selected T/M Plate Shooting Back
Jo Edwards	14	Selected T/M Plates Shooting Back and Forwards
	15	Selected T/M Plates Shooting Forwards
	16	Selected T/M Plates Shooting Forwards on Car
5-17-67	17	Hold T/M Plates - Pits and Grandstand
	18	Hold T/M Plates - Paddock and Grandstand
	19	Hold T/M Plates - Shooting Back with Cars Following
	20	Hold T/M Plates - Shooting Back and Forwards
	21	Camera Car Tests
	22	Camera Car Tests
	23	Camera Car Tests
	24	Camera Car Tests
	25	Exploitation Roll
	26	Exploitation Roll
	27	Exploitation Roll
	28	Exploitation Roll
Jo Edwards	29	Selected T/M Plate - Shooting Forwards (Additional print)
5-17-66	30	Selected T/M Plate - Shooting Backwards (Additional print)
	31	Selected T/M Plate - Shooting Backwards - Printed for Night

— HAVE BEEN SCREENED

Day of the Champion

Robert Relyea

Opposite: Robert Relyea, seen in both photos, was the Vice-President of Solar Productions and Steve McQueen's right hand man from 1966 to 1970.

Bottom right: A list of background footage shot for *Day of the Champion*, a film that Warner Brothers was preparing for Steve McQueen. However, delays on *The Sand Pebbles* forced the studio to shut down production.

It is well known that Steve McQueen didn't like to lose. I saw firsthand one of the few times he lost a race to make a movie, and it wasn't pretty.

I was Steve's right hand man at Solar Productions in the late sixties. I had worked with him before on the films *Never So Few, The Magnificent Seven, The Great Escape* and one you may not have heard of, *Day of the Champion.* That's because it was never made. But it certainly wasn't for a lack of trying.

In late 1964, directors John Sturges and John Frankenheimer had the same idea, to make a movie centered around the Grand Prix race. Anytime you make a movie, you always want to base it on a book so that you're not accused of stealing. In this case, Frankenheimer read Robert Daley's *The Cruel Sport* and talked about adapting it into a movie called *Grand Prix.* Daley was receptive to the idea and Frankenheimer started negotiations with McQueen.

A few days later, McQueen had an argument with producer Ed Lewis, who was going to make the film with Frankenheimer. Steve then contacted Sturges to set up a deal at Warner Brothers for *Day of the Champion.* Since the movie would take some time to prepare, it enabled Steve to first shoot *The Sand Pebbles.*

"You go to Thailand and I'll set up the picture," Sturges told McQueen.

No one in Hollywood wants to make a movie on the same subject, at the same time, as another studio—especially about racing. There might be enough of an audience for one film, but the market could not bear two. It became an ugly fight to see who could complete their film first.

Frankenheimer scored first, when he set up a deal at MGM for *Grand Prix.* He quickly gathered a small film crew for the 1965 race in Monaco. Sturges retaliated by getting studio head Jack Warner to spring for a full-page ad announcing principal photography for *Day of the Champion.* Frankenheimer returned the volley by hiring James Garner for the lead in his film. Garner just happened to be McQueen's neighbor. Don't ever let it be said they play fair in Hollywood.

Sturges dispatched a crew to Brands Hatch and Reims, where he shot loads of racing footage of a man in a green helmet. He also began constructing a script with Ken Purdy, a well-known sportswriter.

The two competing directors were flying all around the world, hiring racing crews away from each other and trading personal insults. Hurting McQueen's cause was the fact *The Sand Pebbles* had gone from a nine-week shoot into a nine-month marathon.

A week before principal photography began on *Day of the Champion,* I received a late night phone call from studio head, Jack Warner, who was in Monte Carlo. Jack loved gambling and never failed to tell me when he cleaned up at the tables. At the end of this particular conversation, Jack said casually, almost as an afterthought, "Oh yeah…pull the plug on the racing picture. We're not going to beat them. *Grand Prix* will be the first to the theaters—I don't want to be second. Shut it down."

"But Jack…"

"Send everybody home," he said without a trace of emotion.

It was heartbreaking for me because of all the time I had put into pre-production. We had been filming second unit shots for almost a year, had a million feet of racing footage in the can and spent close to $4 million. For Steve, I'm sure it was worse. He didn't talk to James Garner for almost two years.

"Saw *Grand Prix,* man," Steve said when he finally bumped into Garner at his mailbox. "Not bad." It was the only compliment Steve could muster.

Steve and I never liked coming in second and to top it off, we weren't good losers. Enough time had passed to where we could finally talk about the subject again. I said, "One day we're going to make that racing film and it will be the death of us all." That movie turned out to be *Le Mans,* and I didn't realize how prophetic that statement would be.

Robert Relyea is retired from the film industry and lives in Westlake Village, California.

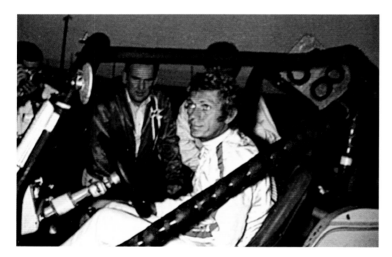

Bench Racing with McQueen

Tom Madigan

Opposite: McQueen and fellow actor and neighbor, James Garner (bottom left photo), take a spin in a "Prinz" buggy at Ascot Park Raceway in Gardena, California, August 1969.

I was introduced to Steve McQueen back in the sixties by my longtime friend Tony Nancy. Steve would appear, often late at night, at Tony's legendary upholstery shop in Sherman Oaks to sit around and "bench race" about cars and motorcycles. As long as the gathering remained private, McQueen was one of the guys, laughing and telling stories. But if a group of strangers or outsiders discovered that Steve McQueen was around, the scene would quickly dissolve, and Steve would make an abrupt personality change, taking on the arrogance of a movie star. Tony, who was well known for his temper, would start telling the gatecrashers to leave his shop before he tossed them out.

However, the good times far outweighed the awkward. Sometimes he would bring his son Chad, or other racers like Bud Ekins to share in the storytelling. Steve always felt secure within the confines of Tony's shop and the two similar personalities became good friends. Tony later became General Manager of McQueen's Solar Plastics Engineering Company for a short period and was also responsible for restoring the interiors of several of his cars. Tony would always defend McQueen against those who spoke ill of him and proclaim how capable he was with cars and racing.

I was editor of *Off-Road* magazine when racing in Baja became recognized as a legitimate sporting event. At the time, Vic Hickey, owner of Hickey Enterprises in Ventura, California, was one of the leading manufacturers of off-road equipment in the country. Hickey had also developed a racing machine called the "Baja Boot" powered by a Chevy V-8 engine. Vic and his wife Lee invited me to tag along with them for the running of the Mexican 1000 Baja Race.

Hickey had persuaded Steve McQueen to drive the "Baja Boot" with one condition—that he acted like a race driver and not a movie actor. Without showing the slightest fear, McQueen slid behind the wheel and took to the dirt with a vengeance. It was not his driving that impressed me, but the fact that whenever he screwed-up or abused the race car, Hickey would chew his tail up one side and down the other. McQueen did not react like a prima donna movie star, but would stand quiet like a child getting instructions from a parent.

About a year before his passing, I met with Steve at his airplane hangar at the Santa Paula Airport near Ventura, California. Several weeks earlier I had shot photos of Steve flying a Stearman bi-plane he had bought from a friend of mine named John Shuebeck. I was returning to Santa Paula to deliver some prints of that flying adventure. Steve gushed over the images—especially when he discovered that I wasn't going to send any of them to the *National Enquirer*.

I noticed that Steve looked tired. He was sporting a scruffy beard, his eyes were dull, and his voice seemed raspy. He claimed to be getting over a bad cold. After some small talk, Steve invited my wife, Darlene, and me into his hangar for a tour and a detailed account of the hundreds of antique toys and auto memorabilia he had there. Then a most unusual event took place.

Possibly feeling protected from the outside world by the closed doors of the hangar, Steve dropped into an old wooden swivel chair and started talking about motorcycle riding, running the Baja, and other random bench racing. He talked about how much he loved flying his airplanes. There was no conversation about his movie roles, just plain racer talk. After a couple of hours, he said he had to close up and head home. We stepped out into a cool breeze blowing from the nearby ocean. Steve thanked me again for the photos. He promised to sign a poster from his movie *Le Mans* that I had forgotten to bring. We shook hands and he disappeared into the hangar. I never saw Steve McQueen again, but that day provided an insight to the fact that beneath the movie star facade there was the heart of a real racer.

Tom Madigan has been a part of California car culture since the fifties. He not only competed against drag racing's pioneers, he has been writing about them as a contributor to Motorcade magazine, a feature editor for Popular Hot Rodding magazine, and the author of several books.

Tailor Made for McQueen

Alan R. Trustman

Above: A natural athlete, McQueen mastered polo in a matter of weeks for his role in *The Thomas Crown Affair* at Myopia Hunt Club, Hamilton, Massachusetts.

Opposite: *The Thomas Crown Affair* brought Steve McQueen out of blue jeans and a T-shirt into three-piece suits and ties. This added millions of females to his legion of fans.

I'll be the first person to admit that I didn't want Steve McQueen to play the part of a distinguished Bostonian called Thomas Crown in a screenplay that I wrote. And I wasn't alone.

Director Norman Jewison didn't want him, and neither did United Artists head Walter Mirisch. I had created the role of Thomas Crown for one man—Sean Connery. If he didn't do it, perhaps Rock Hudson or Jean-Paul Belmondo could pull it off. Steve McQueen wasn't on anybody's radar.

Thomas Crown was tailored three-piece suits; McQueen wore blue jeans and a T-shirt. Crown stirred and sniffed a glass of brandy before tasting it; McQueen liked nothing better than the taste of a beer. Crown played the sport of the bluebloods, polo; McQueen raced motorcycles in the desert.

It was a strange situation. Norman Jewison held in his hand the hottest script in town, and no one was available to play the lead, except for Steve McQueen, who was keen to take it. Finally, exasperated, Jewison gave in and awarded the part to Steve. McQueen's signature on the dotted line meant guaranteed ticket sales. So I went back to work on my script, making adjustments for Steve's acting abilities.

For three days, ten hours a day, I viewed every piece of footage on Steve and made a checklist of what the actor could and could not do. I discovered that if he was comfortable and stayed within a certain range of characterization, he was terrific. The moment he become uncomfortable, you could squirm watching him.

When I first met with McQueen, I explained the character of Thomas Crown and then we discussed his range as an actor. "You can be the new Humphrey Bogart. You are shy and you don't talk too much. You are a loner, but a person with integrity. You're quiet, and gutsy as hell. You like girls, but are basically shy with women. Your smile is tight, just around your mouth, and you don't show your teeth. You never deliver a sentence with more than five or ten words because paragraphs make you lose interest or something goes wrong with your delivery. As long as you stay with that, you can be number one."

The reason my movies made money, I'm convinced, is not due to the quality of the scripts. A movie is made by force of the personality that dominates the picture, and if that person has a clear idea of what is needed for the film, and he is a strong central character, the result is a terrific picture. I went over this with McQueen and he dominated *The Thomas Crown Affair*.

Alan R. Trustman is the screenwriter of The Thomas Crown Affair and Bullitt.

Vicki and Crown
Faye Dunaway

Right: McQueen said *Thomas Crown* co-star Faye Dunaway was the most formidable of all his leading ladies. She in turn said he was an old-fashioned movie star with an abundance of charisma and screen presence.

With Steve McQueen as my co-star, it was my first time to play opposite someone who was a great big old movie star, and that's exactly what Steve was. He was one of the best-loved actors around, one whose talent more than equaled his sizeable commercial appeal. Steve, I loved. He was darling. He was daunting. Steve McQueen was an absolute professional, and he knew what was necessary technically to achieve his performance every time he went in front of the camera.

Steve was all sinewy and tough, but at the same time he had such vulnerability. He definitely had archaic notions about women. If he said it once to me, he said it a million times, "A good woman can take a bum from the streets and turn him into a king." He believed a good woman was terribly important in a man's life.

Steve had so much charisma and he seemed to trigger those nurturing instincts in women. He was a chauvinist—notoriously so—but a chivalrous one to me. There was a strange dynamic between us.

We'd both grown up on the wrong side of the tracks; but by the time I appeared in *Thomas Crown* I'd shaken off anything that might hint of that. I could walk into an art auction or the polo club with absolute confidence. I could order from a menu in French. I knew good wines from bad. Steve, on the other hand, never stopped feeling he was a delinquent and any day he'd be found out.

Steve, friends said, didn't know how to deal with someone like me, who was intelligent and not inclined to the old male-female games that he knew how to win. For my part, I saw him as such an icon. That shade of distance between us ended up working well in creating the relationship between Vicki and Crown. That's what they call chemistry, when the unspoken, underlying realities of the actors—as people—connect with intensity. Steve and I had that in spades.

Faye Dunaway is an Academy Award, Emmy and Golden Globe-winning actress. This passage is reprinted with the permission of Simon & Schuster, Inc. from Looking For Gatsby: My Life by Faye Dunaway with Betsey Sharkey. Copyright © 1995 by Faye Dunaway. All rights reserved.

Con-Ferring with McQueen

John Harting

Opposite: The *Thomas Crown* dune buggy, a six-cylinder Chevrolet Corvair on a VW chassis, has become a movie icon.

The dune buggy used in *The Thomas Crown Affair* was built in the City of Angels and I was lucky enough to work on the team of mechanical "midwives" who helped deliver this baby to the silver screen.

In 1967, I was a twenty-one-year-old student at Los Angeles State University working part-time at Con-Ferr Manufacturing Company in Burbank. They primarily made four-wheel drive accessories and sold new Toyota Land Cruisers with Chevrolet engines.

That spring, owner Pete Condos asked me to find a Chevrolet Corvair six-cylinder engine for a special dune buggy Con-Ferr was making for Steve McQueen's new movie.

Con-Ferr had been involved in the creation and restoration of cars, hot rods and dune buggies since 1961. Back in the sixties, dune buggies weren't fancy. When someone wanted to build a cheap one, they looked for a four-cylinder Volkswagen engine. The VW's were popular because they provided a good floor pan, the engines were air-cooled and they had rear suspension, which meant they had good traction. But McQueen wanted more horsepower, which is why he specifically asked for a Corvair engine. I found one in a wrecking yard and brought it back to the shop where it was steam-cleaned and prepped.

We then attached a VW transaxle and chassis. The body was all hand-laid fiberglass by Eckley Turr, an excellent artist as well as a colorful character. McQueen also asked for additional touches, such as a wraparound windscreen, sunken headlights beneath plastic covers, wide tires on mag wheels and a luggage rack on the back.

The movie star, who was at the height of his career at that time, struck an imposing figure. He came by to check on its progress on two occasions. Both times he drove a red Maserati roadster, wearing a T-shirt and blue jeans. McQueen walked in and said "Hello boys," to the team of people working on the buggy. He seemed to be a private man, but he was laid back and casual, and polite to those he interacted with. He left as quietly as he came.

The car, like so many props in McQueen movies, became iconic to car buffs. Soon after the movie was released, Con-Ferr received several requests from celebrities such as Dick Smothers and Connie Stevens, for custom-built buggies.

It's pleasing to be connected in some small way to a piece of movie history.

John Harting is the Equipment Maintenance Supervisor for the Los Angeles County Metropolitan Transportation Authority and resides in Norco, California.

Two Wheeled Impact
George Derrah

Elegantly dressed for *The Thomas Crown Affair*.

Steve McQueen knew how to make a lasting impression.

I met McQueen in the summer of 1967 when he was in Beverly, Massachusetts, filming *The Thomas Crown Affair*. He came with his two kids one day to our family business, Brown's Bike Shop, looking for some bikes. I was fifteen at the time, fixing flats and oiling up chains. He sure didn't look like a movie star with his sun cap, T-shirt and painter's pants.

"Howdy boys," he said to Mike, my co-worker, and me. I had no clue who he was but Mike certainly did. After working for a minute, he peered around the corner saying that he thought the gentleman was Steve McQueen. "Who?" I asked.

"Steve McQueen, man. *The Great Escape. The Magnificent Seven. The Sand Pebbles.* He's great." Mike was so worked up that some of his enthusiasm rubbed off on me.

My father, who everyone knew as "Brownie," had just finished a transaction with two ladies and introduced himself to Steve. I'm not sure if he knew who Steve McQueen was either, but he held the attitude that Steve should probably know him.

"My name is Steve McQueen and I would like some bikes for my kids. I was told this was the place to come." My father assured him it was and then introduced us to the star.

"Well fellas, this is Steve. What did you say your last name was?" my father asked.

"McQueen," he replied politely.

"This is Steve McQueen. He's from Hollywood," my father finished his introduction. I shook his hand while Mike let him know that he was a big fan, especially of *The Great Escape*.

"Did you do your own motorcycle stunts?" Mike asked.

"Some of them," Steve smiled. McQueen only took credit for what he did.

After we exchanged pleasantries, McQueen picked out a few bikes, a portable General Electric AM/FM radio, and some assorted items. He ran up a sizeable tab of about $350, which was a lot of cabbage in our shop at the time. About twenty minutes later, we loaded the bikes in his car and McQueen wrote out a check.

After Steve and his family left, my dad pulled out the check.

"I don't know if this will clear or not, but at least I'll have something to put on the wall if it does."

George Derrah is the proprietor of Brown's Bike Shop in Beverly, Massachusetts, which is where he resides.

Above: McQueen and Faye Dunaway at Crown's unfinished beach house, Crane's Beach, Massachusetts.

Right: A signed song sheet for "Windmills of Your Mind", the theme music for *The Thomas Crown Affair*.

Summer of '67
Jack Good

In the summer of 1967, I was a twenty-three-year-old college student looking to earn a little extra cash on the side. When it was announced *The Thomas Crown Affair* was going to be filmed in the Boston area, it provided welcome employment for a number of young people as well as the local police.

The movie was filmed in three contiguous communities: the polo and golf sequences at the Myopia Hunt Club in Hamilton, the bank robbery scene in Beverly, the dune buggy and beach sequences at Crane's Beach in Ipswich, located about twenty-five miles north of Boston. It was thought the film would be a wonderful opportunity for tourism.

I was hired as the first-aid man at Crane's Beach, where everyone worked for four weeks on pre-production and three weeks of shooting.

I watched Steve McQueen ride and eat up the sand dunes in his custom-made dune buggy. He was relaxed and seemed much more available on the set than his co-star, Faye Dunaway. While he was open and congenial, she showed up for her shots and then disappeared. The feeling around McQueen was that of a star, but you didn't need to tread too lightly. He went out of his way to make people feel comfortable around him.

There's no question that what kept Steve going was the dune buggy scene. While it comes off as loose and unrehearsed, the cast and crew spent a lot of time perfecting the way they were going to shoot it, especially how the dune buggy approached the camera. It was this scene that Steve cared about the most, and they had to get it right.

Another shot took place with McQueen and Dunaway sitting on the partially built deck of Thomas Crown's beach house. It was a short scene, but it took weeks to prepare the fireplace. The bricks and wood were hauled in by a bulldozer because the set was housed on such a remote part of the coast. The only mementos I have are Instamatic pictures I shot of the set. I find it hard to believe it was more than four decades ago.

It was a positive experience for everyone involved and a boost to the local economy. We've had a few films made in this area because it's so picturesque. Not one, however, is as special or enigmatic as *The Thomas Crown Affair*.

Jack Good is the vice president of the Beverly Bank in Beverly, Massachusetts, where he also resides.

McQueen for a Day

Ed Donovan

Above: McQueen and former Boston police officer, Ed Donovan, 1967.

Right: An honorary badge given to Steve McQueen by the Boston Police Department.

With the announcement that Steve McQueen was coming to Boston to shoot *The Thomas Crown Affair*, the city took every step to ensure his safety.

Whenever a celebrity came to town, the city of Boston was obligated to offer them police protection. Back in 1967, I was a plain-clothes cop assigned to protect McQueen. The first day was uneventful, but on the second day an assistant director pulled me aside and said, "Mr. McQueen's stand-in has taken ill. You're his height, his build and you look like him. Would you mind filling in?" Would I mind being Steve McQueen for a day? Who would turn that down?

McQueen was a man who liked his privacy and wasn't comfortable with fanfare. No matter how much I admired him, I just couldn't bring myself to ask for an autograph. I remember one cop walked up to him and had the nerve to say, "Hey Steve, my wife told me to tell you that she'd love to have your shoes under her bed anytime." Steve smiled, but he looked uncomfortable. Afterwards, I said to the cop, "What is wrong with you? Why would you say a thing like that?"

I had the feeling Steve liked cops. At the time of my assignment, I had to wear a suit and a tie, and in his role as Thomas Crown, McQueen was required to wear three-piece suits all day. He asked me if I ever became accustomed to it.

"Never," I replied. "I can't wait to take them off at the end of the day." Steve was like me—he was more comfortable in blue jeans and a T-shirt even though he cut quite a striking figure in his expensive suits.

I didn't take my big assignment as his stand-in as seriously as I should. The sixties were some of the busiest drinking days of my life. Thoughts of suicide continuously ran through my mind due to depression. I was not only drinking, but was taking Quaaludes as well. I certainly did on that day. I felt I had to appear tough. Of course, who was more macho than Steve McQueen? Well, he noticed my hands were shaking and walked over to me.

"How you doin'? Have a rough night?" No one else knew my torment, except McQueen.

"Frankly, I could use a stiff drink right about now," I admitted. He just smirked and said he could use one as well.

I think McQueen respected me because he knew I was a blue collar worker. I felt he didn't completely trust people and was somewhat a loner like myself. He recognized that I was uncomfortable as a cop, needing help. Though I was outwardly macho, I was lonely inside.

Later, I became an actor and perhaps learned more from watching McQueen than anyone else. He was definitely a proponent of less is more, cutting the dialogue if he could. He would speak slowly and use his eyes to emphasize what he said. He was a master reactor.

McQueen also cared deeply about his craft and was always on the set watching and learning. Many actors disappear or go into their dressing rooms when they're not shooting, but not McQueen. He was the kind of actor who wanted to make sure everything was perfect. He wasn't just part of the scene—he felt he was a part of the movie.

It was a shame that he died so young as there were a lot of good movies ahead. But he had a full life, and I'm proud of my small but personally significant association with him.

Ed Donovan is a retired Boston policeman and a veteran SAG actor. He is also the editor/publisher of In Focus, a magazine devoted to film, television and the arts industry in Florida.

Taking the dune buggy for a spin during a
break in filming on *The Thomas Crown Affair.*

Divided Soul
Haskell Wexler

Steve McQueen was nervous about playing Thomas Crown. He was
not comfortable in a suit and tie, but for the film, he wore one in almost
every scene. Steve never revealed to me his anxiety but it was obvious
to everyone around him that he was feeling the pressure.

I generally only talked to Steve about cars. We went tearing away from
the set in a dune buggy one day and the engine blew up. We were
stranded for about forty minutes and that's when I got to know the real
Steve McQueen. I think he just wished he didn't have to go back to the
set and be Thomas Crown for that day.

*Academy Award winner Haskell Wexler was the cinematographer on The
Thomas Crown Affair.*

A Hot Commodity

John Bartlett

STEVE McQUEEN *in "The Crown Caper"*

Above and right: In the years since his death, Steve McQueen has become a fashion icon. These two pictures taken on the set of *The Thomas Crown Affair* are proof that McQueen's look and image are timeless.

For my first collection with Byblos, in the Spring and Summer of 1999, we wanted to capture the spirit of Steve McQueen. I referred back to *The Thomas Crown Affair* and the idea of him as a playboy who's stylish and sexy but also a little bit dangerous. Much of what made him a great star was his looks and amazing body, but now these qualities are more common in actors, , perhaps as it can now be more easily obtained by surgery.

John Bartlett is a fashion designer who resides in New York City. This passage originally appeared in the March 1999 issue of Interview.

Hipster's Jive
Jacqueline Bisset

Jacqueline Bisset thought her *Bullitt* co-star was jumpy and nervous.

I was brought in to screen test for Steve McQueen for the role of Cathy in *Bullitt*. It was a wonderful experience.

Steve was so enthusiastic. Jumpy and wild and on his toes. He was so hyped up we never seemed to finish any discussion.

He would rush up to me and say, for example, "Hey, you're a soul chick and you go up to these dudes, and man, you really dig the scene?" I would think, what on earth is he talking about. His language was very American.

He was happiest on his bike. He took me for a ride once on the back, and I loved it. Neile came up with the kids and Steve almost seemed fiercely paranoid, so protective about his family and private life. Yet somehow he had this most terrific warmth.

Jacqueline Bisset has been an international film star since the late sixties.

That's Hollywood!
Peter Yates

McQueen deep in conversation with *Bullitt* director Peter Yates.

The William Morris Agency had been trying to persuade me to leave England for a shot at directing films in Hollywood. I had three films under my belt, but didn't want to come to America to shoot a movie called *Bullitt*.

"I'm not coming to America to make that kind of film!" I told my agent. Later, I came to my senses and decided, who was I to say no?

At the time, I didn't know of Steve McQueen's reputation for being hard on directors. I believe my English accent gave me a distinct advantage, because Steve took it as a sign that I was much cleverer than I was.

Steve was always right on the edge of everything and used his insecurity as a testing device. We developed a routine over time: Steve would announce something as awful and I would tell him it was fine. Quite often he thought, if he said he was worried, he could make other people look and examine it. This is something many of the big stars do.

Steve also displayed incredible willpower. I accompanied him in the green Ford Mustang, on one of the hill-jumping sequences to keep an eye on him. After one of the jumps, I had to tell him to slow down because we were out of film.

"That's nothing," Steve replied. "We're out of brakes." McQueen managed to slow the Mustang by switching down the gears and turning the car onto a street that inclined upward. When the car came to a full stop, we roared with nervous laughter.

Bullitt did wonders for my career. I would be hired for a job and be told, "We want a chase scene like in *Bullitt*." It's annoying at times, because people talk more about *Bullitt* than any of my other films. I've had two films nominated for an Academy Award and they still want to talk about that damned car chase. That's Hollywood for you.

Peter Yates' career has spanned nearly fifty years as a writer, director and producer. His best known work is Bullitt, which was added to the National Film Registry in 2007.

Top and bottom photo: Don Gordon co-starred with Steve McQueen in three films, including *Bullitt*.

What's in a Name?

Don Gordon

Steve McQueen and I were close friends, but it took him a while to warm up to me. It took him even longer to remember my name.

Steve drove past my house on his motorcycle when he was doing *Wanted: Dead or Alive*. He recognized me from my work on television and we became friendly. The process was slow, though. At first, he would drive by without even an acknowledgement. Then, he began driving by with a quick wave. Next, he would drive by slowly and wave. Then, almost stopping at a "Hi." Eventually, he would pass by, stop, and give a "Hey, how ya doing?" I knew the son-of-a-bitch a year before he learned my name. Even then, he couldn't remember my first name so he called me every name in the book. Ed, Fred, Dan. Finally, I became fed up. "For chrissakes, it's Don. Think of Donald Duck!"

Steve went from television star to movie star in the span of a decade. He gave my career a big lift when he gave me the part of Delgetti in *Bullitt*, which was my first role in a motion picture. In early 1968, I received a call from my agent to go to Warner Brothers and meet

with director Peter Yates. I had no clue who Peter was or what the movie was about.

"Steve thinks you would be good in this role," Yates said, upon our introduction. Throughout our conversation, I kept thinking, "Steve who?" When I left the Warner Brothers lot, it hit me: "McQueen, of course."

Later, at a party on location in San Francisco, I thanked Steve for getting me the part. He became visibly upset and insisted he had nothing to do with it. That tells you what kind of man he was. He didn't want me to feel beholden to him. He wanted me to be a little arrogant, to have courage and a little chutzpah, and to do the job bravely because he was embarrassed that he had intervened.

Don Gordon worked with Steve McQueen in Wanted: Dead or Alive, Bullitt, Papillon and The Towering Inferno. He resides in Los Angeles, California.

Rehearsing a scene for *Bullitt* at the San Francisco International Airport.

Bottom left: Lieutenant Frank Bullitt was the coolest movie detective of the sixties.

Taking a Bullitt

Barbara Dougherty

About forty years ago, in the spring of 1968, I met Steve McQueen at the San Francisco International Airport during the filming of *Bullitt*.

My father, Joseph Smith, was the film's lighting director and Steve was there with him. The timing was perfect for a family reunion, as my brother, also named Steve, had just returned from his tour of duty in Vietnam. My husband and I drove to the airport from the Simi Valley. I was expecting a baby at the time. It was a happy occasion for our entire family.

My dad introduced everyone to McQueen. To my delight, he talked to each one of us individually, and specifically about motherhood, with me. He told my husband how fatherhood changes a man, and talked to my brother about being a soldier. He was personable and friendly, not to mention easy going and comfortable. McQueen was genuine in what he had to say and interested in us as people. I remain impressed at how congenial he was and not full of himself, like most movie stars. I've met many other stars over the years through my dad's work, and the same can't be said of them.

Barbara Dougherty lives in Simi Valley, California.

Iconic Influence

Andy Armstrong

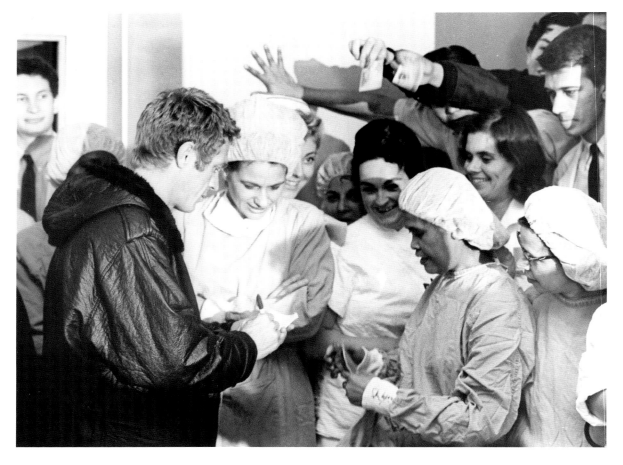

Opposite: Frank Bullitt was the defining role of Steve McQueen's acting career.

Left: McQueen taking a break on the set of *Bullitt* and signing autographs with real doctors and nurses, who served as cast members on the 1968 film.

How can someone I've never met influence my childhood, teen years, movie work and life so exceptionally? Thinking back, it had to be Steve McQueen's iconic presence, courage and tenacity. His passion for cars and bikes didn't hurt, either.

Anything with a motor and wheels has been my own passion since I could walk. Since the age of fourteen, I've competed in motorcycle off-road events and later raced cars. So when I watched *The Great Escape* at my local cinema, I sat there, gaping in awe, as this movie hero slid to a stop on his Triumph in the motorcycle chase. I watched as the actor, not a stunt double, rode fast towards the camera, beginning as a small dot and finishing as a fantastic movie poster moment before looking left and right, then roaring away. It's one classic shot that has stayed with me all these years.

Bullitt mesmerized me as well. Sure, McQueen was doubled for much of the action in his movies, but he had an innate ability to gage what shots he could convincingly pull off and performed them admirably. To persuade an audience that a piece of action is realistic is no small feat. McQueen succeeded every time. No one doubted his presence. He owned every scene. And that's tough to accomplish.

So when I say that Steve McQueen is the absolute benchmark in my own career, I'm not slinging hash. Several of his iconic shots in movies such as *Bullitt* and *The Magnificent Seven,* show in its purest and most beautiful form how to not only make the character believable, but puts you inside that spirit of believability—you have no doubt McQueen is the person he portrays.

The man was clearly accomplished with action scenes and he possessed an instinctive knowledge of what looked realistic. I worked as Peter Yates' Assistant Director, for many years after he made *Bullitt,* and remember Peter telling me how Steve insisted on having real doctors and nurses in the hospital sequences in the movie.

This ability to make a scene look natural was ultimately what made him such a charismatic actor. Whether acting or reacting, Steve McQueen was and still is one of my movie heroes. He made it all look so effortless.

As an action movie director and stunt coordinator, I've looked to McQueen's authenticity on screen to help me create the most natural and convincing scenes I can. From one motor head to another—Steve, if I can call you that, thanks for the helping hand.

Andy Armstrong is a Hollywood-based Action Movie Director and Stunt Coordinator.

McQueen, Marvin and Bruce Who?
David Wolper

McQueen never tested himself for a belt in the martial arts for fear that it would be used against him in a lawsuit. Friends and fellow martial artists say he had no problems handling himself.

Perhaps the most boring evening of my life was when I sat between movie stars Steve McQueen and Lee Marvin at a private dinner party in the sixties.

Sandwiched between the two actors, I listened to them all evening, regale about motorcycles, racing and car engines. They were genial fellows, but not the greatest intellects. It was like listening in on a conversation with a pair of auto mechanics.

I didn't want to be rude, so I smiled and nodded every now and then, to act as if I were a part of the conversation. Near the end of the meal, Steve and Lee finally ended their chat long enough to speak to a few other people at the table. Lee turned to me and somehow we came to the subject of weight and exercise.

"I can put you in touch with someone who can whip you into shape," Lee said, who insisted I give him my number to pass onto his trainer. Steve chimed in and said he was his trainer, too.

A few days later, the trainer called, but I wasn't interested.

"Well, call me if you change your mind," the gentleman said. "My name is Bruce Lee."

Oscar winner David Wolper is a producer, director and writer. He lives in Beverly Hills, California.

The Blog Lloyd Thaxton

Back in the fifties, the perception of the people who rode motorcycles came right out of Marlon Brando's *The Wild One*. They were in scruffy gangs that rode into town on their "hogs" to create havoc; a seedy bunch that no self-respecting citizen would ever want to emulate. In the sixties, one way to pick up a few minutes of fame in Hollywood was to acquire a big motorcycle with lots of shiny chrome. Then you could park it out front of the famous Whisky A-Go-Go and just sit on it. It was even better if you could persuade one of the Whisky A-Go-Go girls to sit behind you, high up on the back. This was the personification of "hip" and the big kick-start for the popularity of ordinary (instead of ornery) folks riding "bikes".

In 1963, *The Great Escape,* starring Steve McQueen, was a turning point. One mighty leap over that fence and the Hollywood crowd jumped right along. Everyone wanted to be him.

I'm not ashamed to admit that I was a member of the Hollywood Angels. We were a rather close-knit group. I bought my beautiful, blue-tanked, chrome-trimmed 1965 Triumph Bonneville from celebrity bike dealer and movie stunt coordinator, Bud Ekins. Bud was the stunt person who made the jump in *The Great Escape* and was a close friend of McQueen. Not too many people were aware of this, but Steve was a motorcycle off-road racer himself. He raced with Bud Ekins' six-man All-American team competing in the International Six-Day Trials in Germany.

My good friend and neighbor, actor Don Gordon, introduced me to Steve. Besides playing Steve's cop partner in *Bullitt,* he also had a starring role next to Steve in *Papillon*. Don invited me to visit the *Bullitt* set in San Francisco and that's where I met Steve McQueen.

At the time, I was living on Mulholland Drive, high up in the Hollywood Hills. Mulholland's sweeping deadman curves went for miles above Los Angeles and presented a considerable challenge for any motorcyclist.

One evening, Steve and Don showed up at my door. They wanted to know if I could come out and play. It was as if I was ten-years old again and my pals were asking me to play ball or catch lightning bugs or something. There would be no ball game tonight, though. They had their bikes parked at my front curb and I was out the door in a shot.

What a night! We rode high above the sparkling lights of Hollywood, all the way to Latigo Canyon, which led us down to the Pacific Coast Highway. Soon we were cruising along, accompanied by the beautiful sound of muted mufflers and pounding surf, bouncing off the sandy Santa Monica beaches. No one said a word. It was a warm, breezy moon-bright night; filled with the wind-in-your-face joy only a lover of motorcycles could possibly understand.

In Malibu, our hunger started and we turned into the first restaurant we saw. The tantalizing aroma of burgers cooking and onions frying filled the air; a scene typical of any hamburger joint you might encounter in the USA. Packed tightly with young people, having a good time, no one bothered to look up as we chose a booth in the back. However, after we sat down and ordered, I could faintly recognize what sounded like my name, coming through the drone of the many conversations in the room. You know how you can make out certain words in other people's conversations? Kind of like, "YadayadaLloydyadayadaThaxtonyada?" I followed the sound to a group of five teenage boys sitting in a booth across the way.

Sure enough, a few minutes later, one of the boys shyly approached our table. He carefully put down five torn-off pieces of paper and asked, "Lloyd, could you sign these for me and my buddies?" He never once looked over or acknowledged that Steve McQueen was sitting directly across from me. I signed my name. He thanked me and went back to his friends.

A few minutes later, I once again started to recognize familiar words from the same booth. This time it was, "YadayadayadaSteve yadaMcQueenyada." It wasn't long until the same volunteer came back to our table and stood facing me while he laid down five new pieces of paper. He then politely asked, "Lloyd, could you please ask Mr. McQueen if he would give us his autograph?"

Why didn't he just ask Steve for his autograph, as he had asked me? And why did he call me "Lloyd," while referring to Steve as: "Mr. McQueen?"

One layer of celebrity was being peeled off, to expose the bigger layer. Steve McQueen, you see, was bigger than life. The teenager saw Steve up there, twenty-feet tall, on that huge movie screen. I, on the other hand, came right into his living room each day on his family's small, more intimate television screen, as his good friend and buddy "Lloyd." Steve was—well, "Mister McQueen".

After the young man went back to his excited friends, neither Steve nor I discussed what had taken place. We simply acted as if it was a most natural occurrence; something that might happen to anybody sitting around having a burger and fries. Our previously interrupted conversation picked up without missing a beat. We finished our burgers, mounted our bikes and rode off into the sunset—Sunset Boulevard.

Steve McQueen was one of the best people I met in Hollywood. He treated everyone with great respect. However, he always knew who and what he was. A few years after this ride-for-burgers outing, I was invited to a pool party at Steve's beautiful home nestled in a rustic canyon. His co-star in the film *The Sand Pebbles*, Lord Richard Attenborough, was in town and Steve was hosting a party to introduce him to his friends. At one point in the afternoon, Steve asked if I would like to see a new bike he had just purchased. I believe at this time his collection included over a hundred and fifty new and antique motorcycles.

As we were looking at his fantastic new toy, I asked, "Are you still a member of the International off-road racing team?" He answered, with genuine sincerity, "No, that's all behind me. From now on I'm going to concentrate on being a movie star." Notice he didn't say, movie "actor". Though he was a remarkable actor, he knew he was more than that. He knew he was a star. He knew he was … Mister McQueen.

Emmy winner Lloyd Thaxton was a writer, producer, director and star of the Los Angeles-based The Lloyd Thaxton Show. He died in October 2008.

Full Flush on the Vegas Strip

Pat McMahon

I've been in show business for most of my life and one of the most interesting dynamics I've witnessed is the difference in perception between television and movie stars.

In the late sixties, I was standing in line outside a Las Vegas hotel waiting to catch a taxicab. Vegas back then wasn't as developed as it is today, and it was a long distance between hotels if you walked. Steve McQueen, a major star, had just entered a cab ahead of me when I received a tap on my shoulder. I turned around and it was a young couple from Phoenix who recognized me from *The Wallace and Ladmo Show*, a popular children's program.

"Excuse me, Mr. McMahon, would you mind signing this for the family?" the gentleman asked.

"I'd be delighted," I said. "But you just missed Steve McQueen." My new friend nodded and acknowledged that he had seen Mr. McQueen but was too nervous to ask him to sign anything.

"Oh, I could never work up the nerve to ask him for an autograph," the gentleman said, knocking me down a peg or two in the process.

That's the difference between a television and movie star—on television you're twelve inches tall and are broadcast into people's living room. But in the movies, you're almost immortal.

Pat McMahon is an Emmy-award winning actor, radio show personality and the host of The Pat McMahon Show. He resides in Phoenix, Arizona.

Bullitt was the film that transformed Steve McQueen from a celebrity to a pop culture icon.

Full Moon Fever
Liz and John Richard Ingersoll

Our dad rarely cursed or screamed. When he did, you knew he had probably just finished talking to Steve McQueen.

Dad was Rick Ingersoll, a longtime publicist for some of the biggest stars in Hollywood. Over the years he worked with Alfred Hitchcock, Mae West, Cary Grant, Grace Kelly, Rock Hudson, Glen Ford, Mia Farrow and many others. Some might have been difficult, but none of them were in the same league as Steve.

Steve was moody, unpredictable, volatile, and paranoid and didn't make my dad's life easy. We both remember the late night phone calls, heated exchanges, profanity and the phone being slammed down on the receiver. This all stemmed from the fact that Steve hated publicity even though he made for great copy. When Steve stopped giving interviews at the height of his career, it placed a major strain on their relationship.

"Whenever there's a full moon, Steve goes crazy," dad often told our mother.

With that said, we always thought of Steve as part of our extended family. We went to his house on numerous occasions, hung out with his kids, celebrated together on special occasions, and circled the wagons when times became tough. Our families were always there for each other.

Despite his love-hate relationship with our father, Steve was nothing but kind to the Ingersoll kids. He was warm and respectful to all children, which shows in the photo taken with our family on the set of *Bullitt*. Steve made sure our trip to San Francisco was special by paying extra attention to us. That's the Steve McQueen we choose to remember.

Liz Ingersoll is a graphic artist who resides in Pacific Palisades, California. John Richard Ingersoll is a businessman and motorcycle enthusiast residing in Arizona.

Opposite top: McQueen with his publicist Richard "Rick" Ingersoll (in shades holding a cigarette) talking with San Francisco city officials.

Opposite bottom row: McQueen meets Richard's children, John and Liz, on the set of *Bullitt*. They say that despite their father's love/hate relationship with McQueen, he was "family".

Right top and bottom: Steve McQueen relaxes by taking a swim in the family pool at his Brentwood home.

A Kiss is Just a Kiss
Carol Ingersoll

All photos: Neile and Steve McQueen during the various phases of their marriage.

Steve McQueen is remembered for many attributes—his blond hair and steely blues eyes, his death-defying roles as a daredevil who raced cars and motorcycles, and his sexy smile. But for me, the essence of the man boils down to a small, yet thoughtful act.

Steve and his wife, Neile, were good friends of ours because my husband, Rick Ingersoll, was his publicist. The McQueens were a delightful couple and exceptional dancers and we often attended social functions, charity events and parties together, including swinging bashes at their posh Brentwood home.

One night, Rick and I accompanied actor Bob Horton and his wife, Marilynn, for dinner. The McQueens were already waiting for us in the bar. Marilynn and Steve greeted each other with a kiss on the cheek. Steve knew I was shy. He looked at me. "And how about you?" It was a small, kind gesture, typical of Steve, who wanted everyone around him to feel special. He was sweet and polite and never lost his Midwestern values or manners.

Of all the movies stars I met over the years, Steve was the most unglamorous. He wasn't caught up in his own hype or what his movies were doing at the box office. Nothing thrilled him more than to talk about cars and motorcycles.

Sadly, when Steve and Neile divorced, his relationship with our family ended as well. Steve moved away from Brentwood in favor of a more laid-back lifestyle in Malibu. His new life didn't include production company employees, lawyers, accountants, agents, publicists or first wives.

Time will never extinguish the fun we experienced, the glamour of that era, or the feelings we had towards each other.

Carol Ingersoll is retired and resides in Pacific Palisades, California.

The Imprint of a Life
Darren Wright

Nearly thirty years after his death, the incredible hunger for Steve McQueen seems insatiable. Imagine his popularity in life!

I'm just a fan and a movie buff. To me, Steve McQueen was a very good actor with an incredible screen presence. He is only one of the several actors I loved to watch—maybe not even my favorite. However, he took on a whole new depth of meaning for me when I picked up and read an old biography by Penina Spiegel, called *McQueen: The Untold Story of a Bad Boy in Hollywood*. Spiegel dished the dirt on Steve, but she also wrote with empathy about a man who's childhood experiences and ensuing emotional suffering touched my heart. His courage and determination in the face of it all thoroughly impressed me. After reading the works of Spiegel, Marshall Terrill (*Steve McQueen: Portrait of an American Rebel*), Neile McQueen (*My Husband, My Friend*) and others, I understood that Steve McQueen was someone special, and why his star shone so brightly on film.

And so I started out to create a comprehensive online record of McQueen's film and TV performances, a list of biographies and documentaries, as well as a section on his little-known humanitarian work for the poor and needy. There's a bit of fun stuff, such as the site's "collectables" section for those who wanted to explore the man in depth. The site was not intended to go much further than this, but the more I learned about Steve, the more he interested me and the site kept growing. It wasn't only my fascination that kept me working on it. Emails from McQueen fans who were thrilled to discover the site and who wanted more, played a significant role in keeping me going. It has been pleasing to experience this passion

and feedback, and to know that the site serves his memory well. That is a big part of why it's still slowly growing to this day.

McQueenOnline.com has opened doors to intimate knowledge and experiences about Steve that I wouldn't have otherwise had, making valuable friends and contacts all over the world. Living in Australia, it's hard to meet these people, but I've spoken by phone or corresponded by email with those who acted with him, raced cars and rode bikes with him, dated him, interviewed or met him at some point in their lives. Probably the greatest highlight of all these, however, was interviewing his first wife, Neile McQueen Toffel.

I've also talked to some of his most devoted fans, such as Donna Redden from Nova Scotia, Canada, who has played an important role in helping me develop the site. Most adore Steve McQueen, or strongly admire him and there is little negative feedback. Frankly, there is much to badmouth for those who are so inclined. My take on it all? I don't idolize Steve McQueen, but I respect and admire him for being a real person with faults and strengths. My website isn't a shrine of worship. Steve was just a man like any other, but he was special in a way that left a positive impression on many—ranging from giving them the will to go on fighting against life's odds to just making them feel good. That is a legacy Steve's family and friends no doubt are proud of.

My favorite McQueen films, in no particular order, are: *Papillon, The Getaway, Junior Bonner, The Sand Pebbles, The Cincinnati Kid, Baby, the Rain Must Fall* and *Hell is for Heroes*. The films I wish he'd made are *Yucatan, The Bodyguard* and *First Blood*. I feel he would

All photos: McQueen played slight variations of himself throughout his career.

Opposite left: *The Cincinnati Kid*.

Opposite right: *The Sand Pebbles*.

This page: Above photo is from *Nevada Smith*; top right is *Bullitt*, middle is Alfred Hitchcock's *Man From The South* with Peter Lorre, and the bottom photo is *Baby, the Rain Must Fall*.

have gone on to make winning films in his fifties, sixties and even seventies had he lived, because he was creating more depth in his characterizations with each film. He was getting better and better right until the end.

So I feel blessed to have come about as close to Steve McQueen as is possible for somebody who never met him. And I hope to take up the invitation to meet a few of the people I've connected with through the site someday, when I travel to the US and Europe.

I don't think I would have found any of the current crop of movie stars interesting enough to devote the time and energy necessary for developing a website as comprehensive as McQueenOnline.com. Brad who? Tom who? Hey, they're impressive in their own way, but after I've left the cinema or turned off the DVD player, they're forgotten. But not McQueen, he stays with you.

Darren Wright is the webmaster of www.mcqueenonline.com

A Special Bloke
Dave Bickers

Even though an ocean separated us, a mutual love of motor sports brought me and Steve McQueen together.

I met Steve McQueen at Bud Ekins' bike shop sometime in the late sixties. Bud's shop was the nexus of the racing world and boasted a wonderful cast of characters. Of course, Steve McQueen was one of many. I found Steve surprisingly laid back but passionate about bikes and racing. Steve knew us Brits were crazy about motor sports and because I had a fair amount of success at that time, he was anxious to learn as much as possible. He did that by basically listening and watching.

Steve once invited me and a group of riders to his house in Brentwood. The home was lovely, with a long and winding driveway, big gates and a security camera. Somehow the subject of pool came up and Steve hinted that he was a pretty good player. A couple of us decided to play a trick on him. When Steve wasn't looking, we dropped a weighted ball on the table—it was one of those balls that travels around in circles. He played with us as if it

was a regular ball and he still beat us! Couldn't believe he never said a word.

The last time I saw Steve he was married to Ali MacGraw. I asked him to ride saddleback on the bike with me, and Ali didn't look too happy. But Steve was game and off we went.

Whenever Steve is on television, I stop what I'm doing and watch him. He was such a special bloke and I love to see him. It's like a visit from an old friend.

Dave Bickers, known as "The Coddenham Flier", was a world-champion motocross rider in the sixties. Today he owns Dave Bickers Motorcycles in Ipswich, England.

Above: All decked out in leather, McQueen races through the desert on a Triumph.

Opposite: Various still shots and behind the scenes photos of McQueen in *Bullitt.*

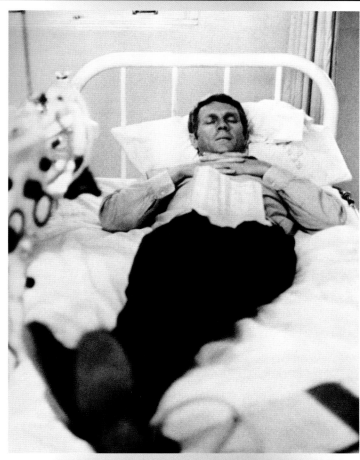

What a Motley Crew of Pumpin' Celebs

Doug McGeorge

Working at the Standard Station on the corner of Sunset and Barrington in Brentwood, around 1969, I bumped into all sorts of celebrities, which made it a fun place to work. Steve McQueen lived just up the hill and was a regular customer. He was always friendly and outgoing.

I remember once, late at night, lending Esther Williams a dime to use the phone. Violinist Jascha Heifetz was a stickler, always wanting lots of service on his Rolls—but he was a bit of a kidder, too. His sister taught piano in Mill Valley, the same town where I grew up. His was the only autograph I ever had—and he volunteered it.

The friendliest cowboy of all was James Arness. He would always leave his car and chat. Clint Walker's shoulders were so wide he had to turn sideways to pass through the door. It is amazing what odd facts stick in your memory.

As for Steve McQueen, on Saturday mornings he would arrive in his pickup truck with a load of motorcycles and fill them all up. Most of the time, he was on his way to the races.

One afternoon a man pulled up, stood up on the seat of his sports car and yelled to me, "Have you seen Steve?"

I did not know he was referring to Steve McQueen, so I yelled back "Steve who?"

"McQueen," he answered. I said I hadn't seen him. One of the others in the station recognized Jay Sebring, the hairstylist who was killed soon after, by the Manson gang.

Steve was unlike other stars of today—down-to-earth, approachable and treated everyone with respect.

Doug McGeorge is retired from real estate management and lives in San Mateo, California, and the Napa Valley. He is the grandson of the founder of Pacific McGeorge College of Law, Sacramento, California.

Above: Having fun with "The Duke" at a Hollywood bash. McQueen held John Wayne in high esteem as one of the all-time film greats.

Opposite top: Steve and Neile McQueen outside of The Factory in Los Angeles with Mia Farrow and Liza Minnelli.

Opposite middle: John Wayne and Steve McQueen enjoying a night of fun and revelry at a black-tie event.

Opposite bottom: With actress Juliet Mills.

McQueen & Dutch

Michael F. Egan

The Steve I knew was a private, can-do man. He was fully committed to his family, auto and motorcycle racing, and his acting career. He reveled in the old motorcycle culture as an enthusiast and collector. I met him through another friend, Bud Ekins, a champion off-road motorcycle racer with a Triumph dealership in the San Fernando Valley. Bud doubled for Steve in the famous *Great Escape* fence jumping scene and hair-raising stunts in other movies. Steve had been in the Marines and I had just been discharged from the Marine Corps in the sixties, when I met him.

Steve was a genuine collector of anything antique and vintage: toys, furniture, fans, Betty Boop curios, guns, knives, memorabilia, motorcycles, automobiles, signs and airplanes. After World War II, he rode an old Indian motorcycle for transportation. Although he had a lot of Indians, he also owned a well-balanced and diverse collection of other American and English motorcycles. He was generous and without fanfare or horn blowing, helped numerous people in need. He kept it quiet. He wasn't interested in a pat on the back.

He relied on Bud Ekins for guidance on the value and desirability of the old bikes he was collecting. Bud heard of a motorcycle collection of about forty pre-WWI bikes for sale back East. He mentioned it to Steve who was interested in acquiring it and flew out with him to check it out. After looking at the bikes, Bud assured Steve the entire collection was rare, desirable and priced right. Steve bought the collection on the spot and told Bud he could buy four motorcycles of his choice in appreciation for the lead and evaluation. Once Bud chose the bikes he wanted, McQueen immediately said, "Okay, I'm going to keep them because I know you would only pick the best." In typical Bud style, he shrugged when relating the story later and added, "At least I made him buy first-class airline tickets." On Steve's death, those motorcycles were left to Bud.

Von Dutch was a popular paint and color innovator in the Southern California custom car and motorcycle circles, well known in the movie prop community for fabricating special effects. He worked on and off for Bud, painting, flaming and pin-striping motorcycles. He had a reputation for being temperamental and unpredictable. Whether it's true or not, Dutch is credited with creating the "Mare's Laig," a sawed-off Carbine rifle with an oversized cocking mechanism Steve used in the *Wanted: Dead or Alive* TV series. Dutch also prepared *The Great Escape* movie motorcycles, disguising them to look like German BMW military bikes, at Bud's shop.

In 1969, Steve made *The Reivers*, a William Faulkner fable, into a movie. It's a comedic coming of age adventure, about a well-to-do southern family's wild and woolly ranch hand, Boon (Steve), their innocent twelve-year-old grandson, Lucius, and Ned, the family chauffeur, who together liberate the patriarch's brand new Winton auto. Without permission, the three joy riders head for Memphis' red light district to see Boon's working girl friend. The movie needed a special automobile and Steve knew Von Dutch had the ability to create a custom model. It had to look like an early open touring car; be able to start, run, and brake under its own power, have an electric starter and be operated safely, by a short, slightly built, twelve-year-old boy.

Steve went to Dutch to inquire if he would build the circa 1910 "Winton Flyer" from scratch in three months. He admonished Dutch that the auto had to be finished and delivered on time, asking what it would cost. Dutch's reply, "$10,000 to build the car, half now in cash, the balance in cash upon delivery." He agreed to be available as the mechanic on location, plus Dutch wanted to have a minor role in the movie as a blacksmith riding an antique motorcycle. Steve agreed to the terms and paid him half up front. Steve knew from experience someone should keep an eye on Dutch.

Since I haven't seen the Von Dutch version of the Winton's story in print anywhere I'm going to tell it as Dutch told it to me. He related that nothing went well at all. He later told an *L.A. Times* reporter that it took him three months working night and day to finish the Winton. What he left out was that for the first ten of twelve weeks, nothing was accomplished except the spending of Steve's money. Anyone Steve sent to check on the Winton job during the first two months was told by Dutch that a tarp covering a pile of junk out back was the Winton. The inspectors reported to Steve nothing much appeared to be getting done. As the deadline loomed, Steve was justifiably worried and angry that the Winton would not be built. He was laying out a large amount of dough on the movie pre-production with a possible missing co-star and more down time.

About two weeks from the deadline, Dutch said he bolted upright in bed, in a cold sweat at three a.m. in the morning. He knew he was in big trouble because he had spent the money and hadn't started the job. He quit drinking and worked like a madman—sometimes twenty-four hours a day—building the Winton in his backyard. He adapted new and old salvaged antique chassis and power train parts, finishing the assembled car with fine pin striping. He had Tony Nancy do the rushed but gorgeous leather upholstery and a plating shop prepared the chrome and nickel work.

When Steve saw the Winton, he went bonkers from disbelief. The big yellow open automobile was ready to go and stunning beyond expectations. The vehicle performed beautifully. It was the regal co-star. True to Steve's promise, Dutch is in the movie riding an old Indian motorcycle for one shot of about three seconds duration. If you blink, you will miss him. I think it is fair to say this was Steve's punishment for Dutch taking him on a perilous and frustrating wild goose chase.

Bud Ekins, Von Dutch and Steve McQueen were all good friends. They're all gone now. We'll never see their feats again. I said, "Goodbye" to three of my treasured friends with their passing.

Michael F. Egan is a writer and resident of Santa Paula, California.

McQueen with director Mark Rydell. Despite the fact the two were acting buddies in the fifties, Rydell says McQueen put him through the wringer during the filming of *The Reivers*.

Opposite: From *The Reivers*' hilarious sequence involving the "Winton Flyer" getting stuck in the mud.

Mark Rydell On The Ropes

Crews, for the most part, respect and like me. Actors do the same. But Steve McQueen had me on the ropes.

I knew Steve in New York back in the fifties when I encouraged him to pursue a career in acting, rather than tile setting. A few years later, he found me a guest spot on *Wanted: Dead or Alive*, and eventually went to bat for me as the director of *The Reivers*.

For some reason during the filming of this movie, McQueen made it difficult for me, until finally, someone whispered that it was because of an attractive girl who was going to be in the picture. She had come to the location and flirted with me, and I had responded. The next day, McQueen was impossible—vocal and negative, challenging every decision I made. The actress was Steve's girlfriend and I said, "I'm sorry. I had no idea." But that wasn't an excuse for Steve's behavior.

We had our big confrontation in a scene where Steve and Rupert Crosse were pushing the "Winton Flyer" out of the mud. There was mud everywhere, and the two stars were sliding and falling, and not having much success at moving the car. I was sitting high atop a crane when McQueen yelled at me.

"Ryyyyydellll, get over here." As I climbed down from the crane, my heart stopped. The crew stood still. McQueen was a physical presence given to brutality. He'd demonstrated to me many times he was a first-class tae kwon do kicker. When I reached the ground, I stood eye-to-eye with McQueen. Steve announced loud enough so the crew could hear, "You know, there's only room for one boss on this picture."

"Yeah, that's me," I cut him off. Inside I was trembling, but he walked away. If he wanted a fight, I was ready.

I've dealt with some major, tough actors. Nobody's had me on the ropes except Steve. But I hung in there and told him I would outlast him. I said, "When you're furious with me, I'm still going to be here trying. I'm not going to fold. And I'm not going to give in to you, because you're wrong." It just drove him crazy, but he did finally surrender.

I miss him as a star and a friend, because he had a wonderful, magnetic personality. He was also difficult and strong-willed. But if I had a chance to work with him again, I would do it, because he had magic—real magic.

Mark Rydell has led eight actors to Oscar nominations and directed Steve McQueen in The Reivers. He is currently the co-artistic director of the Actors Studio West in Los Angeles, California. This passage originally appeared in the December 1991 issue of Movieline magazine.

The Reiver

Sharon Farrell

Left & right: Actress Sharon Farrell was Steve McQueen's co-star in 1969's *The Reivers*. She said working with the superstar was one of the highlights of her career.

Steve McQueen was a gentleman and a real swell guy—for a reiver, that is.

I was born and raised in Sioux City, Iowa, and Steve also hailed from the Midwest. He felt we had much in common despite the fact that we were about a decade apart in age.

"Sharon, we are alike," Steve once said. "You're street smart not book smart. We even look similar. You have a mole just like me. Out of instinct I touched my cheek. Yep, ol' Steve was right. Then again, he was right about a lot of things.

Working on *The Reivers* with Steve was a pure joy and one of the highlights of my career. He was protective and never once let me down. I had a problem with a photography shoot over some silly costume they asked me to wear. It's the kind of thing a real actress doesn't get stressed about, but I was in tears like a big baby and making a mess of my makeup. Steve came to the rescue. He taught me how to stand up for myself and never do anything my gut told me not to do.

"You can always get what you want, Sharon," Steve said. "Stand firm and remember you have about three feet around you that is your space. No one has a right to go beyond that unless you invite them. Think with your body and listen to your gut. Even when it's over something silly, if you don't feel good about it, then it's not right." I wiped my tears away and smiled. I've carried that bit of wisdom with me ever since.

In between shots and scenes Steve took me for several rides on his motorcycle, and even taught me how to drive a stick shift. But after my first lesson he didn't think I should ever purchase a car that had stick. He did get me to shift gears when it came to what I wore. Steve taught me to dress conservatively, not flashy, but proper like a lady. He wanted me to look classy. I listened then, and also when Steve told me to stop smoking Romeo and Juliet Cigars. I developed the habit a decade before, while filming my first movie in Cuba. The cigars were a substitute for my cigarette habit, and I thought, were an improvement. Steve didn't agree.

One time Steve and I ventured out with our *The Reivers* co-star Rupert Crosse, to a funky, out-of-the-way soul food restaurant near the beach. It had everything: sweet potatoes, greens, turnips, grits, fried chicken and catfish. We sang songs, carried on and had a great time. Steve and Rupert ended the evening wrestling on the floor.

Rupert was tall and skinny and stood about six-feet-five; Steve was about five-eleven. Most leading men in Hollywood didn't work with other actors who dwarfed them on screen, but Steve was gutsy. He fought to give that role to Rupert, who eventually was nominated for an Academy Award for Best Supporting Actor in *The Reivers*. Steve wasn't nominated at all, but he was the first person to call and congratulate Rupert, which was a big thing to do.

Everybody I knew loved Steve, and he remained my friend and hero until his untimely death.

Sharon Farrell is a veteran film and television actress, and was Steve McQueen's leading lady in 1969's The Reivers. Visit her website at www.sharonfarrell.biz.

Monkey Business

Randy Burak

According to McQueen, riding motorcycles was his emotional release from the pressures of stardom.

I was a star struck twenty-two-year-old kid when I first met Steve McQueen, who was almost twice my age.

At the time, I was a brash motocross champion and desert racer, and he was the number-one box-office attraction in the world. He may have been a movie star, but he raced like a bronco.

I met Steve racing at Indian Dunes Raceway in Valencia, California, where he was filming *On Any Sunday*. He was a relentless competitor—especially when the cameras were rolling. When they are behind in a race, most riders take the same line. With Steve, good luck. I ended up winning, with McQueen taking third.

Afterwards, he came to shake my hand. He was shocked at how I had modified my helmet so that the front was a monkey face. I had always done this to attract attention during desert races, but McQueen told me I didn't need "that stuff." He offered to buy me a

new helmet if I erased the monkey face. Still, he liked my style and asked me to ride with him.

For the next six months, I rode motocross with Steve at Indian Dunes. Motocross is much more regimented and Steve was really a desert racer, where you turn it up and hang on. With motocross you need to set yourself up for turns and find the right line. Steve would go off the course frequently, but he'd mumble to himself and return to the track. I think he felt confident riding next to me that I wouldn't run him over.

Even though Steve was a huge international movie star, he was always friendly and greatly respected talented riders. He's well missed, that's for sure.

Randy Burak is a former motocross and desert racer and is a chief lighting technician in the film industry. He lives in Southern California.

Steve McQueen with his daughter Terry, whom he lovingly referred to as "the apple of my eye."

McQueen at Speed: A Man in Motion

Kandee Nelson

Right: A free-spirited McQueen in France during the filming of *Le Mans*.

When Steve McQueen was three-years old, he became fascinated by the simple revolutions of a single wheel on his Uncle Claude's trundling wheelbarrow. Before long, he was racing the neighborhood kids for gumdrops on his red tricycle over the dirt bluffs of Slater, Missouri. Deserted by both parents and frequently uprooted, he had only the nurturing of raw instinct to navigate the wheel-bending, desolate track of childhood. Once he learned to read the terrain, the world at large became his circuit. The McQueen approach to everything in life was: Where can it take me? How fast can it go? This is the Steve McQueen I keep falling for. The man who jumped the gates of Hollywood and took the hill climb to stardom like a bump in the road. McQueen in the pits… McQueen at speed… McQueen at altitude. Just the simple revolutions of a man in motion.

My parents were Steve McQueen fans when I was born in 1964. Though I never met him, through the wonder of television his face was so familiar it was already etched in my subconscious by the time I entered grade school. I grew up in Santa Clarita, a town in California near several of McQueen's favorite escapes: Indian Dunes, Santa Paula, the Antelope Valley and Mojave Desert. Local diners like Tipp's Café and Du-par's were regular stops after a day in the dirt or a weekend desert scramble.

I remember running through the hills behind our house in Wallaby boots pretending to be *Nevada Smith,* chasing down the bad guys as I sought my revenge. But I was too young to catch hold of the shooting star behind the role until much later in life. I was sixteen when Steve McQueen made his final great escape, lane-splitting the highway to heaven as he rolled out of town. The news of his death echoed remotely from the rear panel speakers in our Pontiac station wagon. Hanging a faded vacancy sign on a whole generation, who like myself, were not yet old enough to comprehend the indelible mark he would leave behind.

McQueen in Hollywood was like Huck Finn in Wonderland. Only the looking-glass went the other way. Most who crossed his path didn't understand a word he said, what he was doing or where he was going with it all. He was always in trouble with the suits, and amused himself by outsmarting them. A fierce competitor and solitary by nature, he was driven to distinguish his performance from other actors and kept all rivals at a distance. His natural affinity with mechanism and motion allowed him to approach his character roles as he would all his vehicles. He overhauled, modified and customized them to perfection. Audiences couldn't help but stick a thumb out for McQueen; he was always worth the ride.

Sometime in March 1998, I was working in my new home office. In the adjoining living room, a television was muted but visible; droning the nightly news. I leaned back hoping to catch the weather as the image of a young woman along with her name appeared, on the screen. The one steady girl in Steve McQueen's life, daughter Terry, had passed away at the age of thirty-eight,

struggling with chronic illness. Only ten years earlier she had given birth to Steve's granddaughter Molly, days before my twins were born. I sat for a moment drifting. Even long after he was gone the drama of his life continued.

Terry's death sent me into a wave of reconnections. Not only did I want to know more about this man who had somehow become symbolic in my life, I wanted to understand why. The more I read about him the more I understood about myself. No detail ever shocked me. I only grew to like him more and those who tried to own him, less. I found myself drawn to the complexities of McQueen, and hopelessly enamored with the basics.

One of the most intriguing aspects of Steve McQueen's life was that undertow of foreboding that always had him by the ankles. Often seeking the open deserts and endless skies for solace, McQueen remarked one time to writer William Nolan, "Hemingway has his sea and I have mine."

For me, it's the enduring image of McQueen standing on the pegs of his motorcycle, shirtless, golden, his hair and skin taut with velocity that personifies the impossible glamour he maintained chasing his demons to infinity. Just when you think he's gone forever he'll go throttling past your viewfinder, making the scene again. Don't forget to take your lens cap off.

He's still here, you bastards!

Kandee Nelson is a freelance writer and editor who lives in Santa Clarita, California.

Motoring enthusiast Jeff Gamble captured these images of Steve and Chad McQueen (bottom right) and James Garner (bottom left) at Phoenix International Raceway. McQueen raced a Solar-owned Porsche 908. His Cortez motorhome can be seen in the upper right image. The *Playboy* bunnies mentioned in the passage are evidenced by the boot in the corner of the same frame.

A Kodak Moment

Jeff Gamble

The magic of Steve McQueen both on and off the screen captivated many of his fans, myself included.

Several car magazines reported in 1969 that McQueen was making a racing movie called *Le Mans*. The feature film required that he have some race experience in a Porsche 908 Spyder and he was scheduled to participate in events at Holtville, California; Sebring, Florida; and Phoenix, Arizona. Along with my buddy, Sheldon Gingerich and our spouses, we attended the March 1, 1970, Sports Car Club of America race at the Phoenix International Raceway, approximately a two-hour trip from my Tucson home. Built in January 1964, Phoenix International Raceway is an oval that once also included a meandering 2.5 miles road course around Stage Coach hill.

Pit passes in hand, we soon spotted actor and *Grand Prix* star James Garner surrounded by a bevy of beautiful women, who we learned worked at the Playboy Club in Phoenix. Not far from him was Steve McQueen. These were the days before the large private coaches were commonplace; so there was Steve sitting on the back of the Ginther race car transport truck with his son Chad on top of the roof. I recall he had on a cool old leather cap, a dark blue shirt, white pants and light blue windbreaker. He wasn't engaging in much conversation with Garner or anyone else. He was deep in thought and focused on the race.

There was a moment where we did lock eyes. He gave me a quick smile and I was able to catch my "Kodak moment" with the movie star.

The race, a charity event, was a seventeen-lap winter sprint. All proceeds went to The Arizona Boy's Ranch, a reform school like Steve's alma mater—the Boys Republic.

McQueen's race group ran at the end of the day and he proceeded to set a course record, coming in at 1:41:9 on the circuit.

The normal practice for Porsche was to celebrate racing victories by having their in-house artist create a commemorative poster. You can trust that this factory poster "McQueen Drives Porsche" listing the race dates and a photo of the Porsche 908 is on my garage wall to this day.

Jeff Gamble is a retired dental laboratory technician and a world-renowned racing sculptor. He lives in Tucson, Arizona.

Sunglasses at Night
Ben Affleck

Opposite: Classically cool
in Persol shades.

Top right: Biting into an apple
on the set of *The Reivers*.

Bottom right: Arriving at a race event,
Steve McQueen in fashionable clothing.

There's an old adage: Stars don't make movies, movies make stars.
I think Steve McQueen is one of the few exceptions to that rule.

A movie was always more interesting and cooler if he was in it.
There have been a few others with that power, but Steve McQueen
epitomized it. Acting can seem like a pathetic profession,
undignified in a way—but he carried it off with an enormous
amount of dignity and a masculinity that has a timeless appeal.

Cool is an overused word, but in this case it transcends that Corey
Hart, 'I wear my sunglasses at night' cool—Steve McQueen is
someone you'd like to meet. If he gave you advice, you'd probably
take it. You'd want him around if there was a problem, like a burglar
in your house or if you were at war. And I also assume that women
found him sexy. But what elevated Steve above just being a sex
symbol was that he didn't alienate men. Men liked him and found
him appealing. His brand of masculinity was an unassuming,
easygoing toughness that's not bullying or puffing up the chest,
but rather a likable commanding of respect. Appealing, yet
somewhat intimidating. You wanted his respect and not for him to
think you were an asshole if you said something stupid. You could
sit down and have a beer with Steve and talk to someone ahead of
his time and slightly more evolved in his masculinity.

Movie stars are essentially canvases upon which people project
their own feelings, desires and needs. His canvas was broad and
many people could relate to it.

Bullitt and *The Great Escape* and his other movies might look dated,
but somehow you could put his performance right into a movie
today. And in a business as ephemeral as this one, timelessness is
something people strive for and few achieve. There are actors like
him and Paul Newman, but not too many.

I have this watch I stole from the last movie I did because they told
me it was a recreation of a limited-edition watch Steve wore in
Monaco when he was racing. I figured, 'If it's good enough for Steve
McQueen, it's good enough for me.' After I took it, they called me
the next day and said, 'What happened to the watch?' and I
answered 'I don't know. I left it in the dressing room.' So, Steve
McQueen inspired me to commit a crime.

*Ben Affleck is a popular motion picture actor and won an Academy
Award for Good Will Hunting. This passage originally appeared in the
March 1999 issue of Interview.*

Finding an Angle
Richard George

Since my final year as a student at Art Center of Design, I had hung around Dan Gurney's place, photographing anything and everything that was crafted by All American Racers in their Santa Ana, California, shop. My love of photography and race cars, along with the access, parlayed itself into a nice little profession.

Former F1 racer Richie Ginther was a friend of Dan's and in late 1969, was asked to manage a car for actor Steve McQueen who was preparing to make a racing movie, *Le Mans*. McQueen needed some racing experience—enough to enable him to compete at Sebring.

Two former Gurney mechanics, Dick Weber and Haig Altounian, had signed on with Richie to modify and run the Porsche. Word came down that Porsche wanted to photograph the operation, but would not permit the selling of any pictures of the actor "out the back door".

Weber and Altounian knew my loyalty to Dan—I had photographed many of his "new innovations" that stayed new—and they recommended me to the Porsche PR department. The next call was from Porsche's West Coast PR representative, who explained that while Porsche did not want a "dog and pony act" surrounding McQueen, it did want pictures of this venture.

I signed on without hesitation. The next thing I knew, I was blasting down Highway 86 out of lovely Mecca, California, racing past the seemingly never-ending Salton Sea in my clapped-out VW bus. I headed for a rendezvous with McQueen, his family, the Porsche and its mechanics at someplace called Holtville—a name I only knew from reading about a Cal Club race.

Even if today's paparazzi types existed in that era, they would not have ventured out to Holtville to harass McQueen. Picturesque, it was not, but it was an introduction to the man and the machine, and a rehearsal for two subsequent assignments that would come along. I managed to take my pictures, blending in with the typical Cal Club assembly. Most of the racers treated McQueen as one of them and no one made a pest of himself, allowing the actor to become a race car driver.

The next outing was to be at my "home track," Riverside International Raceway. Having cut my teeth there, I felt quite comfortable since I knew the spots around the course for the better actions shots. McQueen's presence, however, was suddenly more of an issue at Riverside, as we were now only a little more than an hour's drive from Hollywood.

In the meantime, McQueen had decided he would enter the Porsche in the 12 Hours of Sebring and a third test event was deemed necessary—Phoenix International Raceway in March for another club event. The Porsche PR rep asked me to accompany the team to take pictures for the sports section of the Phoenix newspaper. We made a deal with the newspaper: I would shoot McQueen in

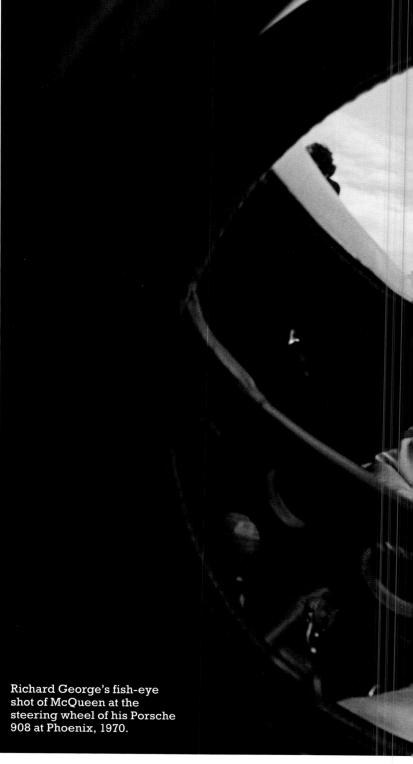

Richard George's fish-eye shot of McQueen at the steering wheel of his Porsche 908 at Phoenix, 1970.

the race, drive the film into Phoenix that night, and using the paper's lab, process, edit and print two pictures that showed our hero and the car. The PR guy had not been much of a race fan prior to this project, but took great pains to tell me the paper wouldn't run a standard picture of the race car—I needed to come up with something unusual. He had seen a photo of a tired race mechanic at an endurance event, looking exhausted, stirring his coffee with a screwdriver. This was the type of photo he wanted.

Great. I racked my brain for a real grabber; something that would satisfy the newspaper. I had to show the editors I wasn't giving them the standard press handout, while promoting McQueen and Porsche. Having observed McQueen's ritual of sitting in the car, methodically pulling on his balaclava, then the open-faced helmet,

I realized if I could mount my camera behind the steering wheel, I would have my shot. Oh, is that all! I remembered a trick my buddy Pete Biro had shown me, which involved a remotely wired Nikon and a very wide-angle lens.

A little Italian fellow shielded McQueen from unwanted public attention; he was quite good at discouraging anyone from bothering the star. I knew protocol required I request permission from him for the shot. Long story short, he said no. In fact, he said, "Absolutely not!" I started to panic. I needed something out of the ordinary, and I needed it right then or my name would be mud with Porsche.

My experience with mechanics had always been that if they trusted you, they'd help you, so I told my story to Altounian and

Weber, and the next thing I knew, I was in McQueen's trailer explaining the shot to him. If anyone in the group understood camera angles, it would be McQueen. He gave me a thumbs up, with a warning that the camera was to be out of the car by the time he started the motor.

The accompanying picture attests to the fact that I made my shot. The unusual-angled photo and a long-lens action shot of the Porsche on a rain-slicked racetrack made the paper—and my day.

Californian Richard George has enjoyed an extensive career as a freelance photographer. He has served countless advertising, editorial and corporate clients and covered a broad range of subjects. His work can be viewed at www.richardgeorgephotography.com.

Reaching the Finish Line
Mark MacVittie

In 1969, Steve McQueen raced at Phoenix International Raceway, where he was the top qualifier and won the race in his Porsche.

In those days, the pits were open and after the race, I walked to Steve's area and congratulated him on his win. He shook my hand, and asked me if I raced. I told him no, but one day that would be my dream.

Over the years, I have become an avid fan of Steve's movies, especially *Le Mans,* which I have seen more times than I can remember, along with *Bullitt* and *The Great Escape.*

As far as racing goes, I finally took the wheel in the late nineties and I'm still racing one of Bob Bondurant's 1996 Orange Mustangs. In 2003, I won the class race series for both the Spec RX7 and the "BondoStangs," as we affectionately called them. I have to say, that Steve was always in the back of my mind, as I put laps on the race track and made it to the finish line almost thirty years after our chance encounter.

Mark MacVittie is an analyst in Chandler, Arizona, and his hobbies include photography, slot car racing, collecting and racing Ford Mustangs.

Top: Neile, Chad and Terry McQueen lending their support to Steve before a race.

Above: McQueen's Bell racing helmet from 1970.

Opposite above and below: Steve, Neile, Chad and Terry McQueen surrounded by race fans, and in the bottom image, also with the mechanic Haig Altounian.

My Cool Letter

Daniel Robin

> Dear Daniel:
>
> I would like to thank you for the interest and appreciation which you expressed in the letter you sent to me.
>
> I hope to continue performing and providing the entertainment which you enjoy.
>
> Sincerely,
>
> *Steve McQueen*
>
> Steve McQueen

Drywood Termite Pellets ▶
Specify **VIKANE**®

The first time I wrote to Steve McQueen, I was fourteen years old. It was 1964 and *Wanted: Dead or Alive* was a big hit in France. Every male from my generation wanted to be him. The French revere cool and Steve McQueen was the essence of cool.

My mother warned me that a man like Steve McQueen was too busy to write to a teenage boy in France, but within a few months, I received a letter from the United States, with the Solar Productions logo. It was a letter from Steve McQueen seen above.

I have always said that Steve McQueen was a great movie star, but he was a much greater man. He was noble and gentle, and took the time to listen and care about others.

Daniel Robin resides in France.

Top left: McQueen in France for the filming of *Le Mans.*

Top right: Letter to French fan Daniel Robin.

Above: Steve McQueen's favorite pen, which he used to sign his marriage license on January 16, 1980 when he and Barbara McQueen tied the knot in California.

Racing is Life
Haig Altounian

A *Le Mans* Gulf Oil racing jacket worn by McQueen.

"When you're racing, it's life. Anything that happens before or after is just waiting." That may have been the best line in *Le Mans*, but it wasn't the most profound thing to come out of the movie.

I was working for Porsche in 1969, when Solar Productions contacted us and said that Steve McQueen wanted to brush up his motor racing skills for the filming of *Le Mans*.

Of course, I had always admired McQueen's movies, but I did not confuse the man with the myth. When he strapped himself into a race car, he was under my watch and tutelage. McQueen had the courage and desire to be a top race car driver, but acting always seemed to get in the way. I remember watching him when I was a teenager, racing at Santa Barbara in the early sixties, in a Cooper Formula Junior. It was hard to miss his ability, even then.

When the Pan Am, Mexican off-road race season ended, we had participated in several SCCA (Sports Car Club of America) races on the West Coast and McQueen did well. He had only one DNF (did not finish), and he was leading the race at the time, when he became a little over aggressive with the transmission. He more than made up for it in his next race at Sebring.

The race took place in March 1970, and he was teamed with Peter Revson, a professional driver, in a three-liter car. The five-liter car was the highest class, but near the end of the race, we found ourselves in the lead. It was a unique situation, and you could feel the excitement of the crowd start to build. A movie star winning a real race would be history in the making. Jack Reddish, of Solar Productions, who was in the pit, made the unfortunate comment to team manager Andrew Ferguson: "I want Steve in the car at the end of the race." Reddish, I'm sure, felt it was for promotional reasons and the movie.

Steve approached me while resting a bit, after his driving stint and asked what I thought.

"You know, Steve, we've a real shot at winning this thing," I said.

"What do you mean?" McQueen asked.

"Winning it overall. Do you know how incredible that would be with a three-liter engine?" I said.

"What do you think it will take?" he asked.

"Well, I just overheard Reddish tell Ferguson that he wanted you in the car at the end of the race," I said, pausing before I spoke again. "Man to man, it's your decision, but if we leave Revson in, that's our best shot to win." McQueen walked away, returning about fifteen minutes later.

"Revson stays in the car."

What an unselfish call. I already had a lot of respect for him and his abilities, but right there, I gained a lot more.

Mario Andretti, who was at the peak of his career driving for the Ferrari team, put on a real campaign, surpassing us with only a few laps to go. We finally finished first in our class, but second overall. From the reaction of the crowd, you would have thought we had just won the Indy 500.

At the end of the race, all of the class winners came up to the finish line. The crowd mobbed us and it was mayhem. They started ripping pieces off the cars. We became concerned about Steve's welfare and we grouped around him as well as we could. Then he stunned me, as he stood on top of the car and gave the peace sign. It was like Moses parting the Red Sea and there was now quiet and a semblance of order.

Although the movie *Le Mans* was deemed a failure when released, I think it has stood the test of time. Every racing person you talk to points to *Le Mans* as the most authentic racing movie ever made, and that's because Steve cared about the racing. All the shots are done at speed, the wrecks are genuine, and the race was woven into the script. The film had to be absolutely genuine—and that was Steve's demand.

That's why there will never be another racing film like *Le Mans*, or another actor like Steve McQueen.

Haig Altounian is retired from the racing industry and resides in Santa Monica, California.

McQueen and his Machines

Matt Stone

Opposite: McQueen loved motors of any kind. The top photo is *The Thomas Crown Affair* dune buggy. The bottom left car is the rare 1957 Jaguar XK-SS at his home in Brentwood, California. And bottom right, revving up for *Le Mans* in a Porsche.

Right: McQueen's Rolls-Royce owner ID card, which was issued in 1978.

Steve McQueen helped build a hot rod before he could legally drive. In the Marines, he hopped up a tank's engine in the hopes of getting it to go faster. As a young acting student, he rode motorcycles through Greenwich Village. In 1970, he nearly won the 12 Hours of Sebring in a Porsche 908, driving with a broken foot in a cast. He raced buggies in Baja, rode motorcycles all over the world, and built entire movies around his love of automobiles and motorsport. He would street race his rare Jaguar XK-SS through the Hollywood Hills at night, then pack a pickup full of pals and dirt bikes and spend the next day busting trails through the California desert. He entered motorcycle races under the pseudonym "Harvey Mushman" so that spectators and the other competitors wouldn't treat him differently than anyone else.

McQueen's story as actor and icon has been told many times. These various books and documentaries often nibble around the corners of McQueen's passions for cars, bikes, and speed, but few realize what a big part of his life they were. Many forget, there was a time in the early sixties, when he was offered a factory ride by the Cooper racing team, and had to decide if he'd continue as an actor or professional racer. He chose acting, as it represented less risk for his growing family, and much higher income potential. But there's no question he would have enjoyed a solid career as a journeyman sports car and motorcycle racer. He once said "I'm not sure if I'm an actor who races or a racer who acts."

McQueen had fabulous taste in cars. He had the interest, and of course the wherewithal, to own almost any car or bike he wanted. He didn't always buy the most expensive pieces, but as with nearly every other choice he made in life, McQueen went with what was cool. He liked to customize his cars a bit; nothing radical, just a few modifications to make them his own. What a collection: three Ferraris, a Corvette, a Mini Cooper S, that fabulous Jaguar, numerous Porsches, old Packards and Hudsons, countless pickup trucks, and a few antique airplanes. There was also around 200 motorcycles, from the latest Husqvarna dirt racers, to old Harleys and his beloved Indians.

It is impossible to discuss Steve McQueen's cars, motorcycles and racing endeavors without considering his movies. In several instances, they are inextricably interwoven. Take, for example, the iconic car chase sequence in *Bullitt*; still considered the best of its genre ever captured on film. It succeeded because Steve McQueen—as actor, filmmaker, car enthusiast, racer, even stunt driver—was involved in all aspects of the scene's makeup. In *On Any Sunday*, he demonstrated his considerable riding prowess. Nor would dashing business tycoon-turned-bank-robber Thomas Crown be ripping around a beach at the wheel of a red, Corvair-powered dune buggy in *The Thomas Crown Affair*, had not McQueen played him. Lastly, there is *Le Mans*, his magnum opus, dedicated to the world's most significant sports car race.

Steve McQueen remains one of Hollywood's most committed and legitimate car enthusiasts. It was always clear how much cars and bikes meant to him, and his enthusiasm for them was genuine. I wonder what he'd be driving today?

Matt Stone is the executive editor of Motor Trend magazine and has been a professional automobile journalist and photographer since 1965.

One Helluva Ride
Mert Lawwill

The three stars of *On Any Sunday*: Bikers Mert Lawwill, Malcolm Smith and Steve McQueen. The documentary was a surprise hit in 1971 and is considered the definitive movie on motorcycle racing.

Steve McQueen's measure of a man?

It sure as heck wasn't social status. Steve cared about people. I learned this by spending time with him during the filming of *On Any Sunday*. I first met Steve in 1970, at the film director Bruce Brown's house in Dana Point, California. We were going to shoot the beach scene on the sand dunes the next day and found ourselves relegated to Bruce's kids' bunk bed. It was funny because Steve looked around and all he saw were pictures of me and Dick Mann, the national-winning motorcycle rider, and a few photos of races. There were no pictures of him in sight.

"Hey, don't you guys go to the movies?" he asked, provoking a few laughs.

If you didn't know Steve was a movie star, you would have never guessed by his attitude and outlook. One time he told me, "You know Mert, you're number one and you've earned that. In my job, I'm just an actor playing somebody else for the day and that's all." It was amazing to me, how insecure Steve felt about his place in society.

Steve was a delightful, easy going person. He was as real as you could get. We used to tease him, "You can't act, that's just the way you are." In reality, all of us had huge admiration for his acting ability but even greater admiration for him as a person.

After *On Any Sunday* was released, I was involved in an accident that completely mangled my hand at a race in Castle Rock,

Washington. The doctor at the hospital said he would have to fuse my knuckles together and I would have a club hand. When asked if there was any alternative, he shook his head. "No, better get used to the idea."

Steve found out about the accident, and arranged for me to meet with a specialist, who happened to be the Los Angeles Rams' team doctor. He looked at my X-rays, and told me a Dr. Robert Stark could repair the injury, but that he was expensive. When I called Steve back, he made all the arrangements for the surgery and allowed me to recuperate at his home in Brentwood.

There were five operations over the course of a year to insert seven pins in my hand, but I never received a bill from the doctor. I later discovered Steve picked up the entire tab.

After recuperating, I was able to ride again and continued with the race circuit. Meanwhile, Steve was making films, and we drifted apart as people tend to do when life takes you in different directions.

I've always held Steve McQueen in high esteem, not just because my hand is relatively free of disability as a result of his generosity. Our time together was one helluva ride. If I could pal around with him today, I'd do it in a heartbeat.

Mert Lawwill was the American Motorcyclist Association Grand Champion of 1969 and amassed 161 AMA Grand National finishes during his fifteen-year racing career. He lives in Tiburon, California.

Racing in Peace
Bruce Brown

Left: Taking a rest from a ride in Bruce Brown's *On Any Sunday*.
Right: Fishing in Alaska, 1972.

Steve McQueen not only gave *On Any Sunday* the green light, he applied the throttle and gave it a little extra gas—which resulted in him being arrested.

I was a surfer obsessed with the surfing way of life, not much into motorcycles. But after I read about McQueen riding in the International Six-Day Trials in *Life* magazine, the sport began to intrigue me. I started going to the races and found that motorcycle enthusiasts are so unlike what you'd expect. Over time, I wanted to do a documentary about their love for racing.

I had made somewhat of a name for myself a few years prior with *Endless Summer*, and I could approach a person like McQueen who had recently turned Solar Productions into a full-scale production company. I met with him in 1969, and told him what I wanted to do.

"That's great, what do you want me to do?" Steve asked.

"Finance it," I said, not missing a beat.

"No, I don't finance movies. I just make them," Steve said.

"Then you can't be in my movie," I said, which caused a burst of laughter.

The next day Steve called. He told me to go and make the movie. He put up $313,000 and was as good a partner as you could ever have.

The picture grossed $10 million in domestic receipts, which was phenomenal for 1971. Even better, the distributor who bought *Endless Summer* also bought *On Any Sunday*, halfway through filming, so Steve received all his money back even before the picture was finished.

After the movie came out, Steve and his first wife, Neile, were in the process of splitting up. He was feeling a little down and needed a change of scenery. I knew a hunting and fishing guide in Anchorage, Alaska, and asked Steve if he wanted to join me and a few others on a rafting trip. His mood lightened considerably and he said yes.

We rented a cabin for about a week and had a ball. My friend, Ron Hayes, owned an Oldsmobile Toronado, which was one of the first cars with front-wheel drive. Steve, who had race car experience, wanted to see if the car would skid the corners. He was driving fast, then slow, and a little crazy at times. Of course, we all had a little too much to drink. Next thing we knew an Alaskan State Trooper was on our tail and flashing the blue lights. One of my friends was egging Steve on. "Steve, you're a race car driver, you can ditch them." Steve drove around the block about ten times—slowly I might add, with the cops in hot pursuit. He finally pulled over and said, "Watch this." Whatever he had in mind, I had a hint it might not be looked upon favorably by law enforcement.

Steve thought the Anchorage police would recognize his face and cut him a break. He didn't know the Anchorage police. They grabbed him and tossed him on the hood of the car, and handcuffed him in one fell swoop. Steve was in rare form, and asked them, "Hey man, haven't you ever seen *The Blob*?" They didn't react. Then he said, "What about *Never Love a Stranger*?" Then he started listing all his B-movies. "*Hell is for Heroes*? *The War Lover*?" The cops finally saw the joke, but they hauled us off to jail anyway. They took all of our mug shots, but Steve decided to flash them the peace sign. His mug shot made all the papers, and is now a part of pop culture history. It was never so much fun getting arrested.

Director Bruce Brown is still a beach bum and resides in Southern California.

Breaking Loose

Tom Biss

McQueen's iconic mug shot was taken in 1972 when he was arrested for reckless driving in Anchorage, Alaska. His arrest is Alaskan folklore and its often rehashed among the natives.

Steve McQueen enjoyed taunting authority, especially after downing a few.

Here's the straight scoop from my father, an attorney and former judge, actor and guide Ron Hayes, and former Governor Ron Cooper, as it was told to me at different times.

McQueen liked to fish in Alaska a couple of times a year, guided by Hayes, who had also directed a few documentaries. After a Sunday supper and a couple bottles of wine at the Crow's Nest in the Westward Hotel, the finest place in town back in 1972, McQueen enlisted Hayes to show him around Anchorage since his plane didn't leave until the morning. Hayes, a client of my father's, obliged, courtesy of his Toronado, complete with Firestone tires—you know, the ones "you couldn't break loose from their grip." Anyone who knows McQueen as a gearhead knows what's coming next, especially with Hayes bragging. Racing around downtown Anchorage they flew, squealing around corners, conspicuous as bugs splattered on a windshield.

It was about 9:30 or 10 p.m. and Hayes was driving as they pulled up to the intersection of 4th and G streets heading north. It was two lanes in each direction and dead center downtown Anchorage. On the right was the 4th Avenue Theater, just beyond that was the old City Hall, down to the left, was 3rd Avenue and the Westward.

Red light. McQueen looked at Hayes and said, "You want to see these tires get broke loose? Move over." Hayes complied and McQueen buckled himself into the driver's seat. They were in the right hand lane.

Black and white. The patrol car pulled up next to them. McQueen glanced to his left, adopted a huge grin, and floored the car right through the red light. He passed the 4th Avenue Theater, the next signal and the old City Hall, turning left on another red, down 3rd Avenue, and sped through one more stop sign before heading in the wrong direction back down 3rd, spun the car around and parked it perfectly at the entrance of the Westward Hotel.

"Where are they?" McQueen said, putting his wrists together, ready for the handcuffs. Eventually, the police came and arrested them. Pa received the call around 2 a.m. "You've gotta bail us out," Hayes implores. So Pa left his bed and bailed them out.

The next day, there was a front page photograph of Hayes and McQueen going through the tarmac at the airport so McQueen could board his plane. The caption read, "*The Great Escape*?" They misidentified Hayes as James Arness since he closely resembled Arness at the time. My dad, who represented McQueen, decided that he couldn't have a fair trial in Anchorage due to the media blitz, and asked the judge for a change of venue. Granted, and the case was moved to Fairbanks, with attorney, and later Alaskan governor, Ron Cooper defending McQueen and Hayes against a charge of reckless driving instead of DUI.

Cooper was all set to defend McQueen as a licensed and certified race car and stunt driver, and planned on showing clips of *Bullitt* and *Le Mans* to the court and jury to prove that McQueen could handle himself behind the wheel of a car. However, before the case reached Fairbanks, McQueen forfeited bail and the case was dismissed. Alaskan police weren't about to try and extradite a heavy-duty movie star on a traffic violation.

Tom Biss is a writer and lifelong resident of Anchorage, Alaska.

Wow, I found Steve McQueen's Husky

Rob Phillips

I firmly believe that everything happens for a reason, and though not a religious man, I also believe a higher power had a hand in helping me find Steve McQueen's 1970 Husqvarna 400 Cross.

Growing up in Scranton, Pennsylvania, I was introduced to Husqvarna bikes by my older brother. Though I would come to own a number of bikes for trail riding, I always had a soft spot for the Husky. In 1976, I bought my first Husky 250 from a local Kawasaki dealer. Over the years, I sold and bought it back several times, until in August 2004, when I decided to restore it. Six months later, it was ready for the road, except now it was of showroom quality. It looked so beautiful that I didn't have the heart to ride it, so I made the decision to sell it for the last time. I had so much fun restoring the bike and making money from its sale, I decided to make bike restoration my new hobby. I continued buying more Huskys and parts, stockpiling as much as I could. That's when I ran into Don Ince, of Vintage Viking.

Don advertised the sale of original dealer invoices for most of the Husqvarnas sold in the United States, during the sixties and early seventies, having acquired all the books from importer Edison Dye, along with many other documents, letters, parts, and memorabilia. I thought it would be interesting for my customers to have an invoice that showed a little history of the bikes.

In this way, I discovered I had restored the first 1970 400 Cross bike purchased by Malcolm Smith, a former world champion racer, who was in the film *On Any Sunday* with Steve McQueen. Completing its restoration, I loaned it to the Motorcycle Hall of Fame Museum in Ohio, where it was displayed for a year in the Malcolm Smith exhibit.

Among the bike collecting community, anytime someone finds a 1970 400 Cross, he tells everyone he has found Steve McQueen's racing bike, and of course, no one believes him—until now.

In late January 2008, a man called to tell me he had a complete 1970 Husky 400 Cross. From the photos, it appeared to be in good shape, so I bought it, and then asked Don Ince to locate its invoice. I learned that the bike came from Temple City, California, which is about twenty-five miles from where Steve McQueen's movie company, Solar Productions, had been based. Three months later, Don discovered the invoice, which revealed it had been sold to Solar Productions.

The invoice and title were dated February 9th, 1970. Just four weeks before the famous Lake Elsinore race took place. I had paid for the bike, almost thirty-eight years to the day, of McQueen's original purchase.

I had Steve McQueen's 1970 400 Cross!

Rob Phillips is the founder of Advanced Racing Technologies and Huskyrestoration.com. He lives in Staatsburg, New York, with his wife Pat and their Westie, Bailey.

Top left: His enthusiasm for motorcycle racing garnered McQueen the cover of *Sports Illustrated* in August 1971.

Top right: Sporting a Husqvarna T-shirt on a motorcycle outing.

Casting Off

Al Satterwhite

Al Satterwhite's photos of McQueen at Sebring are some of the most revealing of the man and racer.

The race is still one of the most talked about victories in Sebring history.

I was at the 1970 12 Hours of Sebring race a few days early, to photograph the drivers in practice. Steve McQueen had entered his open-cockpit Porsche 908 Spyder, in preparation for his unannounced upcoming film, *Le Mans*.

McQueen had broken his foot a few weeks prior in a motorcycle competition, and had it in a plaster cast. He was still hobbling about, barely able to walk, so he used a small mini-bike to travel around the pit area. The image of the larger-than-life Steve McQueen, motoring down pit lane on an itty-bitty mini-bike was so unusual and compelling that I immediately whipped out my camera and started shooting. Known for his aversion to celebrity paparazzi, McQueen didn't mind pro racing photographers. He was interested in racing, and if you were part of that, you were all right in his book. McQueen and I had an unspoken understanding—we would make eye contact from time to time, and he knew I was there to cover the race, not there for him.

McQueen and his co-driver, Peter Revson, were enjoying a leading position three hours from the finish having driven at a safe, steady pace the prior nine hours, as most of their competition dropped out with mechanical problems. The Ferrari team, which was driving a 5.0-liter V-12 engine, was not about to give up the race to a 3.0-liter eight-cylinder engine Porsche, let alone, an actor. Their manager put Mario Andretti in the remaining entry, with clear instructions to "Catch that Porsche!" McQueen was racing so hard that the cast melted off of his foot, and the more experienced Revson took the wheel for the final laps. Phenomenal driver that Andretti was, he beat them by a mere twenty-two seconds, and they finished second overall in the race, taking first in the 3.0-liter class.

McQueen's passion for racing was evident to those who watched him behind the wheel of the Porsche. A driven competitor with a love of cars and speed, McQueen embodied the heart and soul of a winner—at the track and on the silver screen.

Al Satterwhite is a world-renowned photographer and lives in Los Angeles, California.

Opposite top left and clockwise: Steve in *The Sand Pebbles, Never So Few, War Lover* and *Papillon.* Above: *Le Mans.*

Working Class Hero
Paul Taylor

His death was in all the papers, but at just ten-years old, I have no memory of when Steve McQueen died. To me, McQueen was simply a cool actor who jumped a big fence on a motorbike to escape a group of gun-toting Germans.

It wasn't until I watched a television documentary when I was seventeen, that I truly discovered the man and the legend. Steve McQueen's appeal is that he resonates as a working class hero who performs extraordinary deeds. McQueen seemed approachable, carrying none of the Hollywood aloofness.

There has always been an institutionalized class system in Britain, which is why Steve is so revered here. Coming from a working class background myself, there were few similar actors to relate to in England, apart from Michael Caine. Most actors appeared posh, speaking with upper class accents. Being a scouser from Liverpool, I just could not identify with any of them, but Steve was something else—he was cool, he was hip, he was relevant. He represents the ordinary working man, who loves nothing more than to see one of their own become a success and stick two fingers up to authority, as Steve did in *Le Mans*. He gave us a voice, achieving what we wouldn't or couldn't do. He's everything we want to be, but never can be.

As for his love of motor sports, many years ago Britain was a major force in the car and motorbike industry, with companies like Jaguar and Norton. Steve's interest in this field was always going to make him popular here.

As an actor, I've studied Steve's style and how one expression could say more than any words—a certain look in his eye, that great smirk, even the way he would look down at his feet—it all spoke volumes. Working class Brits love an underdog, someone who fights against the odds and triumphs over adversity, which Steve mastered in *The Great Escape, The Cincinnati Kid* and *Papillon*. It was because of Steve, that I wanted to become an actor. He made me feel if he could do it, so could I.

Although Steve has been gone for nearly thirty years, he is still loved and remembered fondly in Britain. I like to think that if I ever met him, that we'd have been friends and shared many a pint in a pub. Steve McQueen was and still is my hero. What more can I say? I just love him.

Paul Taylor is an actor/filmmaker and resident of Liverpool, England.

Le MANS A SOLAR PRODUCTION

October 22, 1970

Mr. Sid Ganis
Cinema Center Films
4024 Radford Avenue
Studio City, California

Dear Sid:

I talked to David Piper on the phone and he is as he says "a bit weak". He has had numerous operations, and, of course, there is his mental state knowing that there is a good chance that he will lose his leg.

I don't think the man is financially fit and he is certainly through with racing one way or another. So many times before in the history of motion pictures brave men have lost their lives and limbs and people have forgotten about it. If David loses his leg, I don't think we should forget about this one. I feel very strongly that we should dedicate the first premiere to David Piper and give all the proceeds to him and his family.

Would you please pass this on to the higher ups, and I do think we owe this to racing for what they gave this film.

My best,

Steve McQueen

cc: Robert E. Relyea
Jack N. Reddish
Bob Rosen

Race for Respect
Lee Katzin

Top: Enjoying a rare moment of frivolity on *Le Mans*, the most intense shoot of McQueen's career.

Below left: An October 22, 1970, letter from Steve McQueen to Sid Ganis, an executive with CBS Cinema Center Films, which financed *Le Mans*. In the letter McQueen makes a plea to Ganis asking him if CBS could raise money for David Piper, a racer and stunt driver who lost his leg in a crash during the filming of the picture.

Below right: McQueen with director Lee Katzin, who was given the thankless job of trying to fill John Sturges' shoes.

"How would you like to go to France?" asked Jim Henshaw, who was my boss at Cinema Center.

"When?" I asked. I was told I needed to be there in three days if I wanted to direct a feature film starring Steve McQueen.

Cinema Center was the movie production arm of the CBS Television Network and had entered the picture business a few years before. *Le Mans*, one of the biggest budgeted films of the year, was bleeding $90,000 a day and had an unfinished shooting script. And, oh yes, the director, the legendary John Sturges, parted ways with McQueen because he would not take direction. I wasn't exactly welcomed with open arms.

"Hello, Steve. Nice to meet you," I said, extending my hand when I arrived on the first day of filming. Instead of taking my hand, Steve grabbed my tie, lifted me up in the air and said he only answered to "Mr. McQueen." It was quite the introduction.

It was a difficult set of circumstances for the first six weeks. Steve would have a blowup and leave, and we'd have to shoot without him until he came back. But that all changed early one morning when Steve spotted me out on the set before any of the cast and crew arrived. He stared at me from his motor home, which was not far from where I was setting up a shot. Finally, he walked over to me and spoke his piece.

"Lee, I am no longer going to be against you. I see what you're trying to do and I'm going to work for you and not against you," Steve said. I had no idea where this came from but from that time on, we hit it off. I was as surprised as anyone.

Lee Katzin was the director of Le Mans. He died in October 2002.

Facing *Bullitt*

John Klawitter

As race car driver Michael Delaney in *Le Mans*.

Knowledgeable people will tell you there are only two kinds of actors: Method actors like Meryl Streep and Dustin Hoffman, who can play anybody, and presence players like John Wayne and Tom Cruise, who can only play themselves. This is interesting, as far as broad and general theories go, but in the life of a star, it can be more complicated. Take somebody like Steve McQueen, surely one of those presence players with his haunting, lonely stare and minimalistic facial gestures.

I worked with Steve in the early seventies and the rumor then, and perhaps still now, was that Steve in life, had taken on the persona of many of his earlier movie characters.

After he played the cool international mastermind in *The Thomas Crown Affair*, the story goes, he was never able to snap completely back out of that role in his real life, and be himself again. Of course, that assumes any of us knows completely who we are, and if you look around, you'll see self-ignorance abounds. Still, when Steve was in big money trouble on *Bullitt*, his classic police detective thriller, he played high stakes financial poker with the studios the way Thomas Crown would have. As the costs soared and the studio threatened to rein him in and shut down the production, he invested his entire personal stake in the picture, gambling every cent he owned on its ultimate success. And when *Bullitt* succeeded at the box office, Steve raked in millions. Suddenly he had the money to go along with the persona.

It wasn't just about money. The legends say that Steve himself raced *Bullitt's* hot Ford Mustang over San Francisco's hilly streets, just as he was supposed to have jumped his own bike for the key sequence in *The Great Escape*. Steve would never deny it, and nobody dared ask him to his face, even though those exploits well may have been created by eager and inventive public relations flacks. (I can call them that, having been one myself.) It is true that people who were on the set for those pictures later told their friends that Bud Ekins jumped the bike in the one picture and handled the hot Mustang in the other. Regardless, Steve once again began to live his own legend as he took to racing cars and bikes in earnest.

So, was there any truth to the rumor that the man was living his movie roles in real life? You decide: By 1968, he had the image of a wealthy, exciting, dangerous and mysterious international loner with a passion for rolling the dice of life and racing fast cars.

It's hard to say exactly when he caught the auteur filmmaker bug that infected so many of us in the "Love Generation". He may have had it all along, that disease sometimes taking a while to become virulent. I do know that by the time he started working on the set of *Le Mans*, where Nikita Knatz and I were set to shoot the feature, *Le Mans and The Man McQueen*, the signs were everywhere. Steve's arms would weave and wave and words like "happening" and "creatively expressive" and "capturing the moment" would come out of his mouth and everything would be a grand mush upon the ears of anyone listening without the cushion of true fan bliss.

Niki and I were to create the story of the making of that particular racing movie, and we did so in a short film that is still considered a classic of the genre. But here's a bit of the real story, a few short strokes from the tale we were never allowed to tell. As he came to France to begin his racing movie, Steve was much affected by the enormously successful Woodstock Festival documentary. He wanted his racing movie to capture the same rough-and-ready, shoot-around-the-clock, 16-millimeter *cinema verité*. That meant that he didn't want to act a role. He didn't want to read what he considered to be phony lines or have a story involved with what he thought were foolish plots. He wanted no heavy human drama getting in the way of what he saw as the ultimate drama of his picture—drivers facing death for glory in the race itself.

So, in Steve's mind, this was going to be a pure documentary, the most realistic movie ever made about racing, which he had begun to refer to as "a blood sport". Unfortunately, that's not the idea he sold to CBS Cinema Center, the people who were funding his dream. That picture was your standard dramatic fare, an exciting grand prix racing picture with just the right dollops of romance, violence and death mixed in. You can see how diametrically opposed that proposal was from the project he set out to create.

Who was going to be in creative control? Well, that was a complex and difficult question. The studio, of course, thought they had control, which they delegated to famous director John Sturges, the man who had given Steve his big breaks in *Never So Few* and *The Great Escape*. With Sturges at the helm, the North Hollywood-based studio could be confident their money and trust was on solid ground and the project would proceed steadily to its successful and profitable conclusion. In reality, nothing would be further from the truth.

Showing up in France at the fabled Le Mans track, second unit director Jack Reddish began shooting racing car footage, the sleek autos flashing through the rural countryside then across the stands area and back into the countryside for more loops. This was dangerous, expensive stuff, and pretty enough on screen, but after some months they had yet to shoot a single frame with Steve in it. And worse, Steve was telling John Sturges more and more exactly how he wanted *his film* shot. After the second unit had filmed 120,000 feet of gorgeous racing footage, he had nearly nothing, Sturges stormed back to the US, claiming it was "the worst experience of his professional life." And the movie went on what the trade magazines politely call "extended hiatus" that lasted eight weeks. Steve returned to North Hollywood to explain it all. He must have been persuasive, because the money men didn't shut the thing down then and there.

Production was resumed with three competing writers, including the famous script doctor John T. Kelly and *Playboy* racing writer Ken Purdy, all three working in adjoining trailers on different versions of what they hoped would be shot the next day—and none of it was much like the script Steve's Solar Productions had originally pitched and sold. John Sturges was replaced by the

Le Mans & The Man McQueen

Written & Produced by JOHN KLAWITTER

Directed by NIKITA KNATZ

Documentary Featurette - 14 minutes 28 seconds
As it originally ran on CBS

In the early 1970's, Steve McQueen went to the Gran Prix track at Le Mans, France to dramatize his love of speed and auto racing in the motion picture Le Mans. Young filmmakers Nikita Knatz and John Klawitter went along to document the experience. Steve's picture is still considered by many to be the 'greatest film about auto racing ever made.' The featurette, titled "Le Mans & The Man McQueen", records the efforts to which the famous actor went to achieve his dream, and the featurette itself is considered a classic of its type in European circles, where it is cherished not only for its historical content, but for the look and feel of what it was like to be on the set with Steve McQueen as he followed his passion for speed and danger.

polished and dapper Lee Katzin, who immediately found himself with the tiger by the tail. Nothing seemed to please Steve, who had taken up residence in a classic French country villa and then had torn up the two-hundred-year-old gardens, turning them into a motocross where he and his friends could jump their bikes.

The mood on the set thickened and turned ugly. If Steve didn't like the new pages, he wouldn't come out of his big motor home, which was parked near the track. He would send out word he was sick. One day, as if to prove his illness, he staggered out looking grey as a slab of limestone. The crew, most of whom had read Forsythe's *The Day of the Jackal*, accused him of chewing cordite to change his complexion. Incredible as it sounds, Steve once roared out of his cabana and towed Lee across the set with a firm grasp on his trademark necktie, yelling for the entire assembled cast and crew to hear that he, Steve McQueen, would kiss Lee's ass in a window of Macy's department store in Manhattan if the footage of him turned out right, but it wasn't. Much to Lee's credit (or discredit, depending on how you think about such matters) he hung in there. Without his tenacity, *Le Mans* would never have been completed.

Viewing it today, you have to be struck by the feeling that *Le Mans* comes about as close to *cinema verité* as can be achieved using huge, bulky 70-millimeter cameras and surly French union camera crews that couldn't seem to take a first shot until eleven o'clock in the morning. But, if you were there experiencing it, the general run of it was grief and agony all around, dissatisfaction and ill will in the air and an overall feeling of gloom.

I'd had a little trouble with McQueen, myself. In spite of Niki's warning (he knew Steve much better than I), I'd wanted to ride along in the tiny passenger seat and film the great man while he was driving. Steve had treated my request like it was impossible, and I must have indicated with a graceless sneer or some other mannerism that it didn't take a superhuman to climb in a race car. That was my attitude problem; I'd been called on it before, and it didn't endear me to our star.

A month went by before I saw him again. Late one night, I was working at our offices on Radcliff near Cinema Center, hunched over a moviola to stick the footage together when Steve unexpectedly walked in. He sat on a stool looking over my shoulder while I ran the trailer for him, and then his hands started going and he described thousands of dollars worth of new footage and expensive optical dissolves he wanted to add to our little epic.

"An eagle," he said, "I see this beautiful slow-motion eagle, wings spread, back-lit by the sun. We cross-dissolve to a shot of me looking into the distance, and then to a shot of the Porsche. You see, we have to somehow symbolize the tremendous feeling of freedom, of exhilaration, of pure, raw energy, that one has when behind the wheel of a racing machine."

"Great ideas, Steve," I said. "But we can't do that."

He stood, and the musing look fled from his face. The creative filmmaker had vanished. I was alone with Thomas Crown. With the dangerous Frank Bullitt. He stared at me. The room grew dark and smoky. All I could see were those flinty, relentless eyes. *I'm in a fricking movie,* I remember thinking. *Steve has put me in a gunfight— only I'm the bad guy.*

I feel embarrassed today that I could be put under his spell so easily, or that I could have acted so foolishly, but his presence was powerful, it just sucked me in. I stood and faced him, knocking over the editor's stool, terribly conscious of my hands at my sides. *As the bad guy, wasn't I supposed to draw first?*

My voice was hoarse, probably from fright.

"Steve," I said. "I can't. We can't."

"Why not, Jack?" he asked in a voice like a whispery knife edge.

"Steve, we don't have the money. And Cinema Center isn't going to pony up."

Opposite: Promotional item for *Le Mans & The Man McQueen*, a featurette that McQueen heartily endorsed.

Above: Steve taking a spin in his Porsche 908 on the wet track in Holtville, California, 1970.

Right: A thank you letter from McQueen to director John Klawitter.

"Oh," he said.

And his mood lightened, shifting us both out of the scene as if a hypnotist in some other dimension had snapped his fingers. No reason for a shoot-out; I wasn't contradicting his creativity. It was just about money.

"You should have said so in the first place," he said, coming over and clapping me on the back. "I'll make those bastards cough up."

Maybe he tried and maybe he didn't. I never heard any more about it. And when Niki and I gathered everybody who mattered in a screening room at the studio and ran the final answer print, a trade term for a version that is color corrected and dubbed with sound, Steve McQueen loved it. At least, whoever showed up that day in the whipcord lean body and behind that enigmatic little smile, said that he did.

John Klawitter is the co-director of Le Mans & The Man McQueen. He lives in Southern California.

Reprinted from Tinsel Wilderness: Lessons On Survival As A Professional Creative Person In Hollywood & Other Extreme Climates by John Klawitter, Double Dragon Publishing (www.double-dragon-ebooks.com), 2007.

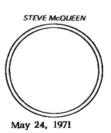

STEVE McQUEEN

May 24, 1971

Dear Jack:

Just a note to let you know that I was terribly pleased with the featurette for "Le Mans", and I'm sure all the people who worked so hard on the film will also be very happy with the results of your hard work as you did a great job.

Many thanks.

Best regards,

Steve McQueen

SM/bc

Mr. Jack Klawitter
11969 Ventura Blvd.
North Hollywood, Calif. 91604

Losing My Lunch
John Wyatt Largo

Opposite: McQueen's Solar Plastics Engineering logo is proudly displayed on the back of his driving suit.

Above: Paul Newman and Steve McQueen sharing a beer on the set of *The Towering Inferno* released in 1974.

In 1970, I was a nine-year-old boy enjoying a hot summer day at the Ontario Motor Speedway. My dad gave me $5 for hot dogs and sodas at the concession stand.

Walking back with my hands full, I was careful not to be elbowed as I worked my way through the heavy crowd. About halfway, I stopped by the fence to watch the stream of high-speed cars shoot by.

To my right were two middle-aged men leaning on the fence. They were wearing sunglasses and baseball hats with racing logos. Both were relatively nondescript.

It was Steve McQueen and Paul Newman.

I tried not to stare. Even above the roar of the engines, I recognized their voices, as they talked shop. Newman was harping at McQueen for not playing the Sundance Kid in the 1969 classic, *Butch Cassidy and the Sundance Kid*.

"You're not going to give me that again!" McQueen countered.

Suddenly, both looked at me and grinned. I stumbled backward, spilling sodas and almost losing my hot dogs. Flustered, I walked away. I scrambled up the bleachers. Halfway up, I stopped and looked back just in time to see both line up for a beer.

John Wyatt Largo is a resident of Phoenix, Arizona.

Opposite top left: McQueen loved Indian bikes as witnessed by his T-shirt.

Opposite bottom left: A 1920 Indian Powerplus "Daytona" racing motorcycle owned by McQueen.

Below: Steve McQueen on a 1941 Indian.

An American Legend
Dennis Bozung

Though he never personally knew him, my dad could never have imagined that that the collection resulting from his life-long passion for an American icon, the Indian motorcycle, would eventually find its way into the ownership of Steve McQueen.

I am one of four sons of Indian motorcycle enthusiast, Al Bozung. Fresh out of World War II, dad began buying up motorcycles and parts around the country. Known as "the man who had what you needed," he collected, rode, restored, bought, traded and sometimes even sold them. When dad died in 1971, he had one of the largest collections in the nation: twenty-six vintage Indian bikes, some rare, some restored to original condition, and parts for most models.

Dad used an old school bus that he had bought to move the bikes and parts from barns, garages and storage sheds of former Indian motorcycle dealerships that had closed after the company went out of business in 1953. They used to say that he could smell an old Indian while driving down the road, even if it was stored in the back of some old garage under a pile of parts. He was one of the charter members of the Indian Four and All-American Indian Motorcycle Club, the oldest Indian motorcycle club in existence today. He remained a trustee until his death at which time Mr. McQueen bought a large portion of his collection.

My dad would have been pleased to know that he had been caretaker of the classics that eventually would come into the possession of another legend, Steve McQueen, who truly understood what it was all about to own a piece of American history, the Indian motorcycle.

Dennis A. Bozung is a member of the All American Indian Motorcycle Club and Chapter President of the Iron Indian Riders Association of Michigan.

A Tough Nut to Crack

Henry Valdez

A matchbook from the El Padrino Room, a bar inside the Beverly Wilshire Hotel that McQueen often frequented.

Steve McQueen probably spilled more beer than most people drank. I would know because I topped off his drinks for more than a decade.

From 1969 to 1978, I worked as a bartender at the Beverly Hills Hotel. The hotel's Polo Lounge was a watering hole for Hollywood dealmakers and generations of celebrities. Throughout the years I had met and befriended many Tinseltown luminaries, including Paul Newman, Robert Wagner, Darryl Zanuck, Evel Knievel and Steve McQueen.

McQueen was a private individual, but he enjoyed the camaraderie of locals while bonding over a brew. It's common for those in the saloon business to frequent other bars, if for nothing else, a change in scenery. I had seen Steve in many local haunts other than the Polo Lounge, including the Zuma Bar in Malibu, the Old Place in Agoura Hills (where I saw him tend bar many nights) and Chez Jay in Santa Monica.

On Ocean Avenue near the Santa Monica Pier, Chez Jay is a nautical-themed restaurant and bar situated in a row of budget motels. Somehow the celebrity "dive" became famous among legends, superstars, out of work writers, tourists, regulars and nobodies. That's because the owner, Jay Fiondella, an ex-Navy man who had bit parts in more than thirty movies, created an atmosphere where celebrities could relax. Jay, who passed away in 2007, was protective of his celebrity clients and banned all cameras and autograph seekers from the premises, which is why this funky, dimly-lit, sawdusted joint has packed them in for more than a half-century. It's a place the Kennedys frequented in their prime, where Henry Kissinger could be found drinking with his friends, where Lee Marvin drove his motorcycle right through the front door and ordered a drink, and where Madonna tracked down Sean Penn many times during their stormy union. It's also where I saw Steve McQueen nearly give Jay a heart attack.

Chez Jay was nearly as famous for its peanuts as its celebrity clientèle. The peanuts were out of this world—roasted in the shell but not too salty. Astronaut Alan Shepard, who was the commander of Apollo 14, had dinner at Chez Jay the night before he left for training in 1971. Shepard told Jay he was going to take a golf ball and golf club with him to the moon. That's when Jay's mind went into overdrive.

"Take a peanut to the moon for me," he asked Shepard. "I want to have the first Astro-nut." Shepard obliged, producing the well-traveled legume a few months later. Shepard even signed an affidavit that it had accompanied him to the moon. The peanut became Jay's prized possession. He carried it around in his pocket and routinely set it down on the bar.

One day I walked into the bar when Jay and McQueen were busting each other's chops. It appeared to me that Jay was taunting Steve.

"Look Steve, you're the highest paid actor in the world and you can have any car, house or woman that you want," Jay said. "But as successful as you are, you can't have this. It's a peanut that's been to the moon."

McQueen, who had cat-like reflexes, snatched the peanut from Jay's hand and popped it in his mouth. Jay leapt over the bar and tried to fish hook the peanut out.

"Don't you swallow that damned peanut, McQueen!" Jay growled. The two wrestled on the ground for nearly a minute until McQueen was too tired to fight the good fight. He was laughing so hard that he finally spat it back out and said, "Jay, you can have the peanut!"

Good thing McQueen didn't accidentally swallow the thing or Jay would've been tending more than bar where the sun don't shine.

Henry Valdez is the owner of Enrique's Mexican Restaurant in Thousand Oaks, California, where he resides.

Wrong Way McQueen
Kathy Swor

Movie veteran Kathy Swor says McQueen was literally hell on wheels when operating a vehicle.

It is well known that Steve McQueen loved his cars and could drive with the best of them. But reading road signs? Well, that seems to be another story.

I was a script aide on the TV show, *The Streets of San Francisco,* when I encountered McQueen in the early seventies. The show was filmed at Samuel Goldwyn Studios in Hollywood. Cramped quarters forced all traffic on the lot to move one way between the stages.

I was driving my two-week old yellow Volkswagen bug around the lot when McQueen's Porsche flew around a corner—the wrong way. We came within an inch of a total head-on collision. That was when my Irish temper flared. I screamed at the top of my lungs, arms flailing wildly, pointing out the one-way signs to the speed demon that had almost demolished my car.

Then the door opened and out popped Steve McQueen.

He ambled to my car, bent down, focused those famous steely-blue eyes on me, and said, "Man, you are cute when you are mad."

Of course, I was still fuming, but what the hell. It was Steve McQueen. Gently patting my car as he returned to his well-tended ride, he jumped back in, and went on his way—still going in the wrong direction.

Kathy Swor resides in Oxnard, California.

Be Who You Are

Kent Twitchell

Opposite: Kent Twitchell's world famous mural of Steve McQueen, which was painted in 1971 in downtown L.A.

Right: Twitchell repainted his mural in 2009 but this time in a studio.

I first discovered the joy of Steve McQueen in the late fifties with the one-two punch of *Wanted: Dead or Alive* and the sci-fi movie classic, *The Blob*. For as much fun as people poke at *The Blob*, many today don't realize what an impact that little movie had on teenagers at the time.

I joined the Air Force in 1960 and McQueen's movies were a must-see for most GI's. We loved them all, even the goofy comedy *The Honeymoon Machine*. *The Magnificent Seven* was forever being argued by servicemen as the greatest western along with *Shane*. He stole *Never So Few* away from everyone else in it, including Frank Sinatra, the film's star. McQueen was our man, our alter ego and we couldn't take our eyes off him. He was so authentic that he didn't seem to be acting at all, but there was always something simmering just below the surface. He was subtle, almost a minimalist, and in his unique way was able to become whatever character he portrayed.

McQueen's war movies were a work of art. He was tough and handled a weapon with the grace of an expert. Then *The Great Escape* put him into the stratosphere.

My exit from the military coincided with the release of *The Cincinnati Kid*, and I continued being a big McQueen fan. When I started college under the GI Bill, *The Sand Pebbles* came out and everyone realized we had a talented actor in our midst.

In 1971, when *The Thomas Crown Affair* and *Bullitt* solidified McQueen's superstar status, I decided I needed to paint him. I was a junior at California State University and I talked my art professor into letting me paint a mural instead of the assigned classroom exercise. I made McQueen two-stories tall on a home on Union and 12th Streets near downtown L.A. When it was finished, media and curious fans called from all over the world to interview me.

That mural helped me find my own way as an artist. As with most students at that time, my paintings were abstract, but I was inspired by McQueen's life to be myself. So I returned to realism, which I had loved as a kid, in spite of the fact that everyone else seemed to think it was dead. Realism was to return with a vengeance and I've been a realist painter now for almost four decades.

During the course of my life, I have matured and learned to appreciate Steve McQueen more and more. Along the way I hope I have learned to be authentic as he was.

Kent Twitchell is an American muralist who is most active in Los Angeles. He is recognized around the world for his larger-than-life photorealist mural portraits, often of celebrities and artists. He resides in northern California.

Changing Fortune
in a Writer's Life
Jeb Rosebrook

Above and right: McQueen showed a softer, gentler side to his acting in 1972's *Junior Bonner*.

"I want to make this movie for Steve McQueen," producer Joe Wizan told me. We were in a screening room at Warner Brothers watching Carol Ballard's documentary on the National Rodeo Finals where an older bull rider named Freckles Brown, was taking on Oscar, a bull that had never before been ridden. Freckles Brown accomplished a ride that eight seconds before had seemed more than impossible.

Joe Wizan, a former agent, was about to produce his first film, *Jeremiah Johnson*. Two Washington State businessmen had given Joe enough money to option scripts he felt were ready for the big screen. A three-page outline titled *Bonner*, the coming-home story of an over-the-hill rodeo cowboy, his family and a bull named Sunshine became their first investment with Wizan.

That was November, 1970. In April, 1971, Wizan and I met Steve. For two-and-a-half years I had tried to earn my living as a writer, and that night in Brentwood, California, would change my life. Because of the character and story I created and the screenplay Joe Wizan had molded with me, I was face-to-face with the highest paid movie star in the world. Within two months we would be in Prescott, Arizona, making *Junior Bonner*. Writers often do not go on location. I did.

So we were in Prescott with Steve, Sam Peckinpah, Ida Lupino, Robert Preston, Barbara Leigh, Joe Don Baker, Bill McKinney, Don "Red" Barry and Ben Johnson, who was soon to win an Academy Award for *The Last Picture Show*.

There were many "Steves". There is Steve in his pickup truck, scouting locations, Peckinpah in the front, me holding on for dear life as Steve challenges every mountainous curve on U.S. 89. There is the quiet, gentle Steve meeting my wife, Dorothy and my four-year-old daughter, Katherine. He places his hand on her head and she is too shy to look up and to this day she will tell you she met Steve McQueen but never saw him! There is Steve, who rarely, if ever shed a tear in a movie, a man without a real father, doing the scene at the Prescott railroad depot, turning away from his movie father, Ace, attempting to bridle the emotion in perhaps one of the most powerful scenes he has ever played. There is Steve, the father with his two children making and selling tie-dye T-shirts. He is proud of them. There is Steve, without the press, enjoying a summer of his own private life. And yes, there is the temperamental Steve, who spends an afternoon attempting to ad-lib over apple pie with Ida, and getting nowhere. "You come back tomorrow," she tells him, "or you'd better be ready to eat a lot of apple pie." He did come back. The two of them are as one, and apple pie becomes incidental.

On the final day of filming, we end up in the old mining town of Jerome, Arizona. Steve, as usual, carries no money. He needs a beer. I buy his beer. He said it was a loan. For me, like that summer, it was a gift.

Jeb Rosebrook is a veteran screenwriter, author and journalist. He resides in Scottsdale, Arizona.

Top Billing
William Pierce

As Junior Bonner, McQueen played an over-the-hill rodeo star who had seen better days.

The Steve McQueen I knew was two distinct people—an intense man when he was in front of the cameras and a regular person when he wasn't in the spotlight.

As a member of the Arizona Film Commission, I had a chance to see both sides of him over a ten-week period when he filmed *Junior Bonner* in my hometown of Prescott, Arizona, in the summer of 1971.

Steve almost didn't come to Arizona because officials from Ruidoso, New Mexico, were lobbying hard for the picture, entertaining movie executives on the taxpayer's dime. That wasn't my style. I told director Sam Peckinpah that his rodeo film would be bogus if it was not made in Prescott. That seemed to grab his attention. A few days later, I received the call that Peckinpah had decided on our location and he was bringing with him an all-star cast of Steve McQueen, Robert Preston, Ida Lupino and Ben Johnson.

As two men who were about the same age and enjoyed the same things in life, Steve and I hit it off. Steve was about as normal as any movie star I've ever met. We were both family men who were heavily involved with our kids, rode motorcycles, liked the occasional beer and bummed cigarettes off each other. I even delivered to Steve several of his $100,000 paychecks, which came once a week over a period of two-and-a-half months.

Once Steve stepped in front of the movie camera, he became a different person—intense, focused and all business.

I was lucky enough to share a scene with Steve at the beginning of the movie. We ad-libbed our lines and nailed the shot in three takes. Steve was surprised that I had never acted before and just about floored me when he told me I was a natural.

"I usually have a problem in my first scene with other actors and I appreciate the fact that you were so relaxed and we got this first one out of the way. I'm ready now," Steve said. He was admitting that even he had first day jitters but I had helped him through it.

I couldn't help him, though, when it came to horses. I noticed he flinched every time he was on a bucking horse in a chute. He admitted that he didn't like working with them, which surprised me given that he had handled horses quite convincingly on *Wanted: Dead or Alive*, *The Magnificent Seven* and *Nevada Smith*. He also had no fear when it came to riding a motorcycle.

"I'm in control then," Steve said. "You can never figure out what a horse might do."

The memories and the friendships that I forged during the summer of '71 have stayed with me. Perhaps the greatest thrill I received was when *Junior Bonner* made its Prescott debut the following year. The movie theater owner, who was a good friend of mine, arranged the marquee to read: *Junior Bonner* starring William Pierce, Steve McQueen, Robert Preston, Ida Lupino and Ben Johnson.

That satisfaction couldn't be bought by one of Steve's $100,000 paychecks.

William Pierce is a U.S. Bankruptcy Trustee and has lived in Prescott since 1960.

My Kinda Cowboy
Barbara Leigh

Opposite: On the set with the gorgeous Barbara Leigh, whom McQueen romanced during the filming of *Junior Bonner.* Hairstylist Kathryn Blondell is between them.

Right: The leading man and lady ready for a big screen kiss.

I met Steve McQueen on a casting call for his movie, *Junior Bonner.* As fate would have it I was given the part of Charmagne, Steve's girlfriend in the film. Off screen, he would become a friend and lover for a short time, but the memories of our relationship and working together on the movie will forever live in my heart.

Steve McQueen was someone almost every woman dreamt to be with, and most every man wanted to be. He was a unique actor who didn't appear to be acting at all. His power came from his facial expressions and his subtle body movements. Only the camera could capture the reality of his work. I remember watching Steve during the filming of the movie and thinking he wasn't acting. But, he most certainly was. Later when I saw the completed scenes I realized that he was a master of his craft.

I learned much from observing Steve and the other actors, such as Robert Preston. I saw that less is sometimes best but I also realized that Steve could be over the top and still make it work. The camera loves certain faces and personalities and one of these was Steve McQueen. The top actors all knew exactly what the camera expected from them and they gave it their best.

Steve could be funny at times, joking around with the crew on the set; but for the most part, I found him to be serious and to the point. He was clear on what he expected from his fellow actors. When the director called "Action!" it was time to work—all kidding stopped.

Steve McQueen was a great father to his children, a friend to all his fans, and a man who loved his women. Good or bad, he was the epitome of the American rebel. For those of us who knew him, he was a gift incomparable to anyone else.

Unfortunately, Steve was a sad person in many aspects of his life, and it took becoming ill to find what he searched for. Himself. He learned only while dying that life was a wonderful gift and I would like to think he made peace with himself and God before he was called home. It's easy to be lost in egos, wealth, sex and relationships. Being humbled by God enlightens us more quickly to the realization of what's important in life. I believe he learned this, and had he been able to beat his illness would have been a stronger person who could have helped others more on a spiritual level. He was a deep thinker, a loving man, father and friend who will be remembered in many ways by many different persons.

When I think of Steve McQueen, I do not remember the movie star, but a special friend who was fun, loving, exciting, and a true rebel. I like to imagine him riding his bike with the wind in his hair and that boyish, crooked smile on his face. I see him drinking a beer, kicking back, letting the world go by, knowing that one day, we will all meet again.

Barbara Leigh is a former model and actress. She resides in Los Angeles, California.

Let the Sunshine In

Buck Hart

I was hired for a small acting part on *Junior Bonner* by casting director Lynn Stallmaster. Even though my part in the movie was eventually cut, I was around the set long enough to see how an angry bull made a sophomoric movie star laugh and drive a foul-mouthed director to nearly eat his cowboy hat.

Steve McQueen's goal in the movie was to ride the meanest bull at the rodeo, ironically named "Sunshine". A precursor to the finale called for McQueen to tweak the bull on the nose while the two were enclosed in a pen. The bull then let McQueen know who the boss was when he stood too close. Director Sam Peckinpah had wisely lined up two Sunshines. One was the meanest, craziest bull in existence, and the other was a docile and good natured look-a-like.

Steve was able to successfully tweak the nose of "Docile Sunshine" but used "Evil Sunshine" to tweak Peckinpah's nose. He was setting up another shot in the center of the ring with the sound and camera crew, when Steve thought it would be funny to release "Evil Sunshine" from the bullpen and into the ring.

I've never seen so many people scatter so fast, and grown men were pushing ladies to escape the snorting beast. It was great sport for the locals, who knew the Hollywood crowd was out of its element at the rodeo. Peckinpah didn't think it so funny; he cursed up a blue streak because not only did the bucking bull push his shooting schedule back a few hours, but it demolished an expensive 35-millimeter camera.

And as they say, that ain't no bull.

Buck Hart is a retired headmaster of The Orme School in Mayer, Arizona. He resides in Chandler, Arizona.

Taking a stroll on the Prescott Rodeo Grounds, summer 1971, during filming of *Junior Bonner*.

Just Your Average Guy

John Allen

You meet the strangest people on the road.

I met Steve McQueen when the transmission on my truck broke down in Prescott, Arizona. It was the July 4th weekend in 1971 and it felt as if I had just entered a Fellini picture.

Every Independence Day, Prescott holds its annual Frontier Rodeo Days, which take place in the city square. That year, Steve McQueen and a cast of characters were filming *Junior Bonner*, one of Steve's finest roles. While I waited for my truck to be fixed, I checked into a hotel next door to the Palace Bar and then went in to hear the house band and have a drink. Steve happened to be standing in front of the bar. With his blond hair, steely blue eyes, red sleeveless shirt, and a beautiful brunette on his arm (actress Barbara Leigh), he was hard to miss.

It so happened that my former wife, Gloria, hailed from Slater, Missouri, and was a childhood playmate of Steve's. When I saw him standing there at the Palace Bar, I wondered if he might remember her. So I walked up behind him and said discreetly, "Slater, Missouri." Steve turned around to face me.

"How do you know about that?" he asked with a puzzled look on his face. I told him that Gloria was my wife and he and she had played together as kids. He remembered Gloria and it was as if her name was a secret pass code into Steve's world. He invited me for a drink.

Before too long, we were carrying on like long-lost friends. We were both from Missouri, served in the Marines and enjoyed racing. We even knew some of the same people in the entertainment industry. Before I switched vocations, I had managed country singer Johnny Duncan and befriended singer/songwriter Jerry Wallace. Steve knew them both.

Steve and I were knocking them down pretty well, to the point where I felt comfortable enough to ask him if he wouldn't mind writing Gloria a little note to say hello. It read:

Dear Gloria,

I'm a little drunk, and your Husband is trying to fight with me. He is good—so I hope all is good with you.

Steve McQueen

Steve invited me to have breakfast the next day with him and Barbara Leigh, and then insisted I go with him to the city's rodeo grounds, where he was filming a scene. It was there that I met director Sam Peckinpah, Robert Preston, Ida Lupino, Ben Johnson and Joe Don Baker.

I'll never forget Steve's generosity those few days I was stranded in Prescott. He was just an ordinary person and that's what he wanted to be his whole life. Looking back, I can say with certainty that he was more than ordinary—he was extraordinary.

John Allen is the mayor of Wood Heights, Missouri.

Opposite: Like his movie character, McQueen was a beer man in real life.

Inset: A handwritten note to John Allen's former wife, Gloria, from a tipsy Steve McQueen.

The Cowboy Way
Frank Kelly

Cowboys don't care who you are, and have a tendency to put people in their place when they stray out of line. That pretty much sums up the start of my relationship with Steve McQueen.

I was a former rodeo circuit rider and was hired by Casey Tibbs to double McQueen in *Junior Bonner*. I was sitting on the meanest bull west of the Mississippi with a silly looking blond wig on my head when Steve made the unfortunate mistake of telling me that he was concerned I might not be the right double for him. He said I had too many scars on my face and wasn't quite what he was looking for. Each one of my scars was a badge of honor as far as I was concerned, and they were earned. Something about his comment set me off and I blew my stack. I told McQueen where he and his movie star looks and attitude could go, and poked him in the chest to emphasize my point. He was certainly taken aback by my straightforward approach.

I stayed on the bull for the full eight seconds, which was the grand finale of the movie, and McQueen came over to apologize once Sam Peckinpah had yelled "cut."

"Frank, I think you took my comment the wrong way," McQueen said, holding out his hand. "I'm sorry if I offended you." Most cowboys have finely tuned bullshit detectors and I only sensed sincerity in McQueen's apology. We shook hands and he was nothing but a pure joy for the next few months.

Over time, Steve came to enjoy the company of cowboys. He liked the fact that we didn't request autographs, ask him to pose for pictures, or fail to put him in his place when he took on a bit of a Hollywood attitude.

In the end, he gave a great performance as Junior Bonner and is one of the true "movie" cowboys of his time. I still miss that son of a gun.

Frank "Machine Gun" Kelly is a former Professional Rodeo Cowboys Association bull rider and resides in Queen Creek, Arizona.

Opposite: Bull rider Frank Kelly and Steve
McQueen got off to a rocky start until the movie
star eventually understood "The Cowboy Way."

Above: This action shot proves that McQueen
did not use a stunt double when it came to riding
horses. Bulls, however, were another story.

Above: *The Getaway* director Sam Peckinpah and Steve McQueen discuss the logistics of an upcoming scene.

Opposite: Having his cake and eating it too— Steve McQueen celebrates his 42nd birthday with co-star and new love, Ali MacGraw.

Giving Props to McQueen
Chalo Gonzalez

My mission was simple: stay one step ahead of Steve McQueen at all times.

That dictate was issued by director Sam Peckinpah, who promoted me from an actor to assistant property master on *Junior Bonner*.

"I'm going to put you in props because McQueen is always playing games and will slow down my movie if he isn't placated," Peckinpah said, looking me dead in the eye. "You're smart, so I want you to keep on top of him."

True to form, McQueen was game. I learned quickly that I had to have within arm's reach at all times three different types of chairs and four different packs of cigarettes. One day he might want a high chair and a pack of Lucky Strikes, or a small stool and some Marlboros. It all depended on his mood. I don't think it mattered to Steve because it was all just a game to him. He wanted me to read his mind and produce whatever he wanted at a moment's whim.

What Steve didn't know was that I befriended his personal driver, Jimmy Hernandez, who tipped me off each morning what his boss was thinking. When I proffered whatever Steve desired, he nodded at me suspiciously but with respect. Steve never could figure out how I had his number, but tried to trip me up again on the set of *The Getaway*, another picture we both did with Sam.

On March 24, 1972, we celebrated his birthday in El Paso with a cake and a Mariachi band. I was asked by a crew member to sing him a traditional Mexican song. Steve must have liked my performance because he called me over to have a word.

"Chalo, you're excellent with props, you're a good actor and a great singer," he said. "If I don't watch out, you're going to take my place in the movie!"

I laughed and took it as a compliment because nobody could ever take Steve's place. He was a great film actor and a fantastic person. And he kept me on my toes.

Chalo Gonzalez is a veteran actor and former prop master who worked with Sam Peckinpah for seven years. He resides in Los Angeles, California.

The Getaway to the Rocket Man Katy Haber

Left: Chad McQueen shakes hands with Elton John while his dad, sister Terry and Katy Haber (behind Elton) look on.

Above: The Elton John Band visits the set of *The Getaway* and shares beer with the shirtless star.

After completing *Junior Bonner* in 1971, we started shooting *The Getaway* early the next year. Steve McQueen hired *Bonner* director, Sam Peckinpah, to helm the film's grueling six-city, six days a week, 62-day shooting schedule. It was not without its glitches.

The prison sequences, shot in the Huntsville Maximum Security and Ellis Unit, used lifers as inmates in the film, all of whom were, of course, wrongly accused and innocent! Ali MacGraw and I entered the prison with me acting as her stand-in for the prison visit. It apparently had been quite a while since some had seen women—we promised like heck we would write and were more than happy to leave.

Steve was not happy either, when he found out that the shower sequence was to be shot in the homosexual unit. I've always wondered why prison authorities felt he would be safer there.

In yet another scene, Steve, along with the other white-clad Huntsville inmates, hoed the ground in a long straight line, guarded by armed guards on horseback and a pack of snarling dogs. When Sam yelled "cut," Steve left the line to walk to the catering truck. He had not been warned in advance that the dogs were trained to attack anything white that left the line. They followed Steve like a flash of lightning, teeth bared. Only the quick action of the guards prevented our star from turning into dog meat.

Our last stop was El Paso. We found the town festooned with posters announcing an Elton John concert on April 20th at the Sun Bowl. Being British, I was the only person on the crew who knew who Elton was. I had grown up in London and attended all his concerts, from the small basement clubs in Soho to his first *Mad Man Across The Water Tour*. Time for some respite. The concert was on a Saturday night and I was desperate to go. I creatively persuaded Newt Arnold, the assistant director, for an earlier call and earlier wrap, secured the crew bus, baked the brownies, booked the tickets and took Steve, Ali, Chad, Terry and the crew to a concert by someone they had never heard of.

El Paso's University Football Stadium, also known as the Sun Bowl, was packed to capacity. Center field held the stage complete with seating. Steve and company were front row center. Elton opened the show with either "Tiny Dancer" or "Levon" from the *Mad Man* album, at which point, everyone sitting at the back of the field rushed forward to be close to the stage.

Steve, thinking that the audience was surging to be near him, grabbed Ali and the kids and left the arena, missing the concert completely. *Ah well,* I thought as I sat alone in the front row, *my loyalty to my friends went only so far.* I wasn't about to leave.

After the concert I went back stage and invited Elton, Nigel Olsson and the band to visit the set, which they did before leaving town. From then on, I never missed an Elton John concert, and many times was accompanied by Ali MacGraw. I have no doubt in my mind that, if asked, Elton would remember that time in El Paso, Texas, almost four decades ago.

Katy Haber, who worked with Sam Peckinpah for seven years on eight of his films, is currently a film and TV producer in Los Angeles. She has served on the Board of Directors of Bafta/LA for nineteen years.

SOLAR PRODUCTIONS, INC.

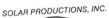

November 10, 1972

Dear Sam:

I wish to hell you hadn't taken off before you saw the film. I just want you to know that all I tried to do was get the click of the guns, the footsteps and the shotgun blasts right. It was just a lot of clean-up work I did for you, and I've done nothing but tell people that this is a Sam Peckinpah film. Just understand that I'm still your friend and I love you and all I am is an errand boy for you in that dubbing room.

You hurt my feelings by not seeing the film. You're a good man and a good director if you don't fuck off, so don't fuck off. Take care of your bones and if you need anything, call me.

Love,

Steve McQueen

SM/bc

Mr. Sam Peckinpah
20 de Noviembre
Durango   DGO
Mexico

9134 SUNSET BOULEVARD, LOS ANGELES, CALIFORNIA 90069 • (213) 278-8600 • CABLE: SOLARPIC

Above: James Garner, Steve McQueen and Sam Peckinpah taking a break during *The Getaway*.

Left: A conciliatory letter from Steve McQueen to director Sam Peckinpah after he abruptly left a screening of *The Getaway*. McQueen had "cleaned up" some of the sounds and special effects without Peckinpah's knowledge, and the letter was an explanation of sorts.

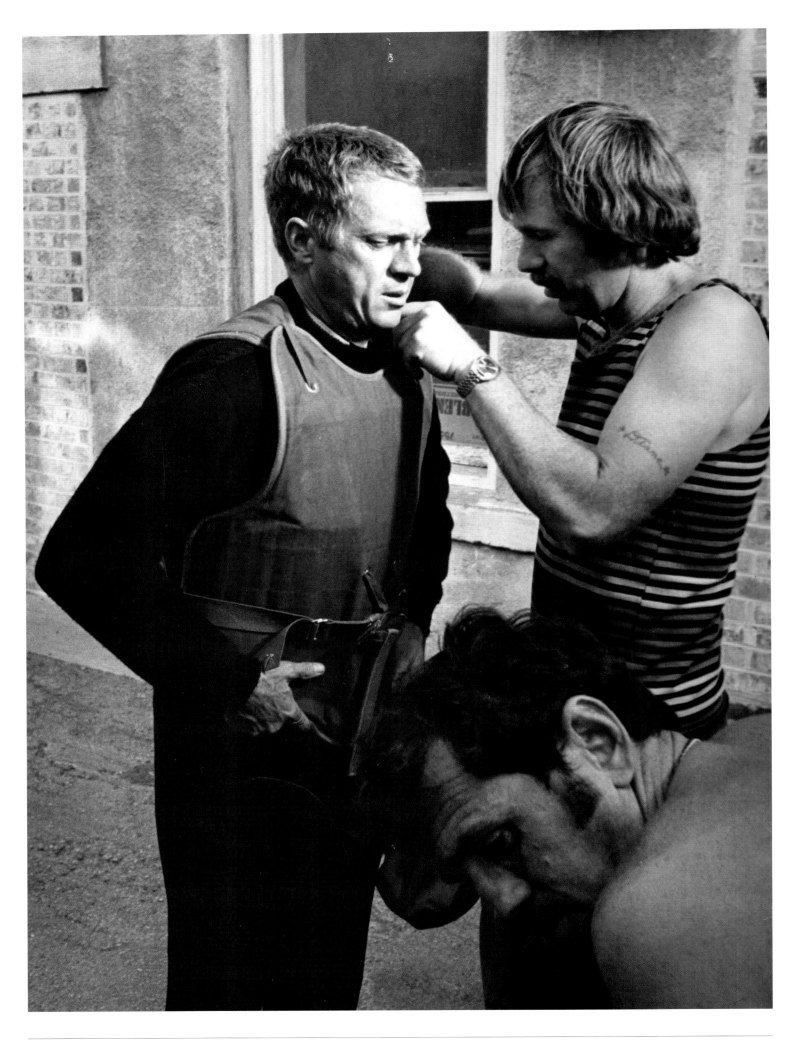

No Shirt, No Gators, No Shit

Kent James

Opposite: Costume designer Kent James adjusting Steve McQueen's wardrobe before a robbery scene in *The Getaway*.

Above: Candid shot of McQueen, with white hair in Jamaica on the set of *Papillon*.

Above right: McQueen and *Papillon* co-star Dustin Hoffman got along just fine until McQueen kicked Dustin's relatives off the set. The two then used an emissary to communicate.

I first met Steve McQueen on the set of *The Getaway,* where I was in charge of wardrobe. I was the second costumer on the film after Steve drove my predecessor away. He had a bad habit of taking off his shirt and dropping it on the ground after each take. When he pulled that number on me, I took producer David Foster aside and said, "I am taking the next plane to Los Angeles. I don't pick up people's clothes. If you want a valet, look in the Yellow Pages under V." Not an auspicious start to our wonderful friendship.

Five minutes later, though, Steve's assistant said his boss wanted to see me. I reiterated to Steve what I told Foster and he apologized. He then asked if I would stay on the show.

"Yes, but I'm telling you right now, don't try to pull any shit," I replied. With that, Steve smiled and we shook hands. We got along well, though not to say that he didn't still mess with me from time to time. Or me with him. Toward the end of *The Getaway* when I knew Steve a little better, I sewed all his pant pockets shut.

About a year later while we were filming *Papillon* in Jamaica, we were going to have dinner one night with Ross Kananga, a stuntman who owned a crocodile farm in Kingston. Steve and I arrived early and hit the buzzer at the entrance gate. No one answered, and Steve became a little antsy. He left the car and announced that he was going to climb over the six-foot wall that surrounded the property and knock on the front door. This was in spite of the fact there was a sign posted on the gate that read, "Beware of crocodiles."

"Steve, don't go over that wall," I warned. "Those crocodiles can burst up to thirty miles per hour on land." He had climbed halfway up the wall when Ross drove up, and confirmed that Steve would have been crocodile meat had he gone over that wall.

Steve got back at me in a fun way the next day at work. It was the scene in which Steve and co-star Dustin Hoffman were required to tackle a crocodile during cleanup detail at the prison camp. For the scene, the animal was heavily drugged and had its mouth wired shut. It was twenty feet long, hissing at everyone and was by no means under control. It gave those who came in contact with it more than they could handle. Steve could tell the razor-toothed reptile gave me the willies and asked if I would bring him a towel to wipe mud from his face. I knew he was messing with me.

I said, "I'm not going down there while that alligator is still alive."

"James, you're a big candy ass," Steve said.

"Yeah McQueen, you got that right!"

Steve also had a soft side to him. While on a beach in Jamaica we asked a local to come to the set and cut up coconuts for the cast and crew. He was using a machete, but accidentally sliced right through the coconut and almost severed his fingers. They folded all the way back, held together by skin. He went off to the local hospital, but Steve insisted this man have the best possible treatment. He arranged for him to fly to Miami where a top surgeon repaired his hand. Steve picked up the entire tab.

As is the case with people who pass on, there's a tendency to miss them more as the years go by. I do miss Steve—the phone calls, riding bikes and giving each other grief. We had such fun.

Kent James was one of the premier costumers in the movie industry when he retired in the 1990s. He and his wife, Carole, divide their time between California and Montana.

The Matchmaker
Ben Johnson

Even though I am a world championship rodeo roper, have starred in more than three hundred movies and won an Academy Award, my most famous claim to fame might be the fact that I introduced Steve McQueen to his second wife, Ali MacGraw. We were at a post-Oscar night celebration in 1971 and Ali asked me to introduce them since I knew Steve from *Junior Bonner.* She was real gung-ho for him, so I arranged a meeting since we were going to film *The Getaway* together.

Steve was a bit of a wild character. He wasn't much different than the characters he played on screen. He liked his talk and his whiskey straight. He also drove straight—into a body of water.

The film company was headquartered in a condominium complex in San Marcos, Texas, just across the way from Aquarena Springs. Steve rented a station wagon, and he and Ali were in the parking lot driving around. All of a sudden, he drove right off the parking lot and into the Springs. All but the back end of the car was submerged. I ran down to rescue them. They stuck their faces out of the back window to breathe, and I helped them escape. Just as we were starting the movie, he was pulling a stunt! I'll never know why he did that.

Steve never took a job he couldn't do. He was a perfectionist. It's what John Ford once said, "If you can put something up there on the screen that everybody wants to do or be, why you've got no problem." Everybody wanted Steve to win.

Ben Johnson won the Academy Award for The Last Picture Show and co-starred with Steve McQueen in three movies. He died in April of 1996.

Actor Ben Johnson says he introduced Steve McQueen and Ali MacGraw backstage at the 1971 Academy Awards. This meeting resulted in their marriage on July 12, 1973.

An Old Fashioned Fella
Carole James

Left: An Associated Press wire announcing the July 12, 1973 marriage of Steve McQueen and Ali MacGraw in Cheyenne, Wyoming.

Above: "If looks could kill", McQueen and MacGraw are startled by the paparazzi in 1973.

Steve McQueen may have been the epitome of cool; but to me, he was just an old-fashioned man at heart. He had a deep respect for people who were grounded as I felt I was. Everything I had was hard-earned, and Steve recognized that trait because it was part of his personality too.

I never worked with Steve and ours was just a mutual friendship through my husband, Kent. We were costumers in the movie business, often working together.

Not so with Steve and his wife, Ali MacGraw. He had a hard time playing second fiddle to Ali when he visited her on the set of *Convoy*. He spent a lot of time hanging out at the pool, pulling a red Radio Flyer wagon filled with ice and Old Milwaukee beer. One day he asked me to go for a walk. Steve questioned how Kent and I could work together during the day and go home with each other at night.

"Our marriage is based on a mutual respect for each other and not putting one person above another," I told him. "We're best friends as well as lovers." Steve's idea of marriage was for Ali to be at home, a wife and mom, but it was evident that she wanted to have a career as well. Unfortunately, Steve found that concept hard to grasp and he and Ali parted ways after the film.

Steve was also old-fashioned when it came to the holidays. One year he invited me, Kent and Sam Peckinpah for Thanksgiving at his place in Malibu. Somehow or other, Steve found out that actor Alec Guinness was going to be in Los Angeles and would be spending the holiday alone. Steve wasn't having any of that. He tracked Alec down and invited him to join the get-together. I've always felt it was such a thoughtful gesture on Steve's part.

When I think of Steve, I remember a man who enjoyed spending time with his friends, riding motorcycles, tinkering with his cars and was just a super fella.

Carole James retired from the movie industry as a costume designer in 1998. She and her husband Kent divide their time between California and Montana.

Beer Buddies
Bill O 'Hara

Opposite: Soaking up the El Paso, Texas sun on *The Getaway*, 1972.

Below right: McQueen as Doc McCoy, a mastermind thief recently paroled from prison.

Steve McQueen and Sam Peckinpah were in town filming *The Getaway*. It was 1972, and I was stationed at Fort Sam Houston, in San Antonio, Texas. I was a longtime fan of both men, so a friend and I went to the train depot to check out the action. There was some security and quite a few people rubber-necking in the parking lot, but no Peckinpah—he was inside with the crew. However, sitting shirtless in a lounge chair facing the sun was McQueen.

True to form, McQueen had a cooler full of iced beer in front of him, although it was only around 11 a.m. My friend, a black kid from Philadelphia, yelled, "Yo Steve" and raised his fist in the power salute. Steve returned the wave and motioned us over, probably because we were young and in uniform. We announced ourselves as big fans of his and told him that we were from Rochester, New York. He responded "Rochester. Isn't that where they make Genesee beer?" When I confirmed this, he described his fondness for the beer and the annoyance of having to import it to the West Coast.

As he told us about *The Getaway* and that Peckinpah was shooting a scene inside with Ali MacGraw, he had a mellow tone. I thought this was a result of the beer, but looking back, I think it was his affair with MacGraw that accounted for his good mood.

McQueen asked what we did in the Army, briefly mentioned that he had been in the Marines and told us to be careful as he shook our hands and bid us farewell.

Not much to tell, but I always thought it strange that he never offered us a beer.

Bill O' Hara resides in Rochester, New York.

Give That Man
Anthony Zerbe
a Cigar

Above: Actor Anthony Zerbe and McQueen, whose acting styles clashed with wonderful results in *Papillon*.

Opposite: McQueen never worked as hard as he did on *Papillon*, which was his acting tour de force.

Although Steve McQueen and I were polar opposites in terms of how we approached acting, our two worlds collided with wonderful results in a scene we did together in *Papillon*.

I am a classically trained actor from the theater world, whereas Steve was one of a line of actors that started with Marlon Brando, James Dean and Montgomery Clift. He came from left field and was so authentic that he seemed to inhabit his roles. He was the perfect actor for the time, although he was not the warmest person in the world. He viewed all actors as competition, especially Dustin Hoffman and me.

McQueen was charismatic and had tremendous presence in all his films, but I felt that he pushed himself in *Papillon*. In our scene together, I played a leper in a French colony who could help Papillon escape to freedom. As a test, I offered him a cigar that had already been smoked and McQueen's character did not know whether I was infectious or not. The cool thing was, I had been chewing on that cigar all day, and I handed him this wet, drooled on, soggy

stogie. This was intentional because I wanted to see what he was made of. It was obviously a challenge.

McQueen, the actor, didn't have to take the cigar that Anthony Zerbe had been chewing on. He could have asked for a replacement during a cut but didn't. McQueen just put it in his mouth and continued with the scene. He delivered one of the most amazing reactions I have ever seen on the silver screen.

Once the scene was over, I looked at him and said, "Oh McQueen, you're something else." He just looked at me and smiled. I thought it was an incredible thing to do and showed how far he was willing to go to bring respect to the part.

When I think of McQueen as an actor, I'm reminded of a star who embodied a certain mythology and brought it to life.

Anthony Zerbe is a critically acclaimed veteran actor and resides in California.

Get Smart
Alec Baldwin

Both pages: A hero for the modern-day man in scenes from *The Getaway* and *Papillon*. Alec Baldwin said Steve McQueen's economy of words sets him apart as an actor.

There are only a handful of leading men in big movies who I believe are successful more because of their brains than anything else.

Watching McQueen, I think the actor is smart as opposed to acting smart. Paul Newman and Jim Garner are two other good examples of this. McQueen was tough, certainly, but he relied primarily on his brains.

I liked him so much in *Papillon*. It wasn't the best movie, but he was incredible in it. It's a movie about people determined to survive. In a way, it's like *The Getaway* which I wanted to remake because it was about a man who had integrity and a sense of honor. He might die, but his honor was what kept him alive in the cesspool of a world.

If McQueen were alive today, he'd be bigger than ever. There are a few actors who remind me of him. Brad Pitt is good, and so is Stallone in his early movies such as *Rocky* and *F.I.S.T.* As with McQueen, there's an overt masculinity, but it doesn't obscure other

features. As far as people accusing him of being a stone face or of not acting, you have to get the bad acting out of the way to see the good acting.

A lot of actors are very animated and they create that expectation in the audience—and then they tire of it. The goal is economizing, and McQueen understood that. The actor almost has to get out of the way. Don't do too much in movies, unless that's your signature. That 'take it or leave it' attitude he had is so compelling. How many men have made a career in the last thirty years of just looking into the camera and saying, 'This is who I am and if you don't like it then too bad. And if you fire me tomorrow, I don't care'. Robert Blake, Sean Penn, you know, all these guys—and McQueen. It's such a seductive thing: "If you don't want me, kiss my ass."

Alec Baldwin is a veteran actor who in 1994 filmed a remake of McQueen's The Getaway. *This passage originally appeared in the March 1999 issue of* Interview.

The Towering Egos

Al Kasha

Opposite: Steve McQueen and Paul Newman
were the two biggest stars of the seventies, but
in *The Towering Inferno*, McQueen established
his screen dominance.

Sometimes it was tough to decide if Steve McQueen's competitive nature was pure ego, talent or a combination of both.

Case in point: producer Irwin Allen was my good friend and sometime employer. Our bond grew stronger when "The Morning After," a No. 1 song I wrote with Joel Hirschhorn, won an Academy Award for Best Song. "The Morning After" was the theme to *The Poseidon Adventure*, which was a 1972 box-office smash and the first so-called "disaster movie".

Irwin enlisted Joel and me to reproduce our magic on *The Towering Inferno*, and invited us to visit the set any time to get a feel for the movie. Johnny Mercer, the American songwriter, once gave me an excellent piece of advice for writing songs for films. He told me to never tell the entire story but only convey philosophically what it is about.

In the case of *The Towering Inferno*, my writing partner and I were moved by one particular scene, when Robert Wagner and Susan Flannery, who played lovers, were about to be engulfed in flames and realized it was the last time they'd be together. We came up with "We May Never Love Like This Again," which gave us our second Academy Award for Best Song.

However, love wouldn't be the word I'd use to describe the relationship between Steve McQueen and Paul Newman. While they respected each other on a professional level, it was evident they were competitive. I sensed this far more from McQueen than Newman who was more cooperative than McQueen in general. I didn't know at the time the history of their film rivalry, which dated back to the fifties. McQueen's first significant movie was *Somebody Up There Likes Me* which starred Newman. Steve was a $19 a day extra. He vowed one day to catch up, but I think he felt that Newman had been given better roles over the years. *The Towering Inferno* was his shot at redemption.

Steve was, without doubt, the image of himself—he rode a motorcycle, loved rock music and was a rebel. He struggled to make it up the Hollywood ladder and once he succeeded, he let you know.

When Steve first read the script, he noticed that Paul had a dozen more lines than he did. He rectified the situation by getting screenwriter, Stirling Silliphant, who was on a deep sea fishing expedition, to return early from his vacation and rewrite the script so the two men had the same number. I remember Steve looking at the playback monitor. He went through everything—line by line, scene by scene—asking to make changes if he didn't like the take. He demanded billing credit over Paul, and requested his own gym and spa on the set when he discovered Paul had one. It was almost comical.

I found it interesting that the two men shared the same agent, a man by the name of Freddie Fields. Freddie was having a heated discussion with Irwin when I arrived on the 20th Century Fox lot one day over who should be billed first—McQueen or Newman. Newman had been a star longer than McQueen, but McQueen was hotter at the moment. Eventually, it was worked out that McQueen had first billing, but Newman's name was higher and on the right. Freddie thought the movie poster should just read, "McQueen/Newman", and even threatened to pull the two stars from the movie, which was too much to believe because they were in the middle of filming.

When I saw the final product, it was clear that McQueen emerged as the film's star. Steve finally got what he wanted—to eclipse Paul Newman.

Steve, as much as he wanted people to believe he didn't care about acting, cared deeply about his craft. In the tradition of Marlon Brando and James Dean, he was a screen rebel. He was perhaps the truest rebel of them all.

Al Kasha is a two-time Academy Award winning composer-songwriter, and has won two Tony Awards for the stage production of Seven Brides for Seven Brothers. He resides in Beverly Hills, California.

Brotherly Love
Pat Johnson

Steve and I developed a special bond. I felt as close to Steve as I did with any of my four brothers, whom I loved dearly.

This bond was based on the fact that our upbringing was similar. We were deserted by our fathers as small children, grew up in poverty and learned to live by our own devices. When one grows up in the streets one tends to put on a false front and protective walls. We both felt that everyone who came along had a "con" and the trick was to figure out what the "con" was so that you would never be "had". You didn't trust anybody or show any weakness but if you did you were vulnerable. The less a person knew about who you were, the safer you were.

Often when I read books, watch TV documentaries or interviews about Steve, he is described as a different individual from the real Steve, and that's how he tried to keep it. Since he and I both came from the same place, we understood each other, and there was no need for any false fronts. He could be honest with me and describe his true feelings without it being seen as a weakness. He often came to me for advice—certainly not in his career, he was master of that—but for personal matters. I could do the same with him. We trusted each other.

This may seem trivial, but the trust was evident when his hit film *Papillon* was released. After arranging a karate workout on the

following day, he asked me about my plans for the evening and I told him that my wife, Sue, and I were going to see his new movie. At that time, all theaters that were showing *Papillon* had lines around the block. He asked me where we were going and when I told him, he said he would call the manager and arrange for us to go in without standing in line. I told him I would rather he didn't as we felt he was worth waiting for. It was about then that he was persuaded that I had no hidden agenda and was not planning to use him to my advantage.

I still miss Steve very much. In trying to describe my feeling on his passing, the right words are hard to come by, but the most appropriate are from a child. When my son Brett was three-years old, I told him how much I loved him and he told me that he loved me too. When I asked him how much, he said, "Papa, I love you so big much, up in the sky, whole world, back down." That describes so beautifully the feeling of loss I still have with the passing of my best friend.

Steve, I miss you so big much, up in the sky, whole world, back down.

Pat Johnson is a ninth degree black belt Tang Soo Do and a member of the Blackbelt magazine Hall of Fame. He was Steve McQueen's martial arts instructor, close friend and trusted confidant from 1972 to 1980.

Opposite: World champion kickboxer Howard Jackson, Pat Johnson, Steve McQueen and actor Chuck Norris at Norris' Sherman Oaks studio.

Above: Pat Johnson, Steve's dog Junior and McQueen taking a morning stroll in southern Arizona, early 1979.

Above: The bracelet was designed and worn by McQueen who later engraved it "For David, love Steve. The Getaway", giving it to producer David Foster after the filming of *The Getaway*.

Opposite: Circa 1972, taking time out from filming *The Getaway*. Note the turquoise bracelet on McQueen's left wrist. It now belongs to McQueen collector Andrew Antoniades, an accountant from London, England.

God Save McQueen

Andrew Antoniades

I first became a fan of Steve McQueen when I was about eleven-years-old and I watched *Papillion* with my father. I was certainly too young for an over-eighteen certificate movie, but not too young to notice Steve's amazing screen presence and magnetism — though at that age I simply summed this up as "cool". Watching the movie was a great father-son experience particularly as I was allowed to stay up late.

The Great Escape was also one of my early introductions to McQueen since the film is an all-time favorite in Britain shown on television every Christmas, and the theme tune is played constantly. One of my fondest memories is sitting with my father watching McQueen tunnel away preparing for the escape and later, after he had annoyed the German guards and was banished to the "Cooler" how he defiantly threw his baseball against the wall. I vividly remember the crowning moment of the film, with my dad saying "Wait for it son, here's the best bit..." The tension was amazing, with McQueen revving his motorbike, looking at the fence, revving it again, then zooming away at full speed, launching himself off the hill to clear the first fence against all the odds. What a moment. This was my personal equivalent of watching the first lunar landing.

After that, my interest intensified. I remember wanting to watch *Bullitt* and being told by my father, yes, we had the tape, but that I had taped over it to copy *Gremlins*. That obviously had not gone

down well since it is his favourite McQueen film. When we finally watched it together, there was another, "wait for the best scene, wait for it!" moment. It was the first film I had seen that really seemed to glorify the star above everything else. Every shot and image was a masterpiece worthy of any photography hall of fame. The build-up to the car chase was tense and it delivered in full.

My father bears a striking resemblance to McQueen. He has shown me photos of when he was in his thirties and forties and the resemblance is uncanny. Now he is in his late sixties, I like to think that this is how Steve would have looked had he lived.

Over the years we watched many more of McQueen's films together. We still endlessly debate "Steve's Top Five", with me usually having to justify why I prefer *Tom Horn*. And I regularly have to show him how to use the DVD player just so he can watch *Bullitt* again. My admiration and respect for Steve has grown and flourished over the years thanks to my father and the moments we shared and still do. I try to collect anything that has an association with Steve. However, our mutual respect of Steve which led to so much bonding between my father and I is perhaps the greatest thing I can take from McQueen's legacy.

Andrew Antoniades, a 28-year-old accountant from London, has been a Steve McQueen fan since he was a boy and old enough to whistle the theme to The Great Escape.

The Purr-fect Star
John Guillermin

Most directors wouldn't describe Steve McQueen as a pussycat, but that's what I found him to be. Of course, it helps when you make your star look good.

Steve came to me before the filming of *The Towering Inferno* with an all-consuming problem: he felt his helmet made him look like an English bobby.

"I look like an idiot!" Steve told me.

The night before filming began I had dinner with a fireman who was serving as a technical adviser on the movie, and spotted an old-style fire helmet sitting on the mantle. I thought it perfect for

Steve, brought it back for him to try and he liked the look. That was a shrewd move and he trusted me from that point on. Filming was a piece of cake.

McQueen was inspired. In one scene in particular, where his character was talking to the fire chief, he just flopped in the corner. He explained, "My character has been fighting this fire all night and he's really tired by now." So he just sat there and chose not to move, which gave it an unusual power. He had a sharp mind and the ability to put his finger on the right atmosphere—in this case, exhaustion.

John Guillermin was the co-director of The Towering Inferno.

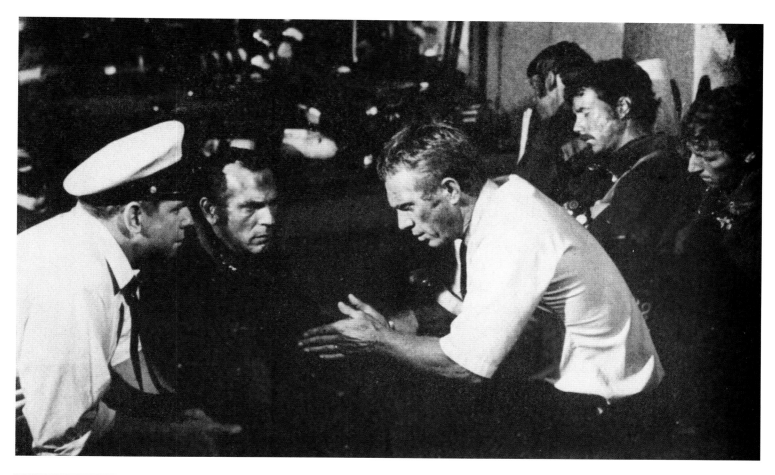

So Long Fire Chief

Richard Baker

When Steve McQueen decided to become an actor, we lost a helluva firefighter.

I knew Steve because of my association with him on the set of *The Towering Inferno*. I was a captain on the Los Angeles Fire Department in late 1973 when the movie started principal photography at 20th Century Fox. I was brought in to consult on some of the action sequences by my friend, Battalion Chief Pete Lucarelli, who served as a technical advisor on the film. Pete knew that I had been working on a rescue harness for the department to be used in various suspended rescue incidents. Even though the harness was only later approved by the department, it was perfect for use in the movie where Steve is helicoptered onto the roof of the burning tower.

Pete and I took Steve to a large soundstage on the Samuel Goldwyn lot off Santa Monica Boulevard. McQueen observed the actions of the firefighters with admiration and told us that at one time, as a young man, he thought he might have liked to become one. Clearly, McQueen did not lack for "balls" as his love of motor sports with high-speed cars and motorcycles demonstrated. I found it interesting though, that when he went to work on the picture, Steve was candid about his fear of heights.

"Ground floor fires only for this firefighter," Steve said. In fact, Steve was never more than twelve feet off the ground during the shooting of the action sequences. He was a pleasure to work with and was always respectful towards the off-duty firefighters working on the movie.

One day he invited Pete and me into his trailer, and I interviewed him, along with LAFD staff photographer Bob Praskin. An edited version of the interview was later published in the August 1974 edition of LAFD's monthly *Fireman's Grapevine* magazine. I didn't realize it then, but by this time in his career, Steve had stopped giving interviews. I think he granted our request because of his respect for the firefighter's profession and because he felt the work we were doing deserved recognition.

Steve was truly a joy to know, however briefly. He was someone I felt comfortable with and admired. So long, Fire Chief.

Richard W. Baker is retired as Chief of the Training Division in 1988 from the Los Angeles Fire Department. He currently resides with his wife in Victoria, Tennessee.

Opposite: McQueen posing with technical directors Los Angeles Fire Department Battalion Chief Pete Lucarelli and Captain Richard Baker, on the backlot of Samuel Goldwyn Studios. Baker said when McQueen decided to become an actor, the world lost a "helluva firefighter."

Above: O'Hallorhan prepares for the blast in *The Towering Inferno's* grand finale.

Interview with "Fire Chief" Steve McQueen

Richard Baker

Richard Baker secures an experimental harness on McQueen, which was later patented and used in fighting fires.

The following Q & A was conducted with actor Steve McQueen on the set of his motion picture, *The Towering Inferno*. It is of particular interest to firemen because McQueen portrays a fire chief in the film which dramatizes a disastrous fire in a high-rise building. Generally, it is also interesting because McQueen had not given an interview in many years but then provided one for the *Firemen's Grapevine* rather than a movie magazine.

Baker: Did you have any interest in the fire service prior to your assignment in this film?

McQueen: Well, I think there's not a kid in the world who hasn't at some time been interested in the fire department. When I was a kid I always looked up to firemen with their shiny red trucks and coats and helmets. It's typical I think to have a hero thing for firemen as you grow up and then it disappears. My adult relationship to firemen, prior to this film, has been in the world of motorcycles, and there I've met a lot of firemen who enjoy riding as I do. I didn't know much about the fire department though, I'm ashamed to admit, and I was naive about it all until Chief Lucarelli had me lose my virginity at the Goldwyn fire. One thing I did know was that the firemen seemed to be steady people, ready to help one another. It wasn't until the Goldwyn fire though, where I had an opportunity to see them in action, that I realized how they had to work together and that their lives depended on the buddy-system.

Baker: I hear that the fire chief's role in the film was originally a secondary one, what happened to attract you to it and make it a major role?

McQueen: Well, I don't know if you heard the whole story or not; but what's happened on this picture is something that rarely happens, especially in Hollywood. There was a writer from New York who wrote *The Tower* and another in San Francisco who authored *The Glass Inferno*, and although written independently, the stories had almost the same plot. Warner Bros. bought one book, and the other was purchased by 20th Century Fox. And, in one of the few times that I'm aware of in my fifteen years in the motion picture industry, they agreed to collaborate, and combined the two books into one screenplay. Now, the part of O'Hallorhan, the fire chief, was originally a fourth lead in the picture; but, it was the part I wanted to play. Maybe because secretly I've always wanted to be a fireman, I don't know. Anyway, dramatically it appealed to me and I also think that part would be good for me as an actor so I took it.

Baker: Chief Lucarelli has told me you've spent a lot of time on research for your part as a fire chief. Is this typical of all of your roles?

McQueen: Well, I try not to take myself too seriously but at the same time they pay me an awful lot of money to do my job and I do everything I can to see that it's done right. I believe that today's audiences are smart and that you have the responsibility to articulate a part accurately. I mean, I don't look at it as play-acting. If I'm going to play a fireman, then for the period of that film—I am a fireman. For three months, or whatever, they own me and I have a responsibility as a professional to do the best I can.

Baker: Speaking of professionals, what's your impression of our firemen who have worked on the film with you?

McQueen: I think they've handled themselves very professionally. They got right into acting, or maybe because they're all playing firemen it just came naturally. We've had as many as fifty of them on the set at one time and they all conducted themselves well. Of course, you know by now that I am impressed with firemen, which is why I've agreed to be interviewed for your magazine. I hope this film will open the public's eyes to what a great job you guys do. I still remember the Goldwyn fire and seeing how you firemen work and the risks that you take. This is what the public seldom sees and I think it's something they should be more aware of.

Baker: In that respect I think this film should have a real impact in increasing the public's awareness of the hazards of high-rise buildings.

McQueen: I hope it will scare them to death. The picture is about three hundred people trapped on the 135th floor of the world's tallest building having a party with a fire raging below them. It presents a lot of interesting problems, which I know you fellas are aware of, such as what happens if the sprinkler systems don't work, the elevators are called to a floor by a fire and trap its occupants, or the amount of flammable contents in these buildings and the toxic gases they can give off. The public is ignorant of much of this but can learn from the film, while being entertained.

Praskin: Speaking as a civilian I'd be interested to know whether the film gives an answer to the problems created by fires in these buildings?

McQueen: That's a good question and in its way I believe the picture attempts to answer it. At the end of the film Paul Newman, who plays the architect, and William Holden, the owner of the building, have a scene with me where we discuss the fire. They ask me how it happened and if it could have been prevented. My last line before I return to the fire station will be something to the effect that—the next time you think about building another one, give me a call. I think that's a start anyhow.

Writer Edwin Heaven had a brief but memorable encounter with Steve McQueen and Ali MacGraw at a Sausalito deli in the seventies.

McCool
Edwin Heaven

Steve McQueen was a nice guy. A cool guy. And a friendly dude.

I met him and Ali MacGraw in Sausalito. At the time I had two Afghan hounds, Benji and Salome, and a huge afro which made me look like I played bass in the Jimi Hendrix Experience. Sweet MacGraw liked my dogs. Cool McQueen liked my attitude. So we chatted for a while and then Steve asked where in this chi-chi town they could find a decent sandwich.

I took them to this little deli and while waiting to order, said jokingly: "I heard you've got a reputation for being fearless, Steve. So go with the pastrami."

He laughed. "And what are you getting, pal?"

"Me?" I said, "Well, I'm chicken-shit. So I'm going with the chicken salad."

This time he roared.

My impression of the man is that in a world of fakery he was the real McCoy. The real McQueen! Probably didn't have a bogus bone in his body. So what was a real guy, a tough guy, like McQueen doing in the mollycoddled world of Hollywood? One look at Ali and one could only assume that acting was a great way to meet beautiful women.

Long live McQueen.

Edwin Heaven is a writer, filmmaker and inventor living in the San Francisco area.

Behind Blue Eyes
Florence Esposito

The man knew how to scale back his visibility. Steve McQueen grew his hair long, sprouted a beard and raced motorcycles. Hollywood ended up a "been there, done that" trip bringing little joy to Steve, so he and wife, Ali MacGraw, moved out to Malibu, practically a world away from the movie industry and all the trappings that came with stardom.

I knew Steve over a three-year period when I worked as a bartender at The Old Place, a funky restaurant and bar nestled in the Agoura Hills on Mulholland Drive. I first spotted him in December 1972 when he brought Ali, Sam Peckinpah and Katy Haber in after the première of *The Getaway*. A week later, he escorted Governor Ronald Reagan and his wife, Nancy, to the Old Place for a casual dinner.

Owners Tom and Barbara Runyon converted the former post office and general store into the coolest place to hang your hat and whet your whistle. The restaurant normally served only steak and clams, but there was stew and sourdough bread on Sundays.

Tom let me run the bar after I proved myself over a period of time. It was a coveted position, even in Hollywood. Actress Katherine Ross wanted my job, even after her star-turning role in *Butch Cassidy and the Sundance Kid*. Steve McQueen also wanted my job and gladly worked without pay. The Old Place was a merging of bikers, actors, beach bums, cowboys and local characters, who made the bar their own. Over the years, I've seen Bob Dylan, Goldie Hawn, Sam Elliot, Ben Johnson, Bill Bixby, Nick Nolte, Mitch Ryan and Doug McClure. Steve, however, made it his home away from home, often joining me behind the bar. Nothing made him happier than pouring drinks to unsuspecting customers.

When you work in such proximity to someone, you come to know who they are and where their heart is and Steve had a big one. During the holiday season, I awoke to the sound of light tapping on my door. It was Steve tacking up a Christmas wreath from the Boys Republic. When I opened the door he said, "You weren't supposed to wake up." Not that Steve cared much for my sleeping habits. On Mother's Day morning, he called at 6:30 a.m.

"Dude, just because you're Steve McQueen it doesn't mean you can call me at 6:30 in the morning," I said, making him howl with laughter.

Eventually I made my way to Chicago while Steve discovered serenity in Santa Paula. I would have taken care of him when he was sick because I know he would have taken care of me. He had that kind of heart. When he loved you, he loved you. When he cared about you, you could genuinely see it in his eyes. And he had the best eyes. Kind eyes you never forget.

Florence Esposito is in the gaming industry and lives in Lake Tahoe, California.

Palm Springs Weekend
Marvin Josephson

The world's biggest box-office star grew his hair long, sprouted a beard and was barely recognizable after *The Towering Inferno* blazed it's way to the top as the highest grossing movie in motion picture history.

In 1974, the International Famous Agency merged with Creative Management Associates and became International Creative Management, one of the largest talent agencies in the world. I acquired the company from former agent Freddie Fields, who stayed on as president for just six months before taking off in a new direction as a producer based at Paramount.

My clients at that time were mostly political figures, including former President Jimmy Carter, Henry Kissinger and Barbara Walters. Steve McQueen's name would add the top of Hollywood to my list.

I didn't inherit Steve McQueen as a client; I had to earn that privilege. A meeting was set up in Palm Springs, California, and I came with ammunition. Underneath my arm was the script of the century. At the time, ICM represented the estate of Margaret Mitchell which had agreed to allow a movie sequel to *Gone with the Wind* called *Tara: The Continuation of Gone with the Wind*. Steve would be awarded the lead role, that of Rhet Butler. It was an entrancing piece of bait.

The meeting was also attended by Steve's business manager, Bill Maher, and the three of us were walking down a busy street when McQueen announced, "Hey, I've got to take a pee." He began urinating. I'm sure that he was waiting for me to be shocked, but I just ignored him. That was his problem, not mine. I realized later that this was one of his tests.

I was struck by many things. For one, you knew you were dealing with a star. He had a certain quality both on and off the screen. He also tested me as he had done with others, and tried intimidating me several times. If Steve thought he could find your weakness, you were dead with him, because he thought you would be the same with other people.

The other thing I learned about Steve was his method of reacting. My background as a lawyer had trained my instincts to be part of an intellectual process. I learned from him that there was another way to react that was also effective in achieving objectives.

Marvin Josephson is the co-founder of International Creative Management. He resides in New York City.

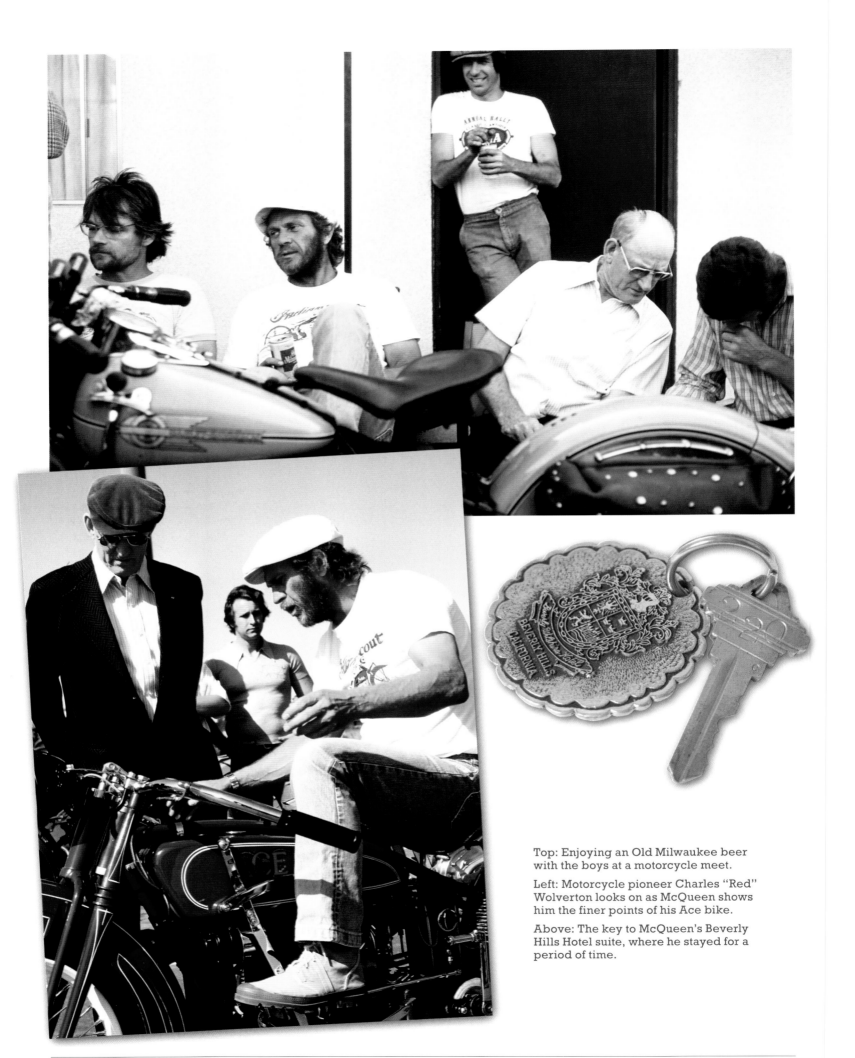

Top: Enjoying an Old Milwaukee beer with the boys at a motorcycle meet.

Left: Motorcycle pioneer Charles "Red" Wolverton looks on as McQueen shows him the finer points of his Ace bike.

Above: The key to McQueen's Beverly Hills Hotel suite, where he stayed for a period of time.

Motorcycle Guy

Mark Rosendahl

No one enjoyed his bikes more than Steve McQueen. I think he became a movie star just so he could buy all those toys.

I met Steve in early 1974 at Starlite Cycle in Fullerton, California. He usually came in with his friend, Bud Ekins, who watched out for him when buying vintage bikes. Bud was the guru of bikes and a hero of mine, and I think he was Steve's, too.

Steve often wandered through the shop, which specialized in restoring Indian Bikes. There are two types of motorcycle people: enthusiasts and consumers. Steve was an enthusiast, a motor-head who loved old bikes. Our shop built two bikes for him. One was a 1918 Power Plus, which is a V-twin bike, and the other, a 1941 Indian Sport Scout, which was originally built as a shop bike, but he bought it before we were finished.

One Monday, Steve rolled up in a '53 Chevy pickup truck, which had a blower and was primer gray. It was ugly as hell but Steve and his buddy seemed to be having a good time. When they opened the doors, a quantity of old Buckhorn Beer cans fell out onto the street. Steve introduced me to actor Lee Majors, and said, "Mark, we don't have any money. Can you buy us a case of beer?" Steve was the most famous box-office star of the day and Majors was the biggest TV star, and between them they didn't have a dime.

So I bought the beer, and sat down on the curb with them while they took turns riding Steve's Indian bike up and down the street. When Steve was riding, I made small talk with Lee, asking him if he rode bikes.

"No, we're just talking" he said. "We're having problems with our wives and needed some guy time." I thought they were out of their minds. Steve's wife at the time was Ali MacGraw and Lee's wife was Farrah Fawcett. Looking as good as they did, it was hard for me to fathom a problem.

A few years later, I saw Steve at an antique motorcycle meet. I had recently picked up a rare Vincent Black Shadow, which Steve ogled and called me later with a request to take another look at it. I had a date that night and told Steve that he could see it, but that my parents would show it to him. My mother answered the door. Steve was sporting long hair and a heavy beard, and Ali MacGraw was dressed in hippy garb. This spooked my mom, who thought he was some hardcore biker dude. She had my dad escort the couple to the garage, where they spent about an hour talking.

When my mom discovered later that it was Steve McQueen and Ali MacGraw who had come to the door, she was cross with me for not telling her and angry at my dad for not making a proper introduction.

We visited Steve once at the Beverly Hilton Hotel with Englishman and motorcycle aficionado, Steve Wright, who restored old bikes for McQueen.

Our task was to deliver a pair of bikes, rolling them through the kitchen and up the service elevator. However, we were hassled by security because Prince Charles, Prince of Wales was visiting the hotel, and we had to drop Steve's name several times in order to make our way to his suite.

His phone kept ringing throughout our visit. He apologized and said it was a couple of young ladies next door. He had spent the night before partying with them in their Jacuzzi. They enjoyed his company so much that they wanted a repeat performance. McQueen, who was feeling rough, wasn't in the mood for an encore.

The last time I saw Steve was at his home on Broad Beach in Malibu when I delivered a '41 Indian Scout to him. He had just purchased an old Mercedes 240D and it was sitting in the garage. It was a piece of junk, but unknown to me, he had a 6.9-liter motor installed with trick suspension. He took me for a ride and just about scared me to death negotiating the winding hills.

Mark Rosendahl is a resident of Chino Hills and has been the service manager for LeBard Underwood for three decades.

Easy Rider
David Clement

Opposite: McQueen and friend Bud Ekins in the California desert on the set of *Dixie Dynamite*, a little known B-film in which McQueen did some stunt riding on a motorcycle.

Above: Steve McQueen's passport.

What Steve McQueen said to me in the summer of 1975 stayed with me all my life and changed it for the better.

Living in La Habra Heights, California, just north of Whittier. I had been riding for about a year and had just started racing. One day, I was invited by a neighbor and his dad to attend an event, along with BSA rider Chuck Minert, who was a friend of Steve McQueen's. I did not know that Steve was going to be there, but it was a chance encounter I will never forget.

Steve had a beard and mustache and looked scruffy, like an old miner. I didn't recognize him as the same person who starred in *On Any Sunday* and *Le Mans*, two films that were influential in my childhood. I don't even remember his particular bike except for its shiny chrome tank. He was polite, not a big shot at all.

Looking back, I think Steve sensed a sadness in me. My dad wasn't around much and he certainly didn't approve of me riding a motorcycle. I worked hard to save money for my bike by mowing lawns, pulled weeds and other odd jobs. After a few hours of riding, Steve walked over to talk to me. Taking my share of falls over the difficult sandy terrain, I explained to Steve that I felt frustrated and inadequate. He listened patiently before putting his hand on my shoulder. What he said was the greatest compliment I had ever received as a kid.

"You're going to be a very good rider someday," Steve said. "Everybody else out here has been at it for years. Keep it up." Anytime an adult male was encouraging, I ate it up. Steve's words resonated with me for years and made me strive to be the best. After that meeting, I felt obligated to see all his movies. Today I own them all on DVD.

I moved up through the amateur ranks over time. In 1983 I won the amateur state championship in the 500 class at Saddleback, and then turned pro. I became a solid mid-level rider on the local race circuit, but at least I was a pro. Steve was right about my potential and it was important that he believed in me.

David Clement is test engineer for Northrup-Grumman and lives in Southern California.

Reunited and it feels so good: McQueen
hounded Bruce Meyer once he discovered the
fellow car collector owned his 1958 Porsche
Speedster. Meyer sold it back to him in 1975.

Hollywood Ending
Bruce Meyer

The resale market for Steve McQueen memorabilia and cars in 1975 wasn't nearly as robust as it is today, which is why I let the actor talk me into selling him back his first sports car.

That was the year that McQueen found out that I owned his 1958 Porsche Speedster, which I believe was Steve's first factory-owned sports car. I bought the vehicle at a Los Angeles car show in 1966 and the owner mentioned when I collected the pink slip that it had once belonged to Steve. That didn't matter to me at the time; I just loved that car.

I had a passing acquaintance with Steve because we both raced motorcycles in the desert, though I was a novice rider. We also shared the same mechanic—Pete Smith, who worked for Bob Smith Porsche-Audi in Hollywood. Pete told Steve that I was the proud owner of his old Porsche Speedster, which Steve quickly dismissed.

"That's just not possible," Steve told Pete. "There was never a moment I recall where Bruce could have seen it." Steve said he had sold the car to a stockbroker and figured that it was long gone. However, something must have nagged at Steve because he called me a few days later.

After we bantered about cars and motorcycles, Steve got to the subject at hand: his old Porsche. Was it his? There was only one way to find out, so we arranged to meet at a location in Westwood, which was almost halfway between his home in Malibu and my place in Beverly Hills.

Steve and Ali MacGraw were already waiting for me when I pulled up with my wife, Raylene. Steve's eyes, which were intense, stayed with the car. He barely met my gaze. I could see the wheels turning in his head. After circling the car, he went behind the driver's seat and ripped up the carpet, which was glued down. I was a bit surprised by this, but when you're Steve McQueen, you can do what you want. Then his eyes became wide as saucers.

"That's where I had my roll bar mounted!" he declared, which proved provenance to him. McQueen quickly suggested we open the hood to see if he could find other clues. He found what he was looking for: there was his original Gardner-Reynolds racing tire. It was a special tread "recapped tire" and everyone that raced in California used this brand.

By this point Steve was as giddy and effervescent as I'd ever seen him. Happy as I was to reunite the two, I had no inclination to sell him back the Porsche. Steve suddenly blurted, "Bruce, I've gotta have this car back. What's it gonna take?" I told Steve that I had fallen in love with it and it was a big part of my life. I also explained that Raylene was very proprietary and would never let me sell the Porsche even if I wanted to. Steve accepted this, we shook hands and that was it—until a few days later when he called.

"Bruce, have you thought anymore about selling me that car?" Steve asked. This routine went on for weeks until Steve wore me down explaining that it was his first love, that he regretted ever selling it and that he would care for it better than I ever could. Finally I came to the conclusion that he loved the Porsche as much as I did and against my wife's wishes, I sold it back to him at market price.

Today there's an enormous premium for a Steve McQueen-owned car. That move, I calculate, cost me at least a half million dollars. But I don't regret it for a second. I reunited a movie star with his first love.

Steve McQueen kept the Porsche for the rest of his life. Six years later I bought an exact twin. Today, Steve's old car proudly sits in Chad McQueen's garage. How's that for a Hollywood ending?

Bruce Meyer is the president of Meyer Pacific, a real estate holding company in Los Angeles. He is also the chairman of the Petersen Automotive Museum and has been a leading car collector for several decades.

Bikers Not Welcome
Mel Haber

Top: This is the man that Mel Haber saw roaring up the driveway of his Palm Springs getaway, not a box-office champion.

Bottom: The denim-clad McQueens step out for a rare night on the town in the mid-seventies.

I'm known in Palm Springs for my restaurant and hotel, and my famous blunders. One of my greatest gaffes? Turning away Steve McQueen.

I celebrated the grand opening of Melvyn's Restaurant and The Ingleside Inn in October 1975. The who's who of Palm Springs showed up, mostly in part thanks to a nineteen-year-old college student by the name of Danny Glick. Danny was a young, ambitious kid who parked cars at a well-known restaurant two blocks away. Danny had assured me that when I opened he would recommend people to visit Melvyn's.

His word was as good as gold. Several people stopped by Melvyn's on opening night, mentioning that Danny had sent them my way. About ten o' clock, I walked outside to have a cigarette just as a scruffy-looking man dressed in dungarees and a T-shirt and sporting a heavy beard pulled up on a Harley-Davidson motorcycle with a pretty lady on the back. *He's certainly not the Ingleside Inn type*, I thought, becoming a little full of myself. He said he had come to see the "new place."

"Please buddy, not tonight!" I begged him. "It's opening night and I don't want any trouble. Come back another time and I'll buy you a drink." He smiled at me, gunned the throttle on the motorcycle and drove off. I was pleased at how I handled a delicate situation so adeptly.

About an hour later, Danny showed up and asked, "Mel, have you been getting all the people I've been sending over?" I told him I had and thanked him profusely. He then asked how I enjoyed meeting Steve McQueen and Ali MacGraw, Hollywood's golden couple. Startled and disappointed that I had not, I said they never showed. Danny said he was surprised because they assured him they would come right over to have a nightcap.

He said, "They were on a big, blue Harley-Davidson motorcycle and Steve McQueen was wearing blue jeans and a T-shirt." Turned out that I'd yanked the welcome mat from under the international box-office champion and his glamorous movie star wife. He never came back.

Mel Haber is the owner of the world famous Ingleside Inn and Melvyn's restaurant in Palm Springs, California. He lives in Rancho Mirage.

The Great Tipper
Dagmar Schuch

Steve McQueen was notoriously tight-fisted, although that doesn't describe the man that I knew.

I worked at the front desk and snack bar at the Hacienda Riviera Spa in Palm Springs in the mid-to-late seventies. Steve and his wife, Ali MacGraw, visited our place a few times a year. Even though Steve had a beard and long hair, I instantly recognized those piercing blue eyes from his movies, all of which I loved. He was one of the few men who ever made me weak at the knees.

Steve was courteous and polite to everyone on our staff. He was also a great tipper. I remember the one time I cooked for him. He had to have his hamburger a special way.

"I want you to put the patty on the grill and then, 'Boom, boom,'" Steve said.

"Boom, boom?" I asked, not quite sure what he meant.

"Once the patty hits the grill, I want you to immediately scoop it up and then flip it over. I like it rare," he said.

It was rare—as well as borderline disgusting. It was the rarest hamburger I had ever served, but I aimed to please. Steve aimed to please as well. He left a $20 tip on a $1.50 hamburger. I wonder what would've happened if I had cooked him a steak?

Dagmar Schuch is the director of administration for the Boys and Girls Club of Palm Springs. She lives in Coachella Valley, California.

Making mashed potatoes was one of McQueen's favorite pastimes. A tabloid reporter wrote that McQueen was fat and hovered at 240 pounds around this time, but this picture shows that he was all muscle.

Above: Taking a break with stunt rider Gary Davis in the hot California sun on the set of *Dixie Dynamite*, a 1976 B-flick that paid $172 a day. It was said that McQueen made close to $14 million in *The Towering Inferno*.

Opposite: McQueen enjoys a moment with members of the cast and crew of Dixie Dynamite. Warren Oates, who was the movie's star, is sitting directly across from McQueen.

Take the Money and Run
Gary Davis

Steve McQueen thought that getting a few hundred dollars for being a stuntman for a day sounded a little more interesting than our usual desert ride.

Here's the scenario: Steve McQueen, the highest-paid movie star in the world after *The Towering Inferno* shattered all box-office records, and I had become friends through one of my mentors, Bud Ekins. We worked on our bikes together at Bud's shop and home fairly often, and developed an easy friendship. Steve was so not-Hollywood and it was truly wonderful. He liked turning wrenches, changing tires, replacing chains and getting his fingernails dirty. He enjoyed the camaraderie of men and was a sincere pleasure to be around.

I received a phone call from him sometime in early 1976, asking if I was up for a ride in the desert the next day. I told him I couldn't because I had a motorcycle sequence to do in a film called *Dixie Dynamite*. In fact, Bud would be there too. Half kidding, I said, "Well, you're welcome to play with the boys as well."

"You know what? That might be kinda fun," Steve gamely replied. The next day he and Bud arrived together and were both put on a Daily Scale Stunt Contract. The base pay at the time was $172 a day. It was said that he was paid close to $14 million for *The Towering Inferno*. You had to admire his sense of humor.

The poor little B-film crew didn't know what to think. Here's Steve McQueen sliding corners, sailing jumps and attacking the woops, staying right with the pack of stunt men. We gave him a planned crash to do called a "Lay Down". He had to land a jump, then lock up the rear brake and force the bike down on his left side. Then, he had to stay down because I had to hit the same jump a bit faster so I could jump over him while he was down. He did everything perfectly as planned. Later I had to wheelie through the pack and take the checkered flag. Steve was so carried away by the atmosphere that he just had to do a wheelie of his own. He miscalculated and looped the bike over on himself in front of everyone. The picture crew was completely freaked. From the panic and concern, it became apparent that he wasn't just one of the normal stunt guys in their eyes. He was truly terrific.

At the end of the day, we informed Steve that he was going to be paid an extra $200 stunt adjustment for the "Lay Down" that he performed. He tried to refuse it, but we told him that we would have trouble justifying our own stunt adjustments if we didn't include him, too. We gave him no choice but to accept.

Afterwards, he took the stunt crew out for a few beers. He probably spent his entire *Dixie Dynamite* paycheck on us.

I respected Steve as a rider, a mechanic, and as an actor, but I loved him as a friend.

Gary Davis is a director and stunt coordinator. He resides in Auburn, California.

Miller Time John Plumlee

A treasured memento of his time on *Dixie Dynamite*, grip John Plumlee saved this scratchy photo of McQueen and himself sharing a beer.

One of the best moments of my life was finding out that Steve McQueen and I were immortalized forever in a photograph.

I was a grip on the set of a low-budget movie called *Dixie Dynamite* in 1976, a drive-in movie at best. Steve's good friend, Bud Ekins, was also enlisted as a stuntman on the picture. We had filmed two days in Santa Ana at the PT Scramble Track.

The movie revolved around Warren Oates' character, who was an old motorcycle rider trying to help some girls win a few bucks. Bud was preparing for a big chase scene involving five riders when a heavily bearded man pulled up in an old pickup truck. He and Bud conversed for a while before Bud walked up to the director, Lee Frost, to ask him if he had $172 in the budget for another rider.

"What's his name?" Lee asked.

"Steve McQueen," Bud replied. Lee, never thinking in a million years it was *the* Steve McQueen, asked if this McQueen guy could ride.

"Yeah, he's okay."

"Hire him," Lee said.

Steve had a ball and got a big kick out of being treated like one of the guys. He was laid back and quiet. He followed direction and did his job. There was no big deal made about his presence, which is exactly what he wanted. The feeling was that the movie executives would have gone nuts over him freewheeling on a bike, so it was kept quiet.

After we wrapped for the day, the Miller beer (Lee's beer of choice) came out and everyone was standing around. I had seen Steve race in Big Sur years before and never had the chance to say hello. We had a brief conversation, but I had no idea that Ben Adams, the still photographer on the set, had taken a picture of the two of us. Several months later at the production office, Ben came in and laid out all his photos on a desk. He handed over a picture of me and McQueen talking over a beer. I was thrilled beyond belief.

John Plumlee is retired from the movie industry and resides in Carmel, California.

Throwin' Back at the Rock
Ed Savko

McQueen with wife Ali MacGraw and her son, Joshua Evans, who don't appear to be thrilled they've been relegated to riding a sidecar.

We've met quite a few characters since my wife, Veronica, and I moved to Southern California from Pittsburgh. You sure don't know what path you're going to take or what people will eventually cross it.

Stumbling across an old stagecoach fashioned from volcanic rock, we decided in 1961 to purchase it and create a small town grocery and gas station in Cornell, California, calling it "The Rock Store."

Located on Mulholland Highway on the outskirts of Los Angeles, the place was desolate because there wasn't much of a population to support the store. When Cornell started to populate a few years later, it forced the development of major roadways connecting Mulholland to the Pacific Coast. Motorcyclists began pouring in from all directions because they were drawn to the windy canyon roads and it gave them the opportunity to test their riding skills. Actors Lee Marvin and Steve McQueen were regular "pit stoppers" and liked being around other gearheads.

Steve usually stopped by the store to grab a beer—or should I say beers—when out on his bike. Once he literally emptied my store of beer when he drank an entire case of Old Milwaukee in one sitting. He came by the next day and raised holy hell when I told him I was all out. I casually reminded him it was he who had drained my supply in the first place.

"Then go and get some more," Steve said with a smile. "I'll be here when you get back."

Steve was a bit of a hell raiser, great fun and a real piece of work. I liked him a lot.

Ed Savko is the owner of The Rock Store, which is a landmark institution for the motorcycling community.

Good Vibrations

Phil Parslow

Opposite: This autographed photo of McQueen in *An Enemy of the People* went up for auction in 2006. The inscription reads: "To Craig – I'm still in Chino! Best, Steve McQueen." Craig, the recipient, is not known.

Above left: Associate Producer Phil Parslow with McQueen. The two developed a fast friendship and a deep bond. The inscription reads: "To quarterback Phil...You're almost perfect like me...Without a nose job. With love and respect...Steve."

Above right: A bespectacled and bushy McQueen with actress and co-star Bibi Andersson.

Actors for the most part are a predictable lot. I've worked with several hundred over the course of my thirty-year career and Steve McQueen was by far the most interesting. I had usually figured them out after a couple of weeks, but I never quite knew what made Steve McQueen tick or what he'd do from day-to-day. Perhaps it was what he said to me when we first met in that cramped Century City office when he was considering me as producer for *An Enemy of the People.*

"I'm crazy. I'm crazy. I think we'll get along great, but just remember what I'm telling you, I'm crazy," he said, barely above a whisper. He also used the word "vibe" often.

Steve and I spent the next eighteen months together and it was the wildest ride of my life. He chose Henrik Ibsen's play as his follow-up to *The Towering Inferno*, which was then the highest grossing picture at the box office. *An Enemy of the People* was a "talkie" about a poisoned spring in a small Scandinavian resort town. Steve, who played Dr. Thomas Stockmann, discovered the spring and disclosed his findings. The only reason the picture was being made at all was out of spite. Steve wanted to stick it to a studio executive who wouldn't let him out of a prior contract, so he picked the most non-commercial project that he could find.

Even though *An Enemy of the People* was not a success, Steve was proud of the picture, especially his performance in which he had to

deliver a three-page monologue—the longest of his career. I know how hard that was for Steve because if he had to memorize more than three lines, it was tough. But he came through with bells on and was terrific.

When Steve asked me to work with him again on *Tom Horn*, I said "yes" without a moment's hesitation. We spent much time on research and pre-production, which meant late night phone calls and bull sessions. During a two-hour conversation on Warner Brothers' back lot, Steve let his guard down. He described the insecurities that he had spent his life struggling to overcome, and how hard he had worked to create his image.

"All to prove that I'm something special, but I'm not sure I have succeeded—at least not to myself," Steve said. The conversation was an eye-opener for me because I didn't realize that Steve hadn't come to terms with himself, even at that age.

But Steve to me will always be the Babe Ruth of box-office champions. His track record on home runs over strike outs is awesome compared to anyone in Hollywood. He carried a mighty big stick and wasn't afraid to swing it.

Phil Parslow was a thirty-year veteran in the movie industry and an associate producer on An Enemy of the People. *He died in July 2003.*

An Unlikely Pair

George Schaefer

Holding an intense and private conversation with
Emmy Award-winning director, George Schaefer.

I met Steve McQueen on a Sunday afternoon at a booth in the Hamburger Hamlet in West Hollywood. He had just come back from a swap meet in Pasadena and proudly showed me some antique auto lamps that fitted one of his many cars.

We were meeting to discuss whether I would direct him in Henrik Ibsen's *An Enemy of the People*. I had seen *Junior Bonner* and a few other films and had always liked him tremendously, but he had never been an actor that I particularly wanted to work with. At the same time, I found the idea of McQueen wanting to do Ibsen intriguing. I think Ibsen would have liked the idea.

Ibsen was an interesting man, an ornery cuss. He wrote *An Enemy of the People* because he was angry with the critics who had panned his play *Ghosts*. He dealt with subjects that were simply not discussed on the stage. Ibsen was a loner. He and Steve in another time would have hit it off.

"I wanna do this," Steve said. "It's something I've gotta get out of my system and if we do it, I want you to hire the best cast in the world. I don't want you to protect me by getting people that I'm not gonna look so good against. It's my funeral if I can't act."

It was McQueen's bravado that won me over, and it was at that moment that *An Enemy of the People* went forward.

George Schaefer directed Steve McQueen in An Enemy of the People. He died in September 1997.

The Defender
Charles Durning

McQueen and fellow actor Charles Durning (far right) struck up an unlikely friendship during their time on *An Enemy of the People*.

I didn't know what to expect when I met Steve McQueen. People told me he was short-tempered and had no regard for anyone. I found him to be completely different. He was loyal to the people that he worked with, even defending them.

I specifically recall an incident on the set of *An Enemy of the People* when one of the actors unknowingly parked his car in a reserved spot for a studio executive. The guard came into the stage area and began berating the actor. Steve interrupted the guard, pulled him aside and said, "Do you realize what you're doing to this man? He's got to go inside and act. Do you know what an actor has to do to prepare himself for a role? Emotions are all he brings to the

job and you have just destroyed his potential to make a living today. If you ever talk that way to an actor again, I will personally see that you are walking the streets."

He was child-like in many ways. He would ask me to come upstairs and watch him perform karate. I was invited on several outings with Steve and Ali. We went to jazz concerts at the Hollywood Bowl and I was surprised he enjoyed such events.

Steve was unique as a movie star because he was down to earth. If he was impressed with your work, he encouraged you to persist. He would stand on the sidelines as I was saying my lines. "Give it more, Charlie. Give it more. Do more there,

Charlie, go ahead," he said, cheering me on. After the scene, he pulled me aside and said, "I don't know when you're going to make it or how, but someday you're going to break through."

The cast of *An Enemy of the People* felt a great sadness when the time came to part ways. McQueen felt such a tremendous bond that he and Ali hosted a wrap party in a posh Malibu restaurant. It was the last time I saw him.

Tony Award winner Charles Durning is one of Hollywood's most dependable and sought after supporting actors who began working in guest appearances in early sixties TV shows.

Your Money's No Good Here
Buckley Norris

Opposite & below: According to an acquaintance, McQueen was a genius when it came to money but his fashion sense was suspect.

Bottom: Steve McQueen needed reading glasses in his later years as evidenced by this Barbara McQueen image.

I only met Steve McQueen once, but he left quite an impression on me. I have no idea what his I.Q. was, but I had no doubt he was a genius when it came to money.

I had been around Hollywood types almost my entire working life because I bonded movies. I was an especially close friend to Jack Webb of *Dragnet* fame.

Jack and I were hoisting a few drinks inside the Cock 'n Bull, a Los Angeles landmark on Sunset Boulevard and Doheny one day in the mid-seventies when Steve McQueen and character actor John Carradine decided to join us.

We downed our ale for a good three hours, laughing, drinking, cursing and trading a few industry stories. When it came time to settle up, we each received separate bills as requested by Mr. McQueen.

I offered to take them to the cashier to pay up. Everybody gave me a credit card, save Steve. He insisted on paying with a check.

"C'mon Steve, you're holding everyone up," I said. "Why don't you just pay with a credit card like everybody else?" Then he absolutely floored me.

"Buckley, I always pay with a check because I know they won't cash them," Steve said with a glint in his eye.

I was stunned for a second. He was the highest paid movie star in the world at the time and he intended on keeping his money. I returned his smile.

"Steve, you're a genius!"

"I get free gas that way, too," he said.

Buckley Norris is a movie industry veteran who lives in Los Angeles, California.

Target practice in the hills of Malibu, 1977.

Hot Times and Cold Beer

Sam Allred

Steve McQueen loved the simple things in life: cold beer, spicy Mexican food, fast cars and the noise of automatic gunfire.

I met Steve through his friend and martial arts instructor, Pat Johnson, who was the chief referee at several of my championship karate tournaments. Pat was so exceptional that his development and enforcement of tournament rules set the bar and were accepted nationally for most meets.

Sometime in the seventies, Pat invited me to one of his private training sessions with Steve. He apparently had been told by Pat that I would be discreet. Steve was athletic, could hit the heavy bag very hard and was not afraid to work up a sweat. We talked during occasional breaks in his workout, but the training was mostly all business. Steve told me that he would be coming to Albuquerque, New Mexico soon to visit his wife, Ali MacGraw, who was shooting *Convoy* with Sam Peckinpah. Steve promised he would look me up, and surprised me when he did.

The first order of business, according to Steve, was locating a case of Black Label beer, which was not available in Los Angeles. After he had found his beloved suds, I took him to a public flea market. Because I was a weathercaster on television, lots of people recognized me and stopped to chat, but not many paid attention to my bearded, long-haired friend save for one lady acquaintance, who asked me a week later if I had been escorting Steve McQueen around town. I was astounded that she recognized him and asked her how she knew. She told me she had spotted him immediately from a mole on his cheek, and then checked his eyes; women pay attention to those details.

We drove all around Albuquerque and the countryside, and stopped for Mexican food at a friend's restaurant called El Comedor De Julia. Steve feasted on enchiladas with red chili, and chased it down with his Black Label beer. We had such a good time that Steve visited me twice again—one occasion centered on a gun collector and the other a car collector. In both instances the case of Black Label beer was iced down in the trunk when I greeted him.

My good friend Don Pakinham owned a large collection of firearms, including a few rare Thompson submachine guns. Steve had never fired a real Tommy gun before and was excited about the prospect of squeezing off approximately 800 rounds per minute and asked Don a lot of questions about them and firearms in general. We decided to shoot in a large unpopulated desert area which was a short drive behind Don's house, at the base of the Sandia Mountains. He also supplied several other exotic weapons for our entertainment. Before we shot up the desert, we went for breakfast. While eating, Steve explained almost apologetically, that he loved wearing jeans but at least they were clean.

The last time I saw Steve, I took him to visit a warehouse, where a casual friend, Phil Coors of the Coors beer empire, maintained some three hundred cars. Steve, who kept his collection to around fifty for insurance reasons, was impressed by the quantity and quality of the many rare and historic vehicles. When we left, around two hundred Coors employees had lined up outside the building to catch a glimpse of Steve. Not a word, not any noise at all. We just entered our car and left.

I seldom spoke to Steve after I moved to Washington, D.C. in late 1977 to take another broadcasting job. I did tell him of a large car collectors' show in Hershey, Pennsylvania and he said he wanted to visit me and attend. However, all communication between us suddenly ceased, and I eventually found out about his heartbreaking condition.

I'll never forget my time with Steve and I cherish the moments we shared. He was just a "regular" guy and anything but a "star". It was like hanging around with a long-time buddy. Í bet Steve would grin as only he could, if he knew that time spent with him more than thirty years earlier was now contributing, in my retirement years, to my "fifteen minutes of fame".

Sam Allred is the founder of the martial art Jukensa Kajukenbo. Allred is also the author of seven self-defense books in Spanish and is a member of the Black Belt Hall of Fame. He resides in Mexico.

A Convoy in New Mexico
Ernest Borgnine

During the filming of *Convoy*, I met Steve McQueen who was married to my co-star Ali MacGraw at the time. He came to the location one day while my stand-in Bobby Herron and I were alone on the set, waiting for someone to give us a ride back to our hotel. Steve asked, "Where's my wife?"

We said, "She's gone ahead to the next location somewhere."

Steve nodded and stood there smoking away. It was marijuana. He made no bones about it. He said, "Listen, it's getting late. You want me to take you back?" So Bobby and I got into his car. Steve was still smoking and now drinking beer. He had three beautiful cowboy hats in the back and he was throwing the empty beer bottles onto them. He drove at a hundred miles an hour at least. Bobby sank low in the seat, as scared as I was. At the hotel we accepted Steve's invitation to have a beer or three, and sometime later, left him in the bar just as he was getting his second wind. I went upstairs and collapsed, feeling as though we were in *Bullitt*.

Steve McQueen was a fine actor. You could tell on the screen that he worked the same way I did, with his heart, but also with his head.

Ernest Borgnine is a veteran actor and won the Academy Award for Marty in 1955. This passage is from Borgnine's 2008 autobiography Ernie: The Autobiography published by Kensington Publishing Corp as a Citadel Press Book.

Opposite & right: Finding a beer in his Ford pickup in "Big Sky Country", Montana, 1977.

Above: Barbara Minty McQueen and Steve McQueen sharing a big laugh at her cabin in Ketchum, Idaho, 1978. Barbara was McQueen's third and last wife and then his widow.

Opposite: An invoice for a bouquet of flowers sent to Barbara Minty from Steve McQueen, when they stayed at the Hilton Inn in Tucson, Arizona in November of 1978.

HARRY FINLEY   FRED GIBBONS   No 9088

Place in room before arrival

FLOWER FASHIONS

One Sixty-Eight South Beverly Drive ● Beverly Hills, California 90212 ● Telephone 275-0159

DATE _11-20-78_

| DELIVERY DATE | AM / PM | SOLD BY |
| M T W T F S S | | |

DELIVER TO _Steve McQueen_
ADDRESS _Hilton Inn_
CITY _1601 Miracle Mile North_
Tuson, Ariz   PHONE

white daisies (1 red rose in center)	30	00
	2	85
TX	1	97
Card Barbara Minty	34	82

CHARGE TO _Solar Productions_   ORDER COMPLETED
ADDRESS
CITY _____ PHONE _836-3000_
_# 1321_

All merchandise taken on memo charge will automatically be charged after 3 days. Due to room temperature and climatic change there is no guarantee on fresh foliage plants after 24 hours.
All accounts are payable 10th of the month following date of purchase.
H-29

Model Behavior

Nina Blanchard

I once owned an agency that represented top models for photography and commercials. One of the models was a beautiful brunette named Barbara Minty. She was in demand by all the best photographers, worked in locations around the world and graced the covers of major fashion magazines.

Barbara was unassuming and not particularly sophisticated. More interested in the outdoors, she was especially crazy about horses, and didn't join the groups that frequented the trendy clubs of that era. I believe she was surprised at her success as a model, and was not completely comfortable in the role.

Steve called me saying that he had seen a picture of Barbara, and found out that I represented her. He wanted to meet her because she might be right to play the part of an Indian woman in his new film. I told him I was aware of the project and there was no such role, but he assured me there was a script revision in the works. Possessed of an agent's mentality, I did not want to deprive Barbara of the chance to appear in a movie. She was not a trained actress, but in Hollywood that didn't necessarily matter and she did have some Indian heritage with her long dark hair and high cheekbones. So, perhaps I should think about it. I told Steve he could meet her if I was present.

Steve was living at the Beverly Wilshire, which is now the Beverly Regent. We met for lunch in the El Padrino Room. Steve and I monopolized the conversation, and Barbara doesn't remember saying more than "Hello." We talked about everything from our childhood to motorcycles. I'm crazy about Harley-Davidsons although I have always been a passenger, never a driver. I think we discussed the movie for a few minutes.

Obviously, I completely missed what silently passed between Steve and Barbara, which would later annoy me as I considered myself perceptive.

In spite of his gruff exterior, Steve was always aware of someone else's pain. He had called me one evening and could tell I was on the verge of tears. He persuaded me to tell him what was wrong. One of my competitors had made some ugly and untrue comments about me in a national magazine. I had never been targeted like that before and I was upset. Steve told me to fix my face, and he would take me out. Over dinner, he described with much humor all his bad press since he became successful, and before long I was laughing. He made me realize what a waste of energy it is to worry about what people say, and since then I have paid no attention to anything negative anyone said about my agency or me. That dinner was a thoughtful, kind act on Steve's part and a lesson I never forgot.

As Barbara and Steve's relationship continued, she did not seem concerned that she was not always available for modeling assignments, and after she moved in with Steve, I sensed that she was very much in love with him and content with her new life.

When Steve and Barbara moved to Santa Paula they lived in a yellow farmhouse and Steve had storage space for his collection of cars, motorcycles and his more recent passion, biplanes. Steve and I had started flying lessons at the same time and kidded each other about who would solo first. I never did finish classes and Steve won the contest. Steve's single-mindedness when he approached a task was astonishing. Everything he undertook he accomplished and never in a mediocre way. He was always the best at what he did, whether acting or motorcycle racing. In many ways Steve was a solitary man, but he had great loyalty to the friends he trusted.

I remember the remark Barbara made to me as we were leaving the Beverly Wilshire after that first meeting with Steve. I asked her why she had said so little at lunch, and she replied, "I'm going to marry that man!" I looked at her in astonishment and thought, "yeah, sure." But she did.

Nina Blanchard is the legendary head of the Nina Blanchard Agency. Today she is retired and lives in the Los Angeles area.

Below: McQueen in front of a blue Ford camper, a vehicle which is sentimentally recalled by Barbara as it was used on many road trips with Steve.

Opposite: Barbara and Steve taking a leisurely ride down the California coast, 1978.

Just Two
Barbara McQueen

If I had to think of two,
I'd always come back to me and you,
The old blue truck
The things we'd do
Me and you
Just two.

*Barbara McQueen is a former model
and the widow of Steve McQueen.*

Opposite: Steve and Barbara outside their Malibu home, 1977.

Top left: A view of the Pacific Ocean from McQueen's Malibu retreat.

Top right: A picture of McQueen's den in Malibu, which includes a library of books and a sliding ladder.

Right: Flashing a peace sign in bed at his Malibu home, 1977.

Breaking a Mother's Silence
Kealoha Rosecrans

When a man is good to your family, you tend to remember him fondly; when a man is good to your mother, he becomes a saint.

Steve McQueen employed my mother from 1977 to 1979, when she was going through a dreadful divorce from my father. Times were tough and Steve became a beacon of light in a time of darkness for my family when he hired her.

My mom, Michelle Elaine Rosecrans, was recommended to Steve by director Leo Penn (father of actor Sean Penn). She had taken care of Leo's ailing father in a Huntington Beach convalescent home and needed extra employment to make ends meet. Steve gave my mother a job cleaning, cooking, and watering the plants at his beautiful Trancas Beach home, on condition that she never talk publicly about him. It was a promise she kept right up to her October 2007 death from breast cancer.

Often she took my brother, Dorian, and me to work because she could not afford a babysitter after school. Steve's life with Barbara

Minty was quiet, but not once we arrived. We enjoyed his two pachinko machines, rolling back and forth on the library ladder and playing at the beach. Steve seemed to have a special place in his heart for kids and welcomed us into his home.

My mother never discussed Steve other than to say how good he was to her. He often gave her a little extra on her paychecks and a big fat bonus at Christmas so that she could buy Dorian and me all the *Star Wars* toys we wanted. But, the biggest gift he gave to my mother was her self-esteem.

So while Steve swore my mom to secrecy, I didn't take the same oath. I am breaking her silence to let the world know what a wonderful human being Steve McQueen was.

Kealoha Rosecrans is a professional skateboarder who resides in Kailua, Hawaii.

Steve and Natalie Wood in *Love with the Proper Stranger.*

Celebrating both Barbara Minty's birthday and her grandfather Chester's in Eugene, Oregon on June 11, 1978.

All in the Family
Linda Minty

Steve McQueen was not only an extended family member, but he just so happened to be my favorite movie star.

It was love at first sight—I was in the seventh grade in 1964 when I first noticed Steve McQueen. A lot of other members of the female gender did, too. That was the year *Love with the Proper Stranger*, a romantic comedy starring Steve and Natalie Wood was released. Steve's nuanced performance as a free-wheeling, moody musician who is forced to do the honorable thing after he gets Wood pregnant, made me weak in the knees.

Fast forward to the summer of '78. Steve McQueen was coming to Eugene, Oregon to celebrate two birthdays—my cousin, Barbara Jo Minty, and my grandfather, Chester A. Minty—who were both born on June 11. Barbi and Steve had been dating for a while and their relationship had become serious enough that it was time to "meet the parents".

Because Steve was such a big movie star and Barbi was an international model, I thought they would arrive Hollywood-style in a large limousine. They fooled me and just about everyone in Eugene by pulling up in an old, beat-up pickup truck. Despite the heights of their respective careers, both were just farm kids at heart.

But if the truck threw me for a loop, I was in for a bigger surprise at Steve's appearance. He was smaller than I had imagined, had wavy, long hair, and wore blue jeans, a T-shirt and a down vest. He was noticeably low-key at the birthday party because Barbi's father, my

uncle Gene, made no secret of the fact that he did not approve of the age difference between them. Steve was so subdued that the kids were not shy to sit on his lap and pose for pictures while the adults peppered him with questions. Everyone was talking about their favorite Steve McQueen movie. He usually replied, "Yeah, I liked that one" or he'd say, "That wasn't my favorite."

When I mentioned that I had fallen in love with him on *Love with the Proper Stranger*, he smiled and rolled his eyes. Legend has it that Natalie Wood was chasing him on that picture and he resisted her advances. Then I added that *The Thomas Crown Affair* was my favorite, and he said that he had lobbied hard for the part and was a big stretch for him as an actor.

What wasn't a stretch of the imagination was how much he and Barbi were in love because they'd steal glances every now and then. Barbi was sweet, down-to-earth, had a good sense of humor and loved the outdoors. He was kind, thoughtful and very loving towards her.

I never saw Steve again, but I do know they visited my grandmother, Vica Minty, upon their return from filming *The Hunter*. Steve gave her an autographed photo and an antique wall clock, or at least, they said it was an antique. Vica had it appraised and discovered the clock was an antique replica. Guess it's the thought that counts.

Linda Minty is retired and lives in Oregon.

Opposite: McQueen's perm was another fashion faux pas, 1978.

Above: Welcome to the neighborhood. A group of kids welcoming McQueen to Corvalis, Oregon, June 1978.

Darth Vader
Wears a Down Vest
Mike Schults

Darth Vader stayed at the Minty house. That's all that I needed to hear.

I had also heard from some of the other kids in the neighborhood that Steve McQueen was staying with the Mintys as well. Our family lived next door to Wilma and Gene, Barbara's parents, in Corvalis, Oregon. It was the summer of 1978, *Star Wars* was the craze, and I was an eight-year old on a quest to find the elusive Vader who was bold enough to be staying right next door to me!

Now, I didn't know who the heck Steve McQueen was, but my friends elected me to snoop around, probably because I was the youngest. So I knocked on the door and Mrs. Minty answered. Being my daring self, I asked for Darth Vader, but she said he wasn't home.

I reported this important news to my friends who promptly sent me back for more specifics. Again, I ventured over and knocked on the door. This time, Steve McQueen answered.

"Is there an actor here?" I asked in all sincerity.

McQueen smiled. "Yes, I am Steve McQueen and I was in *The Towering Inferno.*" I could tell he was amused that I had the temerity to return to the house to ask specifically for an actor.

When the parents found out that Steve McQueen was in their midst, one of them baked a cake and had us sign a card welcoming him to the neighborhood. We then returned to the Mintys with the cake and card. How could they refuse us?

McQueen was pleasantly surprised and invited us in to eat cake with him and take a picture. All the kids—Mike and Lynn Kulm, Caroline Boose, Eric Sorem, Kari Schults, Frank Walters and me— were wet from a water fight we had half an hour earlier. It was obvious by the way he behaved that McQueen liked kids. After we finished with the cake and pictures, McQueen asked us to keep it a secret that he was in town.

I like the fact that McQueen became a Christian at the end of his life—maybe I'll see him again—unlike that elusive Darth Vader.

Mike Schults is a loan officer with Chase Manhattan Bank. He resides in Laguna Niguel, California.

Opposite top: With beer in hand, McQueen points in the direction of where he will build his home on a 400-acre parcel of land in East Fork, Idaho, 1978.

Opposite bottom: Taking a drive around his newly-acquired property, 1978.

Top left: Clearing the land with a tractor, McQueen was going to build a cabin, a guest house and a private runway for his planes and call his ranch "The Crazy M". Unfortunately, illness prevented him from seeing it to fruition.

Top right: Snow Day in Ketchum, 1978.

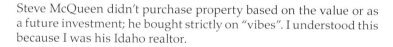

Pass the Ranch

Mike McCann

Steve McQueen didn't purchase property based on the value or as a future investment; he bought strictly on "vibes". I understood this because I was his Idaho realtor.

I met Steve in the early seventies when I was hanging out at Cycle Products West, a motorcycle shop on Pico Boulevard in West Los Angeles. Owner Al Wurtzel was a buddy and one day, in walked Steve, who was married to Ali MacGraw at the time. Steve told Al he had received "a pass from his old lady" to ride bikes, and invited us to join him at Indian Dunes. So we all jumped in a couple of vans and headed out there for a few hours of great riding.

A few years later, I moved to Idaho. The winter of 1977 brought deep snow to the area, and Steve McQueen found a way to make sport of the sticky stuff by plowing his Wagoneer into a snow bank. He was on the side of the road with his new girlfriend, Barbara Minty, trying to figure out how to extract the car, laughing because he was having fun on the ice with producer Ray Stark's car while staring at a hefty repair bill.

After I re-introduced myself to Steve, who remembered our day at Indian Dunes, we became friendly. He said he liked Idaho because there were few people around and he wanted a getaway from the Hollywood rat race. I understood where he was coming from since I had grown up in the film business and was familiar with Hollywood types. Steve did not fit the typical mold. He was such a down-to-earth human being, never bragged about himself, loved people from all walks of life, and was courteous to everyone. Sometimes he got a little crazy, but he was so much fun.

Steve knew I had sold Barbara her home and wanted me to find a place for him as well. It's not as easy as it sounds because eighty-five percent of Ketchum is public land and private property has always been scarce. I found Steve a five-acre parcel in the winter of 1978. He stood on the hood of my Bronco and spotted Barbara's home, which was about five lots away. Then he let out a big smile.

"How much?" he asked. I told him $75,000. He bought it right away. He was going to build a log cabin and call it "The Last Chance". Today it is worth somewhere in the neighborhood of $3 million.

A few months later, Steve came back to me and said, "I'm looking for more acreage." It turned out to be much more. I knew of a hidden 400-acre lot in East Fork, half an hour from Ketchum, which I thought would be perfect. I visited the property, which was owned by a Beverly Hills resident, and drew a map for Steve so that he could inspect it the next day. When Steve saw the directions, he said he and Barbara had already been there—they had an impromptu picnic on the acreage a few hours before my visit. They made plans to build a cabin, a guest house and private runway for his planes, and even had a name picked out for the ranch: "The Crazy M".

Unfortunately, Steve fell ill and never saw the completion of "The Last Chance" or "The Crazy M". I have no doubt that Steve would have eventually moved from Los Angeles to become an Idaho rancher, and I can't think of a more fitting ending.

Mike McCann resides in Ketchum, Idaho, where he continues to sell real estate.

Having It All
Alice Schernthanner

Sun Valley, Idaho, has long been an attraction for celebrities and the jet set. They like coming here because no one makes a fuss over them—and sometimes they're even put in their place if they act too big for their britches. Such was the case with Steve McQueen's son, Chad.

I met Steve and Chad sometime in the late seventies at the Dollar Cabin in Sun Valley. The cabin had been created from a small hut built shortly after World War II and an old ski school dormitory attached to it in 1964. It was where Steve stayed when he visited Sun Valley. Chad was a rambunctious kid, running around the cabin lodge like a windup toy. I wasted no time telling him, "If you want to run, go outside."

"My father is Steve McQueen," he said with a feisty look.

I was pregnant at the time and my hormones were out of whack. This sassy little kid caught me on the wrong day and I let him have it. "I don't care who your father is, you're not allowed to run inside the lobby," I told him. He looked a little chagrined but walked outside, deciding not to challenge me. At that moment, a man stood up, looked at me with those piercing blue eyes and approached the front desk. I thought, *Oh boy, I'm going to catch hell now.*

"Thank you," Steve said with a smile. After that, we became fast friends.

Steve was unlike most movie stars—he was a real person. He enjoyed the company of regular folk and was a kind and compassionate man. He followed my youngest child's birth and always made sure to stop and chat when he came to town. He would drink his coffee, and we'd talk about life in general—our hopes and dreams. I don't think fame or celebrity brought Steve happiness.

"All I ever wanted was a wife and a family and I haven't done well in either department," he once told me.

It wasn't long before he fell in love with Barbara Minty. Of course, he had two children from his first marriage and they were close. I've always felt that in the end, Steve finally did have it all—a wife and a family who loved him.

Alice Schernthanner is retired and resides in Ketchum, Idaho.

Patience is a Virtue
Paul Lovemark

Opposite top left: Steve and Barbara McQueen outside their Santa Paula hangar. Ranch hand Grady Ragsdale is sitting on the left, 1979.

Opposite bottom left: Father and son share a beer in the hangar as Barbara McQueen enjoys the playful banter.

Opposite top and middle right: A Mobilgas sign and Harley-Davidson clock were amongst hundreds of collectibles in McQueen's Santa Paula hangar.

Bottom right: Lavishing love on his antique PT-17 Stearman, 1979.

Top right: A cabinet full of old toys.

Bottom right: An antique Coca-Cola sign.

I've always thought that Steve McQueen was a decent man, but patience wasn't one of his virtues.

I first met Steve in early 1979 when former World War II correspondent, Clete Roberts, introduced us.

Aviation had recently become one of Steve's passions and he was in the market to buy a hangar. I was one of two people at the Santa Paula Airport who owned one.

The hangar was originally owned by Lou Barber, who had a Chevrolet dealership in Ventura. He sold it to a business associate of mine, Bob Schultz, and we were having lunch in a Van Nuys restaurant in 1967 when I bought it from him for $37,000 sight unseen.

My business, Helicopter Rebuild and Welding, employed a handful of people and was doing quite well when Steve McQueen came along looking to buy it from me.

I told Steve I wasn't interested in selling the hangar, nor did I want the aggravation of moving my entire operations. McQueen was persistent to the point of being a pest. Finally, he asked, "Well, what would it take to get you to sell the place?" I threw out an outrageous figure and McQueen told me my price was ridiculous and left. At least I got rid of him. An hour later he came back.

"If you can be out of here in thirty days, I'll take it," McQueen said.

I closed my toolbox and started packing.

Paul Lovemark is retired from the helicopter maintenance business and resides in Reno, Nevada.

The Great Outdoors
Jack Mooseau

Though McQueen's dislike of horses was well known, he could not avoid them thanks to wife Barbara, who was an expert polo player.

A mutual respect for the great outdoors, an appreciation for beer and a love for the state of Idaho was the basis of my friendship with Steve McQueen which had an interesting start.

Barbara Minty was my neighbor in Ketchum and I fed her horses when she was away. One morning I went to the barn and saw a heavily bearded man, who appeared homeless, mulling around. I asked him what he was doing.

"I'm a friend of Barbara's," he said, then walked into her house. Barbara later told me it was Steve McQueen. He respected the fact that I was looking out for her and we hit it off. Our friendship was sealed one night when I let him have the last beer in my refrigerator. My house was seven miles from town and Steve didn't feel like fetching more in the snow.

Ketchum has historically been a second home to many Hollywood stars. They come for the winter but when the snow melts, they discover how beautiful the state is. We rode horses and I taught him how to fly fish and ski. Once, it wasn't so pleasant on the slopes when we stopped for lunch and people started taking pictures of

him. Steve didn't like the attention because his privacy was important to him.

I could possibly be the only man alive who turned down the opportunity to work on one of Steve's movies. He asked if I was interested in some stunt work on *Tom Horn*, but his timing wasn't good. Skiing is a passion for me and I couldn't see giving up a winter to sit around a movie set. What a dummy!

Steve invited my wife and me to visit him and Barbara in Santa Paula, California, where he promised to show us his airplane hangar and take me flying. I initially gave Steve's aviation skills a lukewarm review. Before even taking off, he ran into a pole and put a dent in his wing, tearing the fabric. Undaunted, Steve plopped a Snoopy hat on my head, gave me a leather jacket, strapped me in the open cockpit and up we went into the air. We had a ball.

He is fondly remembered in Ketchum.

Jack Mooseau is a fly fishing guide and bartender. He has resided in Ketchum, Idaho since the seventies.

Yes Man
Fred Weintraub

Behind the camera, setting up a shot. For all intents and purposes McQueen was the real director of *Tom Horn*.

Steve McQueen was the only actor I ever knew who willingly cut his own lines.

The shooting script for *Tom Horn* was the work of two accomplished writers— Tom McGuane and Bud Shrake. Steve also worked hard on it. He would make the script girl stay up until two in the morning, writing new dialogue.

"Steve, all you're going to be doing is saying, 'Yup.'"

"No, no, no," he said. "I have to know the scene."

But then I was amazed to discover that when these new pages were ready, he would take a pencil and cross out all his lines until he ended up with "Yup." But it was interesting how he needed the new dialogue to get to his "Yup."

Fred Weintraub was the producer of Tom Horn. He resides in Los Angeles, California.

Left: Deep in thought during a stockyards scene in *Tom Horn*, early 1979.

Opposite: Despite an Arizona desert location for *Tom Horn,* there were often cold and unfavorable filming conditions.

Double Whammy

Gary Combs

Steve McQueen never had a double as far as he was concerned.

I worked as a stuntman on three of his pictures: *Nevada Smith*, *The Getaway* and *Tom Horn*. For *The Getaway*, I was going to double for Steve, and Sam Peckinpah had asked me to come in for a meeting to discuss the driving scenes.

At the time, I had a problem with my ears sticking out. They looked like two open car doors, and needed to be taped down during my stunts. I was sitting opposite McQueen, who had not seen me in seven years, when he looked at me and pulled at his earlobes and flicked his ears. I did have them fixed later.

Before taking on the job as McQueen's stunt double, I telephoned his other double, Loren Janes and asked him for some advice. He told me that Steve always made him wear a trench coat over his film clothes.

"He doesn't want the public to think he has a stunt double," Loren said. I laughed and quickly forgot about Loren's advice. When I arrived at the set in San Marcos, Texas, I was issued an outfit that matched Steve's, and I noticed later that whenever I put my wardrobe on, Steve would go into his trailer and take his off.

Seven years later I doubled for Steve again in *Tom Horn*. On the first day of filming, Steve patted me on the belly and said half-jokingly, "If you're going to double me Combs, you're going to have to hold your stomach in." Steve, too, had gained a few pounds since I last saw him on the set of *The Getaway*.

"Don't you ever look in the mirror?" was my reply. The comment took Steve aback, who replied that his stomach wasn't that big. He then huffed off and licked his wounds until a few days later on the set, when he caught me slouching. He came from behind and punched me lightly in the back.

"Straighten up, Combs! God, if you're doubling me, you have to improve that posture." I was more than fed up.

"Son-of-a-bitch, you don't look in the mirror, do you?" I said.

While we were exchanging verbal blows, his new lady and future wife, Barbara Minty, took photos of us from a distance. She developed a picture and gave it to me with the condition that I never let Steve know who took it. The photo revealed that Steve had the bigger gut and, in addition, slouched more than me. I later showed it to Steve and grinning widely, casually asked him to sign it.

"Oh my God, where did you get this?" Steve asked. I kept my oath with Barbara, but Steve never did sign the picture. He escaped as quickly as possible.

Gary Combs is a stunt coordinator who resides in Los Angeles, California.

Opposite top: With his dog Junior and John Alonzo, *Tom Horn's* director of photography.

Opposite bottom: With John Alonzo (in black cap) looking on, McQueen checks the sun in order to place the next shot.

Top left: Producer Fred Weintraub worried whether or not McQueen would shave his beard when cameras first rolled on *Tom Horn*. He eventually did.

Top right: Squinting in the Arizona sun.

Heads Up!
Rob Goldman

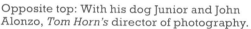

In the spring of 1979, I was invited by my friend and neighbor, cinematographer John A. Alonzo, to visit the set of *Tom Horn* in Arizona.

My first impression of Steve McQueen was that he looked much older than I remembered him on screen. It wasn't until later that I learned he had a terminal illness which perhaps was the reason for his weathered look. Nonetheless, McQueen bounded around the set like a schoolboy at recess.

Being a Western, there were many guns around, and between takes, McQueen enjoyed showing them off to the crew. He liked explaining the intricacies and history of a particular piece. I also recall a special effects man handing him an exploded head he had just constructed for an upcoming scene. McQueen was fascinated by it and showed it off to everyone like a kid with a new toy at Christmas.

During the filming, McQueen and Alonzo dwarfed William Wiard, who was the second director engaged on the set. Apparently, McQueen had run other directors off, including two who had never even stepped foot on location. In some scenes Wiard stood around like a production assistant while McQueen and Alonzo did the directing. They worked well together, for despite their big egos, they had a mutual respect and real chemistry. Alonzo later told me

that McQueen had virtually begged him to work on *The Hunter*, but he had already signed on to another film. I'm sure that had McQueen lived longer he and Alonzo would have made some wonderful films together.

McQueen's positive attitude and passion were infectious. His generosity to the cast and crew made them all want to give their best, and they took pride in pleasing him in a way that wasn't patronizing. It was interesting how Slim Pickens and McQueen joked between takes, talking about the good old days, but when the cameras started rolling, McQueen was all business. Watching him come down the steps during his breakout in the jail scene and observing his facial expressions was something I'll never forget. I learned a lot about film acting that day and about McQueen the person as well.

The McQueen I saw during my brief visit was a man at the peak of his talent. His passion and drive are the reasons the film holds up so well, and, as it turned out, it was McQueen's last great performance. For a twenty-two-year old just out of acting school, it was an unforgettable experience.

Rob Goldman is author of the critically acclaimed Once They Were Angels, A History of the Team. As an actor he was featured in Dances With Wolves, Overboard and JFK.

Me and
Steve McQueen
Joe Brown

I met Steve McQueen in 1979 when he filmed *Tom Horn* in Tucson. I was working as a wrangler and supplied livestock for the production.

To my surprise, I was hired ten days before filming began at Mr. McQueen's request. My duties were to teach him how to rope a horse in a corral. I reported to work every day and practiced my hoolihan loop, but only saw him from afar. His and Barbara's camp at the east windmill of the San Rafael ranch was close to the corrals where I waited, but he stayed away.

On the day of filming, Steve suddenly appeared by my side at the coffee urn, introduced himself, and walked me away from the company. I thought I was about to earn my pay as his teacher, but we talked about books. He said that he and Sam Peckinpah agreed that my novel *The Forests of the Night* was the best book they had read. We talked about my experience in writing it and his in reading it, and then he went back to his work on the set.

When filming began I assumed my regular duties with the wrangler crew, and my son Billy Paul doubled Steve for the scene in which Tom Horn roped his horse. The film company didn't seem to be able to settle on who would direct the film, so Steve took it on himself to keep everybody moving. He made sure that company indecision did not waste any time. Filming happened on schedule. Steve and cinematographer John Alonzo brought the company together every morning before the first scene and kept it busy until it wrapped.

I met Barbara later that first day. She always kept her camera ready. We visited often on the set and have been friends ever since. She took the photograph of me that the publisher used on the jackets of my books *Steeldust* and *Steeldust II*.

Steve and I didn't talk again until the company moved to Mescal for the filming of the scenes in the jail and the execution of Tom Horn. One day I was in the wrangler van about to leave the set, when Steve sent word that he wanted to talk. He and Barbara were waiting for me on a raised boardwalk outside Mezcal's main building. We talked about *The Forests of the Night* and the cowboy life for about an hour. Then he said he wanted me to play Father Brown, the priest who stood by to give Tom Horn the last rites in the jailhouse before his walk to the gallows. I told him I was no actor. He said, "Leave that to me."

I dressed as a priest and stood by every day for a week. Then we did the scene in two takes. That wasn't because I was such a good actor. After the first take, Steve walked over to me and whispered that my leg had shaken all through the scene. "Relax," he said. "Don't let me down. I went to bat for you to do this." Our next take was good enough to print.

After the company wrapped and left Tucson, I figured that my relationship with Steve McQueen was over, but we kept in touch by telephone. One day he said he was at an airport and about to go up in his biplane and practice stunts. He knew I was a pilot and invited me to come to California and fly with him. For me, an airplane was a means to travel from one place to another, preferably in straight and level flight so I declined. Another time he asked me if I would like a part in *The Hunter*, his last picture. I said I wouldn't.

We continued to talk through the trials and treatments that he underwent during his illness. I couldn't help him any other way, although I sent him herbs that I believe might have been of use, but they never got past the buffer zone that surrounds actors of Steve's caliber.

Barbara McQueen took this shot of Joe Brown's cowboy boots.

The more I spoke with him on the phone, the more I became aware of his down-to-earth integrity and sincerity. I didn't have much regard for the actors I knew before him. I'd found that their word was no good. Most could do nothing except imitate the character of men and women who had accomplished real goals, but on account of their fame, they believed they were the last word in everything from rocket science to horsemanship. In reality, the only subject of their conversations was themselves.

Steve changed my opinion of actors. Generally, they entertain us and only have to ply their craft well to be admired. However, Steve passed on the special joy of adventure that he experienced in real life, and showed me that acting can be an adventure too.

He was a man of his word, unassuming and unaffected by fame, and became a respected friend, that I could talk to as a brother. He knew his business and when he worked he tried for a perfect performance, making no excuses and suffering none from others. In my short association with him he put on no pretences, whether he talked about books, granted a favor, prepared to fly high in a stunt plane, or stood up to face the final, most difficult and most futile fight for his life.

Some men are ordinary, some have great style. All good men, like Steve, are extraordinary and glow with style.

Joe Brown is the author of several books and resides in Tucson, Arizona.

Snapshot
Maggie Moore

Behind-the-scenes photos of *Tom Horn* taken by Barbara McQueen.

Imagine the majesty of my first foray into film: the windswept Sonoran desert, dotted with barbed mesquite trees nearly bare in the winter chill, the dry buffalo grass crunching under my feet. The sky looked so big and of such a deep sapphire blue that it seemed to envelope all underneath it in a rich swath of the finest cloth. As a wide-eyed teenager, I could not have foreseen how that scenery and the people involved would forever shape my life. My lifelong vocation, my future husband, and dear friends were all found on that location.

Tom Horn was filmed in the area of southern Arizona where I spent my childhood. The rolling grassland never failed to conjure up images of cowboys—bold, romantic men with a quest to fight for truth. My first sight of Steve McQueen so personified those images that even today I can recall every facet. It was early morning, crisp and bracing, and Steve stood off to one side waiting for a shot to be set up. Gazing over the panorama, he held such a quiet command of all that was around him, he seemed to be ten feet tall. An inner strength and eloquence radiated from him. Often portraying the tough guy and always referred to as a man's man, Steve had a kind heart, and that was never more evident than when he was with Barbara.

I can recall sitting on the director's chairs with Barbara talking about horses, when Steve, having finished a shot, walked up to her and touched the loose strands of her hair that were fluttering in the breeze. The look that passed between them was so exquisite I felt like a voyeur. Even on a crowded set they could look across the scenery and find the other's gaze. It is seldom that two people can share such a serene tenderness.

Steve always wanted everyone to have fun. Although each person on *Tom Horn* worked hard, I think they played harder. I remember the radio-controlled cars that spent more time swimming in the hotel pool than they did running. Then there was the trip to the rodeo. "Fiesta de los Vaqueros" was a big deal in Tucson. Cheers, jeers, a beer or two and sunburn were the order of the day. Another weekend Steve rented a go-cart track to re-create *Le Mans*. Every crew member became a stuntman in his own mind, and by the end of the night there was considerable damage.

One of the funniest incidents occurred on the way to location. The cumbersome grip truck was headed down the dirt road to the set when it became wedged across the bottom of a small gully. The drivers tried every conceivable way to get it across, to no avail. We were nowhere near a pay phone and I am sure that AAA would never have responded to this service call anyway, so some good ol' film set ingenuity was in order. Using ropes and chains, vehicles were hitched together in convoy, until at last, with a mighty heave, the trapped truck bucked loose and trundled off down the road.

Each film set is a microcosm of society, an entity unto itself. I look back on my experiences in *Tom Horn* and realize how fortunate I was to have been there, and to have known Steve McQueen.

Steve was a person who always had time for anyone on the set. When he talked with you, he had a way of making you feel that you were discussing the most important subject possible. His enchanting ability to envelope all those around him in his warmth is what keeps his memory alive within our hearts today. Whenever I think of him, I smile.

Maggie Moore is a still photographer working in film, motor sports and horses. She resides in Middle, Tennessee.

Heaven Sent

Mel Novak

Opposite: No one interpreted the rugged Old West quite like McQueen.

Top left: Applying makeup to the star of the picture.

Top right: The gravesite of Tom Horn in Boulder, Colorado.

I first met Steve McQueen at the home of Pat Johnson, his close friend and karate instructor. Pat's son was having a birthday party and Steve was there.

Of course, Steve was a big star but you wouldn't have known it. He was a friendly, gracious person who gave my daughters a big, warm hug. We talked about life in general, but not much about the movie industry.

At a later karate function, I sat with Steve and Ali MacGraw, who was his wife at the time. After meeting successful actors who are so full of themselves, it was impressive and refreshing to see he was just a good old boy. During this particular meeting, I shared my walk with Jesus Christ and he didn't mock me like some do. As I reflected about our conversation over the next few weeks, I realized that there were wounds underneath. His childhood sometimes haunted him and he had carried this baggage around for years.

I recently met a lifer at the Pelican Bay Penitentiary, who told me that Steve used to come by and talk to the kids in the youth authority camp he had attended. He said, reflecting back, he should have paid more attention to what Steve said.

Around 1976, I was trap shooting with Steven Spielberg, John Milius and Ken Hyman, a studio head, when Steve came walking down. I hardly recognized him as he had grown a full beard and sported long hair, and it was only after I saw his steel-blue eyes that I realized it was Steve. He had never shot trap, but he borrowed my shotgun and was amazingly accurate. He popped one after another, and we were all impressed. He said that Francis Ford Coppola wanted him to play the role that Robert Duvall eventually landed in *Apocalypse Now*. The offer was one million dollars for two weeks' work in the Philippines but Steve passed, saying he didn't want to leave the country at the time.

A few years later, I worked with Steve in *Tom Horn*. He had fired a couple of actors who couldn't handle the dialogue and told producer Fred Weintraub to call me to play the sheriff. By this time, Steve had developed a horrible cough, and it gave me the chills to listen to him.

I'll never forget Steve. He was not only a talented actor who was brilliant in so many films, but he was my brother in Christ.

Mel Novak is a veteran film actor who is also an ordained minister living in the Los Angeles area. He is a traveling evangelist and preaches to the homeless on skid row and in prisons.

Opposite: Barbara McQueen captures her husband enjoying an iced beer, early 1979.

Below: With a mouthful of chaw, McQueen was every bit the cowboy.

I may be the only actor in the world who has worked with both Steve McQueen and Clint Eastwood. They were very different people. Steve was more loquacious and in your face, whereas Clint is laid back. Both were intense and honest in what they were portraying. They were not great actors, but boy, were they movie stars.

Clint once told me that when he was working on *Rawhide*, McQueen was shooting *Wanted: Dead or Alive*. Whenever they bumped into each other at the commissary, McQueen, with his sawed-off shotgun, wanted to fast draw to see who was top gun. Clint regarded it as a joke, but said that Steve took it a little too seriously. He was very competitive.

I worked with Steve on *Tom Horn* and for all intents and purposes, he was the director of that movie. Before we started shooting the outside courtroom scene, in which I faced-off with McQueen, he walked around the set with a ball of chewing tobacco in his mouth and was into everybody's business. "Put that light there. Was it there last time?" he asked the director of photography. "Move this, move that. Put this here. Get that horse out of here." He knew how to take charge of a situation, and put himself on the line whether it was on screen or behind the camera.

Finally there was a call for action, and my back was to Steve. When I turned around for the first time, I saw the full force of Steve McQueen. He was so overwhelming. Those blue eyes were so intense, they were mesmerizing.

Because McQueen and Eastwood both had presence, they were the only two actors I have known who would eliminate their dialogue. They'd both stumble over something in rehearsal and say, "I don't want to say this" and then cross it out. Many actors prefer words because they don't have the wherewithal to stand there and just be. These two definitely could.

Geoffrey Lewis is a veteran actor who has starred in several movies and television productions.

A Reel Movie Star

Dave Friedman

Opposite top: Dave Friedman captures Steve and Barbara McQueen giving autographs to inner city kids on the streets of Chicago on *The Hunter.*

Opposite bottom: McQueen used two modes of transportation on *Tom Horn.*

I first met Steve McQueen at Riverside Raceway in Southern California during the early sixties, when he raced a Porsche 1600 in the SCCA sports car races. I was impressed that he did not put on the so-called movie star persona that was starting to overtake Hollywood. Since both my parents were involved in the industry, I was raised around many of MGM's biggest stars and appreciated how down to earth Steve was.

Our paths crossed several times before I first worked with him as the still photographer on *Tom Horn* in 1979. I remember that film clearly because of the difficult locations during an unusually cold Arizona winter. In spite of the long hours and hard work, we all managed to have a good time. There were the remote control car races around the hotel swimming pool in which many of the cars went for a career-ending swim, and the time that Steve rented out a go-kart track which was totally destroyed by the end of the night because of a shortage of go-karts and an abundance of beer. It was on this shoot that I met the beautiful young lady named Barbara Minty who was to become Steve's wife. It wasn't long before we discovered some common interests, mostly photography, and we became immediate friends.

When *Tom Horn* was about to wrap, Steve asked me to be involved in his next project, which was a large-scale epic film of James Clavell's best-selling novel, *Tai-Pan.* Unfortunately, it never came about due to serious production and financial problems.

A short time later, Steve and Barbara invited me to Santa Paula to visit the hangar and their home. After viewing Steve's incredible motorcycle collection, I proposed publishing a coffee table book about it. My idea was to photograph all the bikes, using many of the wonderful Victorian homes in the Santa Paula area as set pieces, with models dressed in the period in which the motorcycles were built. Steve loved the idea and told me to find a publisher and that we would do it when he finished *The Hunter.* I admitted then that I had already taken the liberty of talking to a publisher of high quality art books based in Switzerland, and that he had immediately green-lighted the project. Steve looked at me for a minute and then we both broke into a good laugh. Sadly, the book would never happen.

We started *The Hunter* in Chicago just after Labor Day 1979. Once again, it was a difficult shoot and we were rushing to complete our work in the Midwest before the cold weather settled in. Although most of us didn't know it at the time, Steve was terminally ill. Being a true professional, Steve never complained and was always first on the set each day.

I recall with much respect something that happened one day when we were working in a poor section of town. The scene where Steve was chasing his quarry through a dilapidated house was being filmed, and one of the extras on the staircase was a poor teenage girl named Karen Wilson. At the time, we did not know that Karen's mother was in the hospital dying of cancer, and Karen was living with almost no family to support her. When Steve found out about her situation, he arranged to have her taken on a shopping spree for some badly needed clothing and other personal items. He also employed her for several weeks as a production assistant on the film. After her mom died, Steve and Barbara took Karen back to Southern California, enrolled her in an excellent private school in Ojai and gave her a life that she could have never imagined months earlier.

When Steve passed away in the fall of 1980, I was working at Culver City Studios on a film called *Lookin' To Get Out.* One of the stars was Ann-Margret, who had worked with Steve on *The Cincinnati Kid.* When I received the call with the bad news, I told her, and we left the stage, hand in hand. Once outside in private, we hugged and cried.

Steve was an honest, true friend who would go to bat for anyone on his crew, and defend that person to the limit. He understood the difference between the reel world and the real world, and those of us who knew him will miss and love him forever.

Dave Friedman is considered one of the best film still photographers of all time. He lives in Southern California.

All photos: McQueen loved motorcycles, but the one manufacturer that won his heart was Indian. Sammy Pierce (in red) was hired by McQueen in 1979 to restore and maintain his fleet of Indian bikes, which were mostly stored in a Ventura, California warehouse.

In Memory of Steve McQueen

Sammy Pierce

One day in the early sixties, I received a phone call at my shop, the American Indian Parts Company in San Gabriel, from a man who said he had found an early 1920s Indian Chief motorcycle, but it was missing a front-wheel brake and he was a little afraid to ride it. I found a front end from a 101 Indian Scout that would work for his Chief, equipped it with a front-wheel brake, and sent it over to him. That's when I found out that the caller was Steve McQueen.

Steve's love of Indian motorcycles and my own enthusiasm brought us to the same meets many times. He would always look me up and we'd talk about his bike and how to make it run better. He told me that he fell in love with the Indian as a kid in Slater, Missouri. Some fellow from his home town bought one and from the moment he laid eyes on it, he dreamed of owning one himself. As a boy, he would go to the Indian motorcycle store in Kansas City and daydream. Oddly, I had worked at the same store not too many years before Steve's visits. It turned out that Steve and I were from towns about two hundred miles apart.

Steve began to collect Indians from all over the United States. Each year, when I was at the Indian Factory Come Home Program in Springfield, he would call me to make sure I picked up any motorcycles he might be interested in. His collection of Indians grew to span the years 1902 to 1953.

Steve also began talking to me about working for him on a permanent basis in order to restore his bikes because some of them were in sad condition. In 1979, he decided to build a museum to house his collection, and I moved to Oxnard where we selected a site for the shop, and I went to work full-time for Steve McQueen.

Steve wasn't a good mechanic, but he had an unfailing ear for a flaw in an engine. A terrific rider, he road-tested everything himself, and if it didn't purr to perfection, he'd let me know about it. But most of the time, he'd come back with a grin on his face which was indication of his approval. He never paid verbose compliments. Once in a while, I'd get a telephone call at home around midnight and it would be Steve complimenting me on something.

We understood each other and got along very well. He liked the way my engines ran and about the only complaint he had was regarding paint color. I automatically painted everything Indian Red. He'd tell me to make one of the Indians green and leave. He'd come back and it would be painted Indian Red. I told him there was never a green Indian. He'd say, "One word from me and

you do as you damn well please, don't you?" But we never had a serious disagreement—he just liked to needle me. Steve would come by when he wasn't working on a movie. I'd tell him I had work to do and he'd remind me with a grin that he was paying me to do it.

Motorcycles were not the only machines that fascinated Steve. He had a passion for old pickup trucks and had about forty in his collection. He also owned restored airplanes, old slot machines, gas ranges, music boxes, antique signs and ceiling fans, cast iron toys and other collectibles. All of them were to have been displayed in his museum.

Steve wasn't an armchair collector. He could ride, drive or fly anything he owned. Not only did he race cars for Porsche, but he was an excellent airplane pilot. When he first set up shop in Oxnard, he'd come flying overhead in his Stearman and buzz the shop.

Every Christmas, we left a space on our door for the inevitable arrival of Steve's Christmas gift—a wreath that had been made by the Boys Republic in Chino. He was a quiet contributor and supporter of that organization and paid the boys in Chino personal visits as often as he could, quietly bypassing the front door and any attention, and going directly to their living area. He was genuinely concerned about youth and their problems.

Steve was as great a humanitarian as he was an actor, and he never sought publicity. In fact, he avoided it. He said, "If you're good at your business, you don't need all that." Wherever he went, he spent a lot of time dodging cheap news magazine reporters who hounded him relentlessly. He wasn't always successful in keeping photographers at bay, as so many of the phony magazine stories that made print will attest.

Steve's absence has left a huge gap in the world of motorcycles, cars and airplanes. He was a meticulous historian and saw to it that his collection was authentically restored. His was one of the greatest collections in the world.

More than that, though, is the loss that all of us feel who knew his friendship. Steve was a classic. One-of-a-kind. I would have gone to hell for him.

Sammy Pierce, known as "Mr. Indian," was Steve McQueen's friend and mechanic. He originally wrote this piece in May 1981 for his family and friends.

AKA "Mr. Indian"
Glenn Pierce

Opposite top left: Indian mechanic Sammy Pierce (pictured in the middle) was kept on retainer by Steve McQueen to fix and maintain his antique motorcycle collection.

All other photos: Glen Pierce's Oxford, California shop, which was about fifteen minutes away from Steve McQueen's Santa Paula hangar.

Dad started buying Indians for Steve McQueen in the late sixties. They included whole bikes, basket-cases and odds and ends. But soon the sellers were tipped off that he was Steve's purchasing agent, which usually meant they could be counted on to add a little "movie star tax".

Steve collected anything old; new items were not his thing. About 1977 Steve finally convinced dad to move from Fresno to Oxnard and complete the "Iron Horse Corral" which was his version of Harrahs. It would be a restoration shop, with display areas and storage for all his collectibles. After buying a home in Oxnard, dad finished the shop, and then he started sorting through Steve's stuff—a lot of stuff. The Harleys were lined up in the rear of the building, catalogued by year and model, with the year painted in white on the front fenders. The Indians, Flying Scout, English and German bikes were lined up waiting to be arranged like the Harleys.

One end of the shop was littered with globe-type gas pumps, ice boxes, some of them in mahogany, and somewhere in the midst of the mess lay a large pile of motorcycle parts Steve had acquired. He told me to separate the good from the bad, but not to throw anything out. The man rarely parted with his treasures.

Steve also had a hangar at Santa Paula Airport with more toys: airplanes, cars and even more bikes, most of which were restored. His Pitcairn biplane had a U. S. mail sidecar that dad made from wood and metal painted to match the plane. And of course, Steve's house was across from the airport, making for a short commute.

After sorting out the Iron Horse Corral, dad began restoring some of Steve's bikes. He took Steve's Chief Chopper and rebuilt it to riding condition, fixing the oil and exhaust leaks. Steve went berserk and dad had to return it to its old ratty chopper state, complete with leaks, tape and wire. Dad painted red only, but Steve liked different colors. There was much arguing about this and who would have the last word!

Dad also built some benches on wheels that were two feet high with tie-downs, to help with the restorations. He could start with a chassis, build the bike and roll it around the shop. Steve would change his mind often: for example, fix a Chief, then later a Scout, then request a different color for the Chief! It was quite a challenge for dad to figure out what was next.

Once, dad was in Fresno when Steve called and said "head back to Oxnard and get some trail bikes" because he was off to Mexico. Dad left and found some small trail bikes for Steve to use.

After Steve died, dad continued working at Iron Horse Corral. He died March 27, 1982, but still was on the payroll.

"Mr. Indian" and "Mr. Blue Eyes" will always be remembered by those who knew and loved them.

Glenn Pierce is the son of Sammy "Mr. Indian" Pierce and has been around motorcycles and cars since birth. Pierce is married and has four children and eleven grandchildren. Now semi-retired and living in the Fresno area, he still owns three of his father's original Indian bikes including a 1926 Scout his father rode from Los Angeles to Kansas in 1930.

Who's Steve McQueen?

Sammy Mason

Above: A pair of antique model airplanes owned by McQueen.

Right: Preparing for a day of flight at the Santa Paula Airport, 1979.

One evening in 1979, I received a phone call from Steve McQueen, asking me to teach him to fly.

Somehow, during the conversation, I formed the idea he was either the attendant at the service station where I filled up my car or the butcher. I concluded that he must be the latter because he could afford to fly.

At the time I had more students than I wanted and turned him down. However, I said that my son, Pete, was available and a good teacher. He insisted that he wanted me to be his instructor, and was willing to pay me more money. "*Those butchers,*" I thought. "*They scalp their customers so they can afford the luxury of flying! No, Mr. Butcher, you'll just have to get another instructor.*"

Whoever this McQueen guy was, he was stubborn, and wouldn't take no for an answer. He called me back several nights in a row. I couldn't remember our butcher being so persistent. Finally, out of curiosity to see what he was like, I agreed to meet him at the airport.

Even behind the heavy beard, those bright blue eyes and infectious smile gave him away. Of course! Steve McQueen, the famous movie star! I liked him, and because I didn't initially leap at the opportunity to fly with him, he accepted me. I learned later that he was always suspicious of someone until he got to know them. Steve was looking for genuine people with whom he could become real friends. He did agree to take part of his flight instruction from Pete. As a flight student he was well coordinated, but at times, stubborn and hardheaded.

As our friendship developed, he began to relate some of the significant events in his past. He told me that an uneasy feeling had kept him from the Tate home that night in August 1969 when the Charles Manson gang slaughtered pregnant actress Sharon Tate and many others.

Although I quietly witnessed my faith in Christ to Steve, I never argued with him when his opinion differed, or put pressure on him in any way. Finally, he asked about attending church with me. Of course he could! He expressed the desire to slip in and out without being noticed to avoid any special attention or to distract from the service. He thought the focus should be on the Lord and not Steve McQueen. Within a few weeks, the power of God's word began to take effect in Steve's life. He realized that Christ had not only taken his sins but also his guilt. His peace and joy was apparent.

Eventually, when Steve walked into the Ventura Missionary Church on a Sunday morning he brought an entourage, including his girlfriend, Barbara Minty, who later became his wife; right hand man Grady Ragsdale, and others who worked on his ranch. It was generally expected that when Steve went to church, everybody went!

Within a few months of his conversion, Steve began to complain of pains in his chest and back. X-rays revealed a spot on Steve's right lung—it was a massive tumor—and inoperable. During the next few months, I watched Steve's once agile and healthy body waste away until he was nearly an indefinable shadow, but his crisp, blue eyes still revealed a deep inner strength. He said he was going to fight to the end, but no matter what the outcome, all was well between him and his Lord.

Sammy Mason was a former acrobatic flyer and engineering test pilot for Lockheed. He died in 2002.

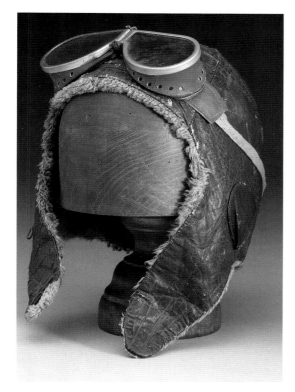

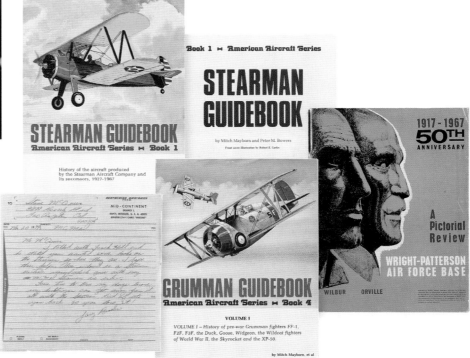

Top left: A pair of aviator goggles and brown leather cap, given to McQueen by friend, Pat Johnson.

Top right: Waxing the wing of his prized Stearman.

Above: McQueen with flight instructor and former acrobatic flyer, Sammy Mason, who taught the actor.

Right: McQueen devoured these aviation books in order to become a proficient pilot.

The Heart that Flies
Wendell Dowling

Opposite: In one of her favorite pictures, Barbara McQueen said that Steve reminded her of a World War II aviator.

Right: McQueen receiving flight instruction from Sammy Mason, who threw in life lessons for free.

Remember watching planes as a kid? You just watched them sail through the air with big eyes and a smile as part of you sailed right along with them. It was the spring of 1979 and the "King of Cool" decided to recapture that feeling by learning to fly.

Sammy Mason, Steve's instructor, was my father-in-law. I just happened to be with Sammy and his son, Timmy, when McQueen asked us to accompany him to check out a piece of aviation history, a yellow Stearman. I had the sense to take a camera.

Steve had heard about the plane from Mike Mason, Sammy's oldest son, who was working at the Camarillo Airport for the Ventura County sheriff and fire air unit. Mike's neighbor, Joe Shubeck, was about to put the Stearman up for sale.

The plane was a very desirable aircraft. Approximately 9,700 Stearmans were produced by Boeing in the thirties and forties and they were primarily used as a training biplane during World War II. In the immediate post war years, they became popular as crop dusters and sports planes. Steve, who had recently purchased another plane, but was having it restored, had just started his lessons with Sammy and wanted a plane of his own to train with. When Steve wanted something, he wanted it right away.

We didn't talk much at first, but I found Steve personable. He also allowed me to chronicle him taking the Stearman for a test flight. When Steve soloed, I painted a picture of him with the plane and presented it to him as a gift. He later asked for another painting to give to his daughter, Terry, and he commissioned me to paint his third and last plane, a silver and blue Stearman.

Eventually we developed an easy friendship. I'd visit him in his hangar, which, to me, resembled a museum. He had a Kentucky Fried Chicken bucket full of old pocket knives sitting on a work bench. Steve told me to help myself. "I hate to break up the set," I said, and didn't take one.

I spent most of my time with Steve at Ventura Missionary Church. The Mason clan sat up in the balcony with Steve and Barbara. There weren't too many people up there, so he was able to keep himself apart from the congregation. Steve later held Bible studies out at the hangar with Leslie Miller, who was an associate pastor at the church. He was private about his relationship with God, but it was evident to those who knew him.

I once took my family to visit the McQueens at home. While Barbi showed my wife, Lynn and the children the animals, Steve and I lay on his backyard lawn like a couple of kids and watched the planes fly overhead. It was one of those rare, quiet times. Steve said he'd rather be at the airport than anywhere else in the world. His motorcycling days were over and I think he found the same camaraderie with the aviation crowd as he once did with his biking friends. He instantly became a part of the Santa Paula community and we protected him. We continue to preserve his name and reputation to this day.

Smooth flying, Steve.

Wendell Dowling is a noted graphic artist and muralist, who lives in Santa Paula, California.

Repentance on the Wings of Birds
Pete Mason

"C'mon, Pete, I told your dad I'd get you to church on Sunday," Steve prodded as he stuck his head into my motel room. It was early in the morning on May 27, 1979, and I obediently walked with him along the quiet streets of Monterey, California.

Suddenly he broke away, running like a kid, waving his arms to scatter birds in a park we were passing. After making sure they had all flown away, he rejoined me on the sidewalk where I was watching with amusement. He was breathless after his exercise, but managed to say that if he was a bird he wouldn't spend so much time on the ground. He must have thought I was wondering why he was so out of breath. Steve explained that in his racing days he was in a fiery crash and had inhaled super hot air, searing the inside of one lung and that he only had partial use of it. I made a mental note to hold my breath if that ever happened to me.

We went into the first church we found which happened to be Catholic. I was raised Protestant so I had to follow Steve's lead. He dipped his hands into a bowl of water and made the sign of the cross. Then he knelt at a pew and began to silently pray. I did exactly the same and after a few minutes, we rose, crossed ourselves again and walked out. Now that's my kind of church. Go in, repent, pray, leave, ten minutes tops.

I don't remember the conversation on the way back to our motel except Steve interjecting one memorable line, "Pete, there are two things in this world I'm never giving up and that's beer and women." Why that sticks in my head, I don't know, but that was Steve in a nutshell.

Pete Mason is an active pilot and lives in Santa Paula, California.

Checking out the hardware at the Watsonville Fly-In and Air Show with Pete Mason, who also gave McQueen flight instruction, May 1979.

One Stop Shopping

Mike Dewey

Opposite top: Pilot Mike Dewey, McQueen and another pilot, Perry Schreffler.

Opposite bottom: McQueen taxiing on the runway in his PA-8 Mailwing.

Steve McQueen was looking for the right pilot to train him and the right airplane to fit his personality, and he found it all in Santa Paula.

My first exposure to Steve was in the spring of 1979. He rented a 1600 square-foot hangar from me and my partner, Doug Dullenkopf, when we co-owned Screaming Eagle Aviation. Even though he was worth millions, Steve flinched at the $300-a-month rent. "Ouch!" he said, but he rented the space anyway.

Soon after, he asked me to accompany him to St. Louis to help him evaluate an extremely rare Lockheed Vega airplane that was for sale. We planned to fly the airplane back to California if he made the deal. This long-range model Lockheed was famous for the number of record-breaking pilots who had flown in it, primarily Amelia Earhart and Wiley Post. The asking price was $100,000, and this time Steve didn't flinch. In fact he had a crumpled cashier's check in that amount in his pocket.

The plane, which was constructed of wood, was in good restored condition and showed well. However, the cockpit arrangement was unique in that the pilot flew the plane from a single tiny compartment that was forward and above the relatively large passenger cabin. To enter the pilot's compartment you had to open a door that also doubled as the back of the pilot's seat. Steve liked the airplane as a collectable but was concerned about flying it since there was no room for an instructor or dual flight controls.

"I'll take the thing off, climb to cruise altitude, set the trim, climb down from the cockpit, trade places and you take over until it is time to land, when we reverse the process," I suggested. But, Steve, as usual, was thinking ahead and wisely realized that as a new pilot he might not be comfortable soloing the airplane at this stage in his flying career.

Steve never told me why he took up flying at forty-nine years of age in an old World War II biplane, but he was the first aviation student I had met who wanted to learn in such a plane. I had heard rumors that his dad was a barnstorming pilot and perhaps he was trying to recreate the experience.

He had a quiet determination to succeed, and doubled up on his lessons, flying for hours at a time with both Sammy and Pete Mason. He was a quick learner and had good eye-hand coordination from racing cars and bikes, and was talented, athletic and focused on flying, so he was easy to teach—and fearless too.

I was standing among a small group of onlookers the day Pete Mason soloed Steve, on May 1, 1979. It was an amazing feat considering Steve broke from the norm by flying a challenging aircraft rather than a more docile modern-day trainer.

I can only surmise that Steve became hooked on flying for the same reason every other pilot does—that sense of pure freedom and the feeling of accomplishment. Taking an aircraft off the ground and returning safely is one of life's greatest pleasures. Once airborne, it's just you and the sky and some of the most beautiful sights imaginable.

Mike Dewey is a retired movie stunt pilot, and currently sits on the Santa Paula Aviation Museum board.

Cliff Notes
George Santillo

McQueen was a folk hero to fans and he is seen here with two in Utah.

I had the pleasure of showing certain properties in the Santa Barbara area to Steve McQueen. It was an honor to work with this kind and considerate man.

I had a breakfast appointment with Steve at the Miramar Hotel restaurant. He was driving one of his antique cars from Malibu, had a minor problem along the way, and had to stop at an Oxnard service station for repairs. Concerned that he would be late for our appointment, he telephoned his office and asked them to page me at the Miramar and apologize for the delay.

Looking at acreage in Santa Ynez Valley, Steve showed his wonderful sense of humor as we were traveling downhill, by the edge of a cliff, on a dirt road that appeared narrower than our four-wheel drive car. Steve said, "Relax, George—there are always two wheels on solid ground." He was totally calm.

Afterwards, McQueen wrote an appreciative letter, thanking me for my continuing efforts and hard work.

This passage was written by George Santillo in November 1980 and originally appeared in the Santa Barbara News Press.

Brass Appreciation
Blanche Hernandez

Top right: The front of Steve and Barbara McQueen's Santa Paula home.

Bottom left & right: Many antiques, including a lot of brass and iron, filled the McQueen home.

Steve McQueen and his new bride, the former Barbara Minty, walked into a Santa Paula boutique where I worked in early 1980. The local paper had mentioned that the two had recently married and were remodeling an old Victorian home they had just purchased.

Steve McQueen was one of my favorite movie stars, so when he walked through the door, I instantly recognized him despite the beard, from those steely blue eyes. I made eye contact, and though it was unspoken, he knew that I knew who he was. The people of Santa Paula respected his privacy, which is why he liked living here.

He asked if our store carried brass door handles. I told him we did not, but that he was welcome to browse. The two stuck around for about fifteen minutes, but didn't go away empty-handed. I gave him the address of an antique store in nearby Oxnard where I thought they had what he was looking for.

He smiled and said, "Thank you. You are most helpful."

Sometimes a simple deed or kind word can go a long way. In the case of Steve McQueen, it has lasted for more than three decades.

Blanche Hernandez, a retired housewife, was born, raised and resides in Santa Paula.

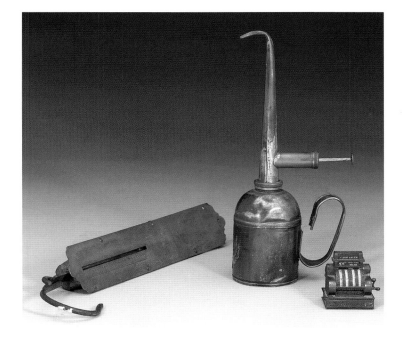

San Pedro Beach Bum

Brad Martin

Opposite: Cruising on his favorite motorcycle, a "Rat bike", assembled from different parts, Santa Paula Airport, 1980.

Below: Looking intense during an Idaho sunrise.

Glamorous movie star wouldn't be the words I'd used to describe Steve McQueen when I met in him 1979. He looked more like a San Pedro beach bum.

I was eating at a sandwich shop in Port Hueneme, California near Santa Paula when a waitress casually informed me that Steve McQueen was next door at the antique shop. I was about twenty-five-years old at the time and idolized McQueen, having seen *The Great Escape* many times. For years, I rode motorcycles dressed like him with the sleeves of my sweatshirts cut off. My friends and I often emulated his jump over the barbed-wire fence in *The Great Escape* on our Stingray bicycles. I hurriedly paid for my sandwich so that I could walk next door to meet him. I couldn't believe the long-haired, heavily-bearded man standing before me was my childhood hero.

He was pondering the purchase of an Indian motorcycle when I introduced myself. "Hi, Mr. McQueen. My name is Brad Martin and I wanted to tell you that *The Great Escape* was a big influence on me as a kid. My friends and I made many jumps on our bicycles as a result of the movie." He smiled, shook my hand and said, "Nice to meet you. I'm glad you liked the movie. I hope you kids didn't hurt yourselves."

It was as if I broke the ice for a dozen kids also in the store, who milled around asking for an autograph. Steve good-naturedly talked to all of us and made sure to sign whatever was placed in front of him. He decided to purchase the bike and asked me if I'd help him roll it out to his truck. After we had hoisted it in the back, Steve shook my hand and thanked me. He was gracious and behaved like a normal person. He certainly wasn't the persona he played in *The Thomas Crown Affair*. I rushed home to tell my mom, who was also a big McQueen fan, and gave her a blow by blow report of the encounter. When I finished, she had just one question.

"Are you sure it was Steve McQueen?"

Brad Martin lives in southern California.

It Takes a Hero
Armando Gomez

Outside his Santa Paula hangar.

Hero. That is the best way to describe Steve McQueen. He was a hero to the end. He was also a gentle, soft-spoken man who had room in his heart for all, and everyone in turn, liked him.

Because of his success in the motion picture industry, he had been labeled a "star," one of those egocentric, above-the-rest people. But Steve was the embodiment of everyman—a simple, quiet, peaceful man who cared about his friends, sometimes more than himself. Steve was a star in some ways, though. As a racing car and motorcycle enthusiast, he drove in many high profile competitions with some of the top-rated racers in the United States.

Steve also collected old cars and motorcycles, antique toys and vintage aircraft. He was a fine aviator who fitted in well at the Santa Paula Airport where he was known and liked, and he welcomed anyone who took an interest in walking through his hangar. It was on lazy Saturday afternoons that one could find Steve working there, but he always had time to sit and talk. He was not "Steve McQueen" the movie star, but Steve McQueen the fellow aviator.

I first met him through a telephone conversation. Word had been spread that Steve was planning to marry again and I wanted confirmation for my column. Steve gave permission for me to release the report and we talked for roughly fifteen minutes about everything under the sun. *What "star" would take the time to do that,* I thought, *Steve McQueen must be a very special man.* Although he hated publicity and interviews, he always gave me something to print in my column. We were friends.

I visited Steve often on those Saturdays and they were special. There was an air of joviality as Steve told stories, with his bride, Barbara smiling effervescently in the bright sun-bathed hangar. There was always something to do. He would work on the airplanes, check the motorcycles, or just sit outside enjoying the day.

Steve liked Santa Paula where he was treated as a normal resident. There were never any crowds when he walked down Main Street, only "Hello's" and "Hi's" from friendly passers-by. He was home here, never bothered, always protected. When a reporter from the *National Enquirer* came to Santa Paula asking about Steve, mum was the word as he was known for fabrications.

When *Tom Horn* opened, I asked Steve why he made the film. He said, "It's a film about a hero, and there are few left in this world."

Steve, you will always be a hero.

Armando Gomez was a former columnist with the Santa Paula Daily Chronicle.

The Six Million Dollar Friend
Lee Majors

McQueen and actor Lee Majors celebrate McQueen's first solo flight by sharing a beer, July 1979. Majors prefers the taste of Coors while McQueen sticks to Old Milwaukee.

Steve McQueen was a wonderful friend and a great actor. Although most of his characters were cool and tough, underneath there was a soft and humorous side to him.

We both lived in Malibu so we would spend time together. When I called Steve he would turn to his son, Chad and say, "Fill up the cooler, Lee's coming over." Off we'd go in his pickup truck with a cooler full of Old Milwaukee beer heading to tiny, out-of-the-way antique stores up the coast.

I don't know why he liked Old Milwaukee beer because it gave him gas—and he wasn't afraid to release it on our journey. When we were looking at junk and antique objects, we always outbid each other for the same pieces. For example, if a toy cast iron car or truck was marked at $30 and he knew I intended to buy it, he'd offer the owner $35. I would say $40 and so on. The store-owners loved to see us coming and they would watch in amusement. Plus, they made a few extra bucks. Towards the end, Steve had to limit his beer to one or two, but he might add a hit of grass, for "medicinal purposes", I'm sure.

I was amazed when Steve showed me his penthouse apartment in the Beverly Wilshire Hotel. Behind the couch was a beautiful, shiny Harley-Davidson motorcycle. I bet the management was nervous when they saw that going up the elevator. Steve also kept a small fleet of antique and new cars in the parking garage.

I took my son who was a young teenager at the time up to Santa Paula where Steve kept his hangar full of motorcycles, most of which were Indians that had been correctly restored to match their original condition. I will never forget how Steve took him through the rows of bikes and explained each one's history. That was a wonderful act of kindness.

The picture of Steve and me taken in front of the yellow bi-plane was on the day he made his first solo flight. We celebrated with a cold beer.

He was a loner and I came from the same mold. I miss Steve, but I'm sure he's up there giving the good Lord a little bit of trouble.

Lee Majors is a veteran actor with more than four decades of film and television experience. His most notable role was as Col. Steve Austin on ABC's "The Six Million Dollar Man," which ran from 1974 to 1978.

The Pilot and the Preacher

Leonard DeWitt

"Welcome to another day in paradise." That was the slogan McQueen used when describing his lifestyle in Santa Paula.

"Daddy, did you know Steve McQueen was in church this morning?"

I didn't. My children and I speculated why he was worshiping with us at the Ventura Missionary Church in 1979. The following week I learned that he had purchased a couple of airplanes and one of our members, Sammy Mason, was giving him flying lessons. Over the years, the Lord has put many wonderful people in my life. Now I could count Steve McQueen among them.

Steve had always been one of my favorite actors. I didn't know much about him personally, but liked the way he portrayed the characters in his films. When I heard that he was taking flying lessons from Sammy, I chuckled because I knew that he had met his match. Sammy was not one of those people who rammed his religion down your throat. Rather, his faith was so much a part of his life, that if you were around him for any length of time, it was going to rub off on you.

It did not take Steve long to realize that Sammy was different from any man he had ever met, so when he was invited to worship with Sammy's family, it was easy for him to accept. He respected them and felt safe in their company.

This rugged actor liked the church. He asked to be treated the same as the rest of the congregation. People respected that and did not ask for autographs. Steve was coming to the house of God to seek the Lord and worship. Everyone wanted him to have the privacy he needed.

After he had been attending for several months, he asked if the two of us could have some time together, and we met at the Santa Paula Airport. For two solid hours, he fired one question after another about Jesus Christ and the Christian faith. Finally, he sat back, smiled, and said, "Well, that about covers it for me."

At that point I said, "Steve, I have only one question to ask you."

He obviously was anticipating this and said, "You want to know if I'm a born-again Christian." I assured him that this was my primary interest. Then he recalled a particular Sunday morning when the Holy Spirit had touched his heart. He said, "When you invited people to pray with you to receive Christ, I prayed. Yes, I'm a born-again Christian." In the months that followed, Sammy and I took turns introducing Steve to the Christian faith. He had a real interest in spiritual matters.

A few months later, Steve called again. He told me that he had just learned he had cancer and was immediately beginning a treatment program.

His spirits were high even though his condition was worsening. I will never forget the day he said, "Leonard, I want to live. I believe God could use me, but if He doesn't hear me, it's okay because I know where I'm going." Many of us prayed for the Lord to heal Steve, but it was not God's plan.

Leonard DeWitt was the senior pastor of the Ventura Missionary Church for twenty-five years. He is semi-retired and resides in Ventura, California.

Obscene Phone Caller
Mort Engelberg

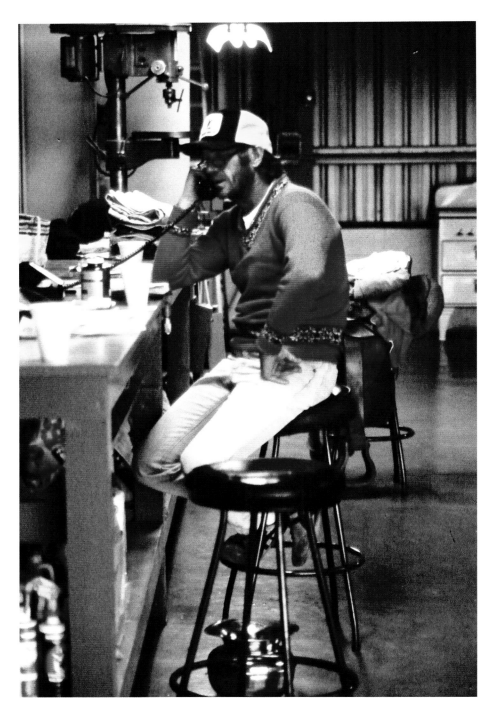

"Steve McQueen on line one," my secretary said nonchalantly to me one morning in 1977. Thinking it was a joke, I picked up the phone and said rudely, "Yeah?"

"Mort, this is Steve McQueen," said the voice on the line. "I read your script and I'd like to talk to you about it." Assuming one of my friends was clowning around, I became even ruder.

"Fine, when do you want to come to Burbank to talk about it?" I asked.

"Well, you know, I'm staying at the Beverly Wilshire and it would be hard to go over there."

"If you're serious about this, come to Burbank."

Then it hit me: I had been in contact with McQueen's agent, Marvin Josephson, who had promised to pass a script called *The Hunter* to his client, but I never entertained the idea of landing McQueen. He was too big a star for this project. And then I had a vague thought that perhaps it might be Steve McQueen. I asked him for his number and told him I would call him right back. When he answered, my heart skipped a beat.

"Mr. McQueen, I'll be right over," I said, hoping he wouldn't change his mind.

When I got to his suite at the hotel, I spotted a stack of scripts five feet high in the corner of the room. Out of all of the scripts he was sent, he liked *The Hunter* the best. It was like winning the lottery.

Mort Engelberg was the producer of The Hunter. He died in 1992.

Steve McQueen often conducted business from the work bench inside his Santa Paula airplane hangar, 1979.

The real Ralph "Papa" Thorson and Steve McQueen in a movie still for *The Hunter.*

Papa and Steve
Wally Emery

Steve McQueen and Ralph "Papa" Thorson had nothing much in common except for the desire to tell the same story.

I knew both men but I was close to Ralph, since I was in his employ for a few years as a fellow bounty hunter. We kicked in a few doors and rounded up many fugitives in our day, some of whom didn't come along as easily as we would have liked. Ralph had an amazing interface with humans: he could talk to street people, criminals, police, lawyers, businessmen and the Hollywood set.

Ralph's home life was accurately depicted in *The Hunter.* His North Hollywood abode was small and messy, but inside it was always teeming with action. All-night card games, bull sessions and a stocked bar made visitors feel welcome. It was nothing to see law enforcement officials, bounty hunters and criminals all playing a friendly game of poker. and I suspect Steve McQueen felt Thorson's thrilling career and quirky lifestyle had all the ingredients for a compelling motion picture.

I met Steve when I left the bounty hunting business and went to work teaching karate for Chuck Norris. He was personable and invited me to ride motorcycles with him at Indian Dunes. I wasn't much on a bike, but Steve was gracious and promised to show me how to ride. During one of our conversations, I told him about my life as a bounty hunter and my many exploits with Ralph.

"Now that's a man whose life story would make a great movie," I told Steve. Our exchange must have resonated with him, and I later heard that he had devoured Christopher Keane's biography of Ralph in a single night.

Despite their difference in size and appearance (Ralph was 6'2" and 300 pounds while Steve was 5'11" and tipped the scales at 170 pounds), Steve nailed Ralph's character. Steve was too ill to concern himself with *The Hunter* when it was released, but I can attest that Ralph was thrilled with the movie and the way Steve McQueen portrayed him.

Wally Emery is a former bodybuilder, bounty hunter, karate instructor and William Morris agent. Today he runs his own health company in Northern California.

Above: Steve McQueen riding Chicago's famous "L" in his last motion picture, *The Hunter*.

Opposite: Intimate shots of McQueen on the set of *The Hunter*.

The Day I Met Steve McQueen

Christopher Keane

My introduction to the Hollywood we all dream about came on the day I met Steve McQueen. I rode the elevator to the eleventh floor of the Beverly Wilshire Hotel, where some of the top movie stars kept their private suites when they were in town.

It was a heady time. I was in my twenties and Steve McQueen, the number one box-office star and my childhood hero, had just announced that he was about to turn my book, *The Hunter,* into his next movie. I wasn't that nervous. Not much.

Ralph Thorson, the bounty hunter and subject of the book, Paramount movie producer, Mort Engelberg, Steve and I sat for five hours discussing how Steve saw the book becoming the movie.

I couldn't help notice in the next room, a beautiful high-backed, Victorian chair, with a hole blown out of the back, and the stuffing spread all over the floor. After a while I mustered enough courage to ask about it. He said a director whom he had hired for the picture turned out to be such an insufferable bore that he wanted to teach him a lesson.

"I told him to sit in that chair," Steve explained, "and explained what a huge mistake I had made in hiring him, that he was an imbecile, and thought far too much of himself to direct this or any other picture. I said that he made me so mad I wanted to shoot him. Instead, I instructed him to get up out of the chair and stand over by the bar.

"When he did I pulled this out." Steve reached down beneath the table and came up with an ancient .45 caliber hog-leg revolver with a long barrel. "I aimed at the chair and pulled the trigger. I informed him that I would have shot him if I could have gotten away with it, but in this case I just killed the terrible aura he carried around, and to get the hell out of my sight."

A long silence filled the room. Was I supposed to laugh?

He laughed and said that the most important thing in this business was focus and the reason he fired the director was that all his attention was on himself and not where it should have been, on the making of the movie.

I learned that afternoon what focus was all about. Everything we discussed, whether it seemed important or not, Steve grabbed onto and fed into a greater power—the motion picture he was about to star in. Nothing else mattered. Not him, not the bounty hunter, the book writer or the producer. It was the story, and the script to follow, and not runaway egos that ensure pictures are made.

I've carried that with me ever since.

Chris Keane is a veteran author and screenwriter. Steve McQueen opened Hollywood's door to him.

Getting Better All The Time
Buzz Kulik

Opposite; Nearing the age of 50, McQueen starred in his last motion picture, *The Hunter.*

Top left & right: On the mean streets of Chicago in *The Hunter.*

Steve McQueen and I crossed roads at the beginning and end of his career.

The first time we met I directed him in an episode of *Climax!* in 1958. It was not a good experience. Steve was a folk hero at the time, being heralded as the new James Dean, but, to be honest, he was a real pain in the ass. He had great instincts, but he was undisciplined and unfocused, insecure and totally unprofessional.

A few years later I bumped into McQueen on the Four Studios lot. He had just landed the role on *Wanted: Dead or Alive.* We were making small talk while I was waiting for my car, and Steve told me, "Buzz, I'm going to be a big star." When I arrived home, I told my wife what he had said, and the two of us had a chuckle. But Steve had the last laugh and I directed his last picture—*The Hunter.*

By then Steve had mellowed quite a bit. He seemed gentler, less driven. He settled on scenes faster than he did in the past. He knew he wasn't in good shape before the film and he revealed that to me. He told me that he had spent too much time in the water in *Papillon* and it had done something to his breathing. We originally had a shower scene between McQueen and Kathryn Harrold, but Steve worried about getting water in his lungs. In another scene, after McQueen had chased a criminal down the block, he had to lean against a brick wall for support, and was breathing heavily.

His acting, however, was as strong as ever. McQueen needs just one word and he's magic. He had a degree of naturalism along with a danger within. You never knew what he was going to do next. He still had a lot of that Los Angeles kid in him. His acting talent was a gift from God.

Buzz Kulik was a World War II veteran before he became a film and television director. He died in January 1999.

Up to Snuff in Aroma

Norman Grimsley

Opposite: McQueen on location for *The Hunter* in the wheat fields of Kankakee, Illinois.

Top right: Making friends with an inhabitant of Aroma Park, Illinois.

Thanks to *The Hunter's* advance crew and the Kankakee County Sheriff's Department, Aroma Park was one of the most exciting small towns in Illinois in 1979.

By the time the set builders came to look over the property where they were going to build a cabin, we all thought we would be asked to co-star with Steve McQueen. With the completion of site location development, reality came to all of us. We weren't co-starring. The Fire Department instead was asked to supply emergency medical personnel (EMP) and an ambulance whenever anyone from the studio was on location in Aroma Park.

So we pestered the crew who built the cabin for inside information about film stars they had worked with. Even so, everyone from the movie treated the EMP crew with respect and humor. The one consistent comment was that Steve McQueen was a great person to work with and for. He treated everyone as an equal; just one of the guys. It was clear to us that everyone liked and respected him as an actor and a person.

On the first day, they were filming the scene where Steve was fighting a huge guy who was running from the law. We had all hoped to meet Mr. McQueen, but it was a closed set and we had to stay by the ambulance on the periphery, and the Sheriff's Department had told us that we were not to try to talk to Mr. McQueen.

We were just sitting around hoping to see a real actor when a man walked up to us and asked if he could have a chaw. We were amazed to see that it was Mr. McQueen who was asking to share some chewing tobacco. We found out later that he had quit smoking but still chewed on occasions. He sat down with us while the crew set up the next scene. We talked about fishing in the area, cars, places to eat, types of emergency calls we have gone on and nightlife or the lack of it. Everyone felt as if they were talking to someone who had a real interest in what we do and felt that it made a difference.

Picture a group of mostly young guys talking to a person of Steve McQueen's stature. We were all trying to make an impression with him and Steve was listening to us as if we were the most important people in his day. Of that group of people, each felt as if they had made a new friend. We realized that making movies is a tough job from the beginning to the final frame of film. When we saw Mr. McQueen on the job, we smiled an insider's smile, knowing what he had to do to do it well.

Norman Grimsley was an EMP on the set of The Hunter and recently was the mayor of the village of Aroma Park, Illinois.

The Steve McQueen You Didn't Know

Loren Janes

Left: Using a stun gun to incapacitate a bail jumper.

Opposite: *The Hunter* director Buzz Kulik, Pat Johnson, Loren Janes and Steve McQueen, Chicago 1979.

Steve McQueen was an excellent martial artist, a disciplined athlete, and a world-class motorcyclist and driver. He was very intelligent, and one of the all-time great actors. He could communicate more with his face and body language than most actors could with words. For several years running, he was the biggest box-office attraction in the world. Almost everyone knows most of this.

Here's something you didn't know. While filming on location in a small rural town, Steve noticed the town's park had no playground equipment. A week after we left, a large truck arrived at the park and installed swings, slides, monkey bars, teeter-totters, and a small merry-go-round. No one ever knew who paid for it—except for Steve and me.

During filming on another location, Steve heard of a boys' club trying to raise money for a clubhouse. A local contractor anonymously received the funds to build it.

While scouting locations for his last film, *The Hunter,* we happened to be in the ghettos of Chicago when a small group of boys playing football in a large dirt lot recognized Steve and threw him the ball. He showed it to me before throwing it back. It was old, torn, stuffed with rags and held together by wire. I looked at Steve and said, "Here we go again." He nodded yes.

He handed me a few hundred dollars in cash and I went to a sports store and purchased one hundred footballs, baseball bats, mitts, and baseballs. They were delivered to the dirt lot the next afternoon. Steve and I hid in a van and watched the kids rip open the boxes, screaming to their friends in excitement. I looked over at Steve and his eyes were moist.

I could share many other such stories about the soul of the man you didn't see. I miss and loved Steve. I will never forget him.

Loren Janes was Steve McQueen's stunt double for two decades. He resides in Canyon Country, California.

On a Chicago rooftop during *The Hunter's* climatic action sequence.

Father Figure

Karen Wilson Brunk

Mom was at the hospital receiving chemotherapy that hot summer day I met Steve and Barbara McQueen. I was walking home from school and saw many people, trailers and police parading in my street. This was definitely unusual on my block. I walked past one particular trailer and felt something tug at me, the same way your heartstrings are pulled when you connect with something in an inexplicable way. I heard later from Barbara, that at that particular moment, Steve had stretched up from where he was sitting in the trailer and turned to look at me through the window. Somehow, our spirits connected.

At home, my sister informed me that Steve McQueen was filming *The Hunter* in our apartment building and begged me to throw on a white T-shirt, take a black marker, find him and make him sign the back of the shirt. Boy, did we get more than we bargained for!

My friends Venus, Bobo and I decided to go outside, but filming had begun in the stairwell and we were told to wait. Steve walked past some men who were gambling and said to put one of us kids in the scene. Venus wasn't wearing the right clothes, Bobo made it too many boys in the scene. I went up and Steve said, "Just right—perfect!" Here I was in my cutoffs and white T-shirt. Well, they wanted me to give them some attitude. I was fifteen, growing up in a very poor neighborhood where you had to learn to survive on the streets and act confident even when you didn't feel it. I stood with my hand on my hip and my foot up behind me on the wall and exuded attitude. I was hot stuff!

After filming wrapped up, I met Steve and Barbara. He said that I was a natural and Barbara said something about paying me for the part and asked what I'd do with the money. I told them that I would give it to my mom because she was very sick. I was on cloud nine as I went back into the apartment, but my sister was furious because the T-shirt had not been signed!

Later, Steve came over to visit mom when I was out with friends. My sister nearly fainted when she answered the door with cleaning gloves on and saw Steve standing there. He asked mom about taking me on a trip for a couple weeks to help him with the filming. Mom agreed, and later I visited Steve because he wanted to talk to me. I was given a black T-shirt printed with the word STAFF and handed a stack of autographed pictures of Steve to give out to the people outside the barriers. Steve asked me tons of questions about my life, and what I wanted to do when I grew up. One thing led to another and Steve and Barbara "adopted" me that summer of 1979. It was the best two weeks of my life. Then they invited me to go to school in California so that I could get out of the neighborhood and do something good with my life. He was a father to me and I will never forget it.

I lost mom and Steve the next year. But I found the courage to work through the pain and sadness and take the opportunities that I was offered. And for this I will be forever grateful.

So thanks, Steve and Barbara, for looking past the attitude and for believing in my future.

Karen Wilson Brunk works at an escrow company in the Los Angeles area. She has been married for nearly 20 years and has four children.

The Last Interview

Rick Penn-Kraus

When Steve McQueen walked past me one day in 1979, I had no idea that in only a few minutes he would graciously agree to grant me an exclusive—and what would turn out to be his last formal interview.

Ready to head home after a track workout, I spotted trailers in the main quad area of the Alexander Hamilton High School and approached some of the movie crew who were on break. I asked them what movie was being filmed, and McQueen's stunt double, Loren Janes, said, "*The Hunter*. Steve McQueen is starring in it." Did he think McQueen would pose for a photo and agree to let me interview him? Loren laughed. "He hates when people take photos of him, and he never, ever, gives interviews."

Armed with this intimidating information, I followed McQueen into the food trailer and cornered him there. "Excuse me, Mr. McQueen. I write for the school newspaper here. Would you be willing to let me interview you and take your picture?" As a young and inexperienced reporter who had not yet entered the professional world, I assumed the direct approach was best.

"Sure," McQueen said. "Write up some questions for me, and come back later. We finish filming around 6 p.m." I returned to school that night with a list of questions. Shooting was concluding in the science building, and when McQueen saw me in the shadows, he stopped the production and waved me over. We sat on the steps, and McQueen told me to ask my questions.

As I started the interview, I looked around and to my surprise, saw that his entire crew was seated in a circle around us, listening. I later learned this was the first interview Steve McQueen had agreed to in more

than ten years, and this group—his crew, agent and friends—wanted to see it for themselves.

McQueen answered all my questions. He was shy talking about his early movies, and proud of his successes. When I concluded the interview he taught me one of the most valuable lessons I've ever had, and it started in the form of a question: "Do you mind if I add something more?"

He put his arm around my shoulders and walked me down the hall, away from everyone else, and proceeded to tell me about his upbringing, and the importance of youth and staying in school. It had never occurred to me to ask about this subject when I was preparing my questions, but it clearly meant so much to him. Then he posed reluctantly for a photo and autographed one that was handed to me.

Opposite & above: Alexander Hamilton High School student Rick Penn-Kraus snapped these photos of McQueen, who graciously allowed the teen to interview him for his high school newspaper, *The Federalist*. Occurring in September 1979, this was McQueen's last formal interview.

Right: Profile shot of the media shy McQueen on the set of *The Hunter*.

Only later did I learn he had turned down cover stories for the biggest magazines in the world, including *Time*, *Life*, and *Newsweek*. He agreed to my request because he had a high regard for young people. The interview showed me what I was capable of and made a huge impact in my life, as the exclusive nature of the scoop by a high school student became as much a story in the national press as the interview itself. Steve McQueen could have declined. It's what everyone expected. But by agreeing, and taking the time to share his thoughts with me, he added a facet to my life that continues to make me smile. His gesture of respect to a young student showed qualities that other people—not just celebrities— would be wise to emulate.

Rick Penn-Kraus is the owner and creative director of RPK Designs in Los Angeles, California. He is an illustrator, photographer, writer and musician.

Steve McQueen Interview 1979
Rick Penn-Kraus

Q. What was your first movie?

A. (Before McQueen could respond, one of the crew yelled out, *The Blob*. Steve was slightly embarrassed.) Let's not talk about that. I don't want to talk about that movie. Next question.

Q. Do you have any plans in the near future for any more movies?

A. That's a big question mark. When I finish this film I'd like to sit down and enjoy breakfast for once and then see from there. I'd like to make my next picture an action-adventure film. I enjoy variety. I liked *Love with the Proper Stranger*, which was a comedy. I had fun making *The Sand Pebbles*, which was mainly drama, and also *Bullitt*, an action film. So you see, I like different types of roles. The first film I was in was *The Blob*—and no, I wasn't the "Blob". I played the part of a young boy. That was when I was about twenty-five. I was a late bloomer in the acting world.

Q. What about your background?

A. A lot of stuff I got into trouble for when I was a kid, people wouldn't even blink at today. I got into trouble with robbery and booze, but not drugs, because they weren't considered bad at the time.

Q. Does being famous disrupt your private life?

A. Yes, it does. The important thing is to have your identity, but never blow your obscurity. That's the key to the kingdom—but the money makes me feel better.

Q. You have not been in the public eye for the past few years, but even when you did make movies, you didn't give any interviews. What was the reason for your silence?

A. For one thing, I don't have anything to say. Also, I think the press is full of shit. But I do have a certain respect for youth, and that's why I agreed to do this interview for your paper.

Q. When was the last time you were interviewed?

A. How long is a decade? (Someone blurted out "ten years.") Then it's been ten years. I don't even remember who interviewed me.

Q. What advice do you have for young people today who want to get into acting?

A. It's very expensive to act, in both time and money. I don't advise going into acting at all. I'm one of the lucky ones. But if you decide to go into acting, be prepared to give all else up and live a straight life. That includes eating and sleeping right. You should see something of life, and put it to use in your acting. Learning stuff on the streets helped my acting a lot. I'm not a "studied actor". You've got to be prepared to be rejected five times a day. That's where the importance of family comes in. The family gives you your rock strength.

Q. Who were some of your idols when you were a teenager?

A. Well, I don't think you'd remember any of my idols.

Q. But teachers read our paper, also.

A. But this isn't for the teachers. It's for the students.

FILM 5063　　　　　KODAK SAFETY FILM 5063　　　　　KODAK SAFETY FILM 5063

→12A　　　→13　　　→13A　　　→14　　　→14A　　　→15

KODAK SAFETY FILM 5063　　　　　KODAK SAFETY FILM 5063

→15A　　　→16　　　→16A　　　→17　　　→17A　　　→18

Opposite top: Scanning the hallways of Alexander Hamilton High School in Los Angeles.

Opposite bottom: McQueen can barely smile when just asked for an autograph.

Above: More shots of McQueen from the camera of Rick Penn-Kraus.

The McQueen Method
Kathryn Harrold

I was on a river trip on the Colorado deep in the Grand Canyon when I was contacted by my agent to report to Los Angeles right away. Steve McQueen wanted to meet me for his new film, *The Hunter*.

I was all wet and muddy, just completely messy after being in the outdoors for a week straight. Although terrified of flying. I left the Grand Canyon for Flagstaff, Arizona, then to Los Angeles on a private two-seater plane, all arranged by Steve McQueen. On landing in Los Angeles, I was met by director Buzz Kulik, who drove me to Santa Paula, where Steve was living in a hangar. All of this seemed very strange.

Buzz did most of the talking, while Steve stared at me and occasionally threw in a few remarks out of nowhere.

"You look like Grace Kelly," he blurted out suddenly. My hair at that time was lighter because of my week in the sun in the Grand Canyon. Steve asked if I could possibly darken my hair. He explained, "I am only attracted to dark-haired women."

During the conversation I mentioned that I happened to be a graduate of the Neighborhood Playhouse, Steve's acting alma mater. Even though Steve claimed to be a Method actor, I had the feeling he was just teasing me. I remember doing a scene without

him, and he was on the sidelines watching me and shaking his head as if to say, "You Method actors." This gave me something to play with and as a result our relationship was occasionally combative during the film.

Another time we were doing a scene that I considered dramatic in which we were fighting. I kept thinking, "He's not giving me anything. He's just saying his words. Nothing." Then when I saw it on screen, I couldn't believe what came over. I think that was my first real experience with what a great film actor he was. It's like a magical thing that just leaps up into the camera. You can't see it with the naked eye, but the camera picks it up. Steve had that more than any other actor I've ever worked with.

One particularly cold day during shooting Steve offered me his jacket. The night before I had had a dream in which I died. Well, Steve was dying of cancer but didn't know it then. We hardly ever talked to each other but for some reason we were standing together on the set, and I brought up the dream. I then asked, "Are you afraid to die?" Steve's reply was firm.

"No, I'm not."

Kathryn Harrold has more than fifty acting credits and was Steve McQueen's co-star in The Hunter.

CONTINUED: (3)

> HOVSTAD
> We'll have it ready for tomorrow's
> edition...

He gestures to Billing, who hurries off with the
report to the typesetters.

> THOMAS
> ~~And, listen,~~ Mr. Aslaksen, do me
> a favor, will you? ~~You run a fine
> paper, but supervise the printing
> personally, heh? I'd hate to see
> the weather report stuck into the
> middle of my article.~~

> ASLAKSEN
> Don't worry, there won't be a
> mistake this time!

> THOMAS
> ~~This is only the beginning. We'll
> go on to other subjects, and expose
> every lie we live by! What do you
> say?~~

yes, I'd like to expose every lie we live by.

> ASLAKSEN
> Just remember...

> BILLING & HOVSTAD
> 'Moderation.'

> ASLAKSEN
> I don't see what's so funny about
> that!

> BILLING
> Doctor Stockmann... I feel as
> though I were standing in some
> historic painting. Someday this
> scene'll be in a museum. Entitled
> 'The Day The Truth Was Born.'

His rhetoric embarrasses the other three men.

> THOMAS
> ~~Well...~~ I've got a patient half-
> bandaged down the road.

Distracted, he tears out. Aslaksen gestures to stop
him.

(CONTINUED)

Above: A letter from Stephen Pitcairn, president of the
Pitcairn Aircraft Association, asking McQueen if he can
obtain color film footage of his antique plane.

Right: For *An Enemy of the People*, McQueen slashed through
the script, illustrating that he preferred less dialogue.

Below left: McQueen adjusts his watch before flying.

Below right: McQueen enjoying a cup of coffee at a dive
motel with friends Ted Petersen (far left in blue denim jacket)
and Chuck Bail (far right in brown leather jacket) before they
attended the Watsonville Fly-In and Air Show.

The Last Ride
Chuck Bail

Left: A leather bound script for *An Enemy of the People*, which McQueen gave to Chuck Bail in 1979.

Steve McQueen and I had a unique relationship. He thought he walked on water, and I didn't.

In spite of different personalities and contradictory temperaments, we managed to maintain a healthy respect for each other. Barbara McQueen will tell you that he complained about me more than once. During a conversation at the height of his career, Steve bragged to me that he had two hit movies coming out (*Tom Horn* and *The Hunter*) to which I replied, "Why not let the movie-going public decide what's a hit and what's not, you egomaniac?" Steve abided my less than flattering comments as I did his because of our history together. I was hired as an actor on Steve's series *Wanted: Dead or Alive* in 1960 and this is where I first met my 800-pound gorilla. In 1961, I had another acting part on this series but it would be twenty years before the two of us met again.

The fateful day was sometime in 1979 at Santa Paula Airport, California. I had just landed my Stearman and was enjoying my lunch at the restaurant. Steve approached me and said "Don't I know you?" I shook my head, paid my bill and left him scratching his head. A month later, we repeated the drill. "C'mon Chuck, quit screwing around," Steve said. "I know it's you." Steve had a fifteen-acre ranch in Santa Paula, his Stearman in a hangar at the airport and was taking flying lessons. He eventually became a very good pilot. For whatever reason, we started hanging around together, flying side by side in our antiques to air shows. At a show in Porterville, California, Steve spied me sitting by the hotel pool, furiously working on an original screenplay called *The Last Ride*. The script tells the story of a handful of former Hells Angels now in their forties, who get together for "one last ride". Sherry Lansing at Columbia Studios liked the screenplay and a deal had been set up.

The next day at the air show Barbara McQueen told me that Steve's feelings were hurt because I didn't ask him to read the script. I gave him my copy and the next morning on his way to church, he showed up on my motel doorstep at 6 a.m. A cup of coffee in one hand, he was waving the screenplay in the other. Immediately getting down to brass tacks, he said, "This is the worst piece of shit I've ever read in my life." I shut the door in his face. A month later he called me, we had lunch and he informed me that he'd do my movie if I could get someone to do a good rewrite. "I've already got the deal going, Steve" I said. "I don't need your muscle." He was flabbergasted. Here was the highest paid actor in the world, getting incredible film offers, and I was telling him I didn't need him for my movie. What was I thinking? Steve was offering to do me a very, very big favor. I came to my senses and began to reconsider my position. In addition to my deep appreciation for this gift, Steve's name on the dotted line would change my status from a "B" movie director to an "A" director.

The Columbia executives went nuts. Getting McQueen was like winning the lottery. They pulled out all the stops, including tapping famed screenwriter Walter Newman to do the rewrite. They also upped my salary and changed my credit from director to director/producer. The movie was chugging along and Columbia was sinking several hundred thousand dollars into pre-production costs.

In late December 1979 I got a phone call from Steve requesting that we meet right away. "Can you keep a secret?" he asked me. I told him that I could not as I knew he had undergone tests at Cedars-Sinai Hospital recently and was not well. "Don't tell me," I said. "I'm the biggest blabbermouth on the planet."

"Chuck, I can't do the film," he told me quietly. "I'm sick." Morally, I was now in a dilemma—if I told the studio, the word would get out about Steve's condition, which he wanted to keep quiet. I stalled the studio as long as I could but a few months later, it was revealed in the tabloids that Steve had cancer. The film was put on a shelf and has remained there ever since. I kept my promise to Steve not to tell, which is exactly what he would have done for me.

You always knew where you stood with Steve for he said exactly what he thought about you or a situation. That sometimes led to more than a few arguments, but deep down I respected him as an actor and a friend. He was a good man, a class act. And I still miss his Scottish mug.

Chuck Bail is a retired stuntman, stunt coordinator, and director with five decades of film experience.

Massages, Buddhism, Billy and the Greatest Escape

Annie Martell

Those intense blue eyes bored right through me.

"Where are you from?"

"Boulder, Colorado."

Steve snorted. "Nobody's from that Hippy Dippy town. Where are you from?"

"I was born and raised in Missouri."

He smiled. "That's better. I think we'll get along just fine."

Steve McQueen was already quite ill when I met him that day at the cancer clinic in Baja. As a registered nurse, I assisted him with all the usual medical procedures. However, what I believe he appreciated most was the pain relief that he said he received from massage. I spent hours massaging his feet, back, neck and head.

We spoke about life and death. Steve's myriad emotions about dying were typical of those with late stage cancer. He didn't want to give up and in his heart and mind, he still hoped for that motorcycle ride out in the country or flying his plane. He knew all too well that the odds weren't in his favor, his cancer was too advanced, but true to his spirit, he never gave up.

We talked about life after death, wondering at the mystery. He asked me about Buddhist philosophy and its notions of reincarnation and karma. We discussed Christian beliefs, too. These heart-felt, serious explorations often occurred while I was massaging his feet.

The Reverend Billy Graham came to visit Steve while we were at Steve and Barbara's ranch in Santa Paula in early November, 1980. The minister had just returned from his first preaching tour of China and gave Steve his personal Bible from that trip. Billy Grahams' name was stamped in gold on the cover, and he had written notes for his sermons on the inside pages. Steve was cheered by that visit, and said something like, "Well, whatever happens next, between the Buddhists and the Christians, I've got myself covered."

It was in the middle of the night when Steve made his final great escape. I was in the room when he took his last breath and feel honored to be part of the team of people that Steve and Barbara invited into their lives.

Annie Martell is a registered nurse residing in the Seattle, Washington area.

The Last Crusade
Billy Graham

I had never met Steve McQueen before, but I recognized him immediately from his pictures, even though he had lost considerable weight. His eyes were bright and shiny when he sat up in bed and greeted me warmly.

He told me of his spiritual experience. Apparently he had been led to Christ by Sammy Mason, a pilot he had hired to teach him to fly a vintage airplane. He saw something in Sammy that he admired, and asked what made the difference. Sammy had carefully explained his beliefs, and Steve subsequently accepted Christ as his Savior. He had started going to church, reading his Bible, and praying. This total transformation of his thinking and his life occurred about three months before he knew he was ill with a fast-moving and possibly incurable cancer. While this was a shattering blow, his new faith became his resource for extra strength.

I sensed during our conversations—interrupted only when the nurses came to give him shots—that he was happy and totally at peace. He informed me that he was leaving for an undisclosed destination for an operation to remove the last tumor. His treatment so far had removed all the tumors except a rather large one in his stomach, and he pulled up his pajamas to show me. He thought that when it was removed his chances would be good for recovery, although he admitted, "I have about a 50 percent chance of surviving the operation."

I read him a number of passages from the Scripture and prayed with him several times.

After two hours I left to give Steve a bit of a rest and went out to the kitchen to talk to the nurses, housekeeper, and Grady Ragsdale. About an hour later, I was informed that he wanted to see me again, and we had another period of spiritual discussion, Bible reading and prayer. I was then informed that it was time to go to Ventura County Airport in Oxnard where a private Learjet was waiting to take him for his operation.

There was a large comfortable couch in the vehicle used to transport Steve over some rather rough roads to the airport. We talked, but I could see he was tiring so I suggested that he lie back and rest a few moments. When he felt he had gained a little strength he would sit up again and ask some more questions.

The plane was parked at one end of the field, quite a distance from the small terminal where people might see what was going on, and Grady pulled the camper as close to the plane as he could. Steve wanted total privacy because there had been a great deal of speculation in the press. Steve walked, mostly under his own steam, to the plane where there were two reclining seats for him to partially lie down. Then he called and asked if I would pray with him again. It was at that point that I gave him my Bible and inscribed it to him.

I look back on that experience with thanksgiving and some amazement. I had planned to minister to Steve, but as it turned out, he ministered to me. I saw once again the reality of what Jesus Christ can do for a man in his last hours.

Evangelist Billy Graham has preached to more than 210 million in 185 countries and has counseled generations of U.S. presidents and world leaders.

Barbara McQueen's photo captures an intimate moment of her husband drinking coffee and reading the paper in the backyard of their Santa Paula home.

Opposite bottom: The Bible that Evangelist, Billy Graham, gave to Steve McQueen just days before his death. It is inscribed: "To my friend Steve McQueen—may God bless you and keep you. Always—Billy Graham."

To My Friend Steve McQueen
May God Bless You and
Keep You Always — —
Billy Graham
Phil. 1:6
Nov. 3 '80

BILLY GRAHAM

The New Testament
of Our Lord and Saviour
Jesus Christ

Funerales Santa Rosa

"Funerales a precios económicos"

16 de Septiembre y Colombia

Porfirio Díaz y Chihuahua No. 2439 — Col. Melchor Ocampo

Teléfonos 4-09-22 y 3-09-26 — Cd. Juárez, Chih.

Ladislao Quintana G.
Gerente

FACILIDADES DE PAGO

SERVICIO DIA Y NOCHE

FUNERALES AL ALCANCE DE TODAS LAS POSIBILIDADES

CONEXIONES CON LAS FUNERARIAS DE EL PASO, TEXAS ESTADOS UNIDOS Y PRINCIPALES CIUDADES DE MEXICO.

Estados Unidos Mexicanos — Secretaría de Salubridad y Asistencia

CERTIFICADO DE DEFUNCION

El suscrito Médico Cirujano, con cédula número **73977** de la Dirección General de Profesiones y con título registrado en la Secretaría de Salubridad y Asistencia, bajo el número **23740** (1) o Práctico con autorización número _____ de _____ CERTIFICA que en la casa Núm. **1886** de la calle **V. Guerrero. CLINICA SANTA ROSA, S. A.** **CUARTO No. 13** (2) falleció (3) un individuo del sexo **MASCULINO.**

CAUSA DE DEFUNCION (4)

Fecha aproximada en que se inició la condición patológica **Agosto de 1978.**

I

Condición patológica que produjo la muerte directamente * Condiciones morbosas, si existiera alguna, que produjeron la arriba consignada, mencionándose en último lugar la considerada como básica o fundamental.

II

Otras condiciones patológicas significativas que contribuyeron a la muerte, pero no relacionadas con aquella que la produjo.

*No quiere decirse con esto, la manera o modo de morir por ejemplo: debilidad cardíaca, astenia, etc. significa propiamente la enfermedad, lesión o complicación que causó el fallecimiento.

a) **INFARTO AGUDO DEL MIOCARDIO**

b) **POST-OPERATORIO CIRUGIA MAYOR**

debida a (o como consecuencia de)

c) **MESOTELIOMA MALIGNO DE TORAX con**

d) **METASTASIS MULTIPLES A HIGADO y ABDOMEN**

Lugar y fecha en que se expide el certificado, Cd. Juárez, Chih., **a 7 de Noviembre de 1980.**

Nombre completo y firma del médico: **Dr. César Santos Vargas. Tel: 2-59-66**

Domicilio del médico y número de su teléfono: **V. Guerrero 1886. Tel: 2-59-66**

DATOS DEL DIFUNTO RECOGIDOS POR EL MEDICO (5)

Nombre del fallecido: **TERRENCE STEVEN McQUEEN**

Día y hora de la defunción: **7 Nov. 1980 3:50 Hs.** — Ocupación habitual (7) **ACTOR**

Edad: (6) **50 años** Estado Civil **CASADO** Nacionalidad: **NORTEAMERICANO.**

Clase de negociación, empresa o institución en donde trabaja: **SOLAR PRODUCTIONS.**

Lugar de nacimiento: **INDIANAPOLIS, INDIANA.**

Nombre del padre: _____ Vive? **no.**

Nombre de la madre: **Julian McQueen** Vive? _____

Nombre del(a) cónyuge: **BARBARA Jo. MINTY McQUEEN** Vive? **si.**

Sobreviven al finado **su esposa y dos hijos: Terry Leslie y Chadwick McQueen.**

Lugar habitual de Residencia del fallecido, calle y número de la casa **8899 Beverly Blvd. LOS ANGELES, Ca. (90048.)**

Localidad: **Cd. Juárez, Chih.,** Municipio: **DISTRITO BRAVOS.**

Entidad Federativa **CHIHUAHUA** País (si es extranjero) **MEXICO.**

Los datos fueron proporcionados por: **Barbara Jo Minty McQueen.**

Domicilio en **8899 Beverly Blvd. LOS ANGELES, Ca. (90048) E. U. A.**

Nombre completo y firma del médico. — Nombre completo y firma del informador.

(8)

Dr. César Santos Vargas. — **Barbara Jo Minty McQueen.**

15 Minutes to 12

Dr. César Santos Vargas

Left: Barbara McQueen snapped this photo of her husband during a visit to Mexico. She has not picked up a camera since his death.

Opposite: Steve McQueen's death certificate, which was signed by Dr. César Santos Vargas, the man who bravely chose to operate on the superstar. The move tarnished his practice but not his reputation as a caring doctor.

"Thank you for telling me the truth," Steve said. "I do not want to hear false hope. Should I have an operation?"

"Yes, you have to," I said. Steve asked to see my hands. I held them out, palms up, feeling as if I were on trial. He grabbed my wrists and examined my hands to see if they shook. He stared at me for a while, searching my face for answers.

"I will trust you because you are honest," he finally said. "I want to live and I am counting on you. Would you please perform my operation, doctor?"

It was a difficult situation because his operation had little chance of success. More than likely it would not end well for him and tarnish my reputation. I was under heavy pressure, but I did not regret my decision. He was a sick man in need and it was my duty as a doctor and as a person to help him. I could not do anything less than that. His honesty and courage would not let me.

Steve checked into the hospital as "Samuel Sheppard" but it fooled no one. Several television stations parked cameras outside shortly after his arrival. Despite the poor prognosis, Steve was full of hope. His operation took three-and-a-half hours as I removed tumors from his abdomen and neck. I was relieved when it was over, and checked on Steve several times. He mostly slept, but the one time he was conscious, he looked at me and smiled.

"I did it," he said weakly, raising his thumb. He seemed tired, but also excited. I told him to sleep and to get well.

A few hours later a blood clot lodged in his heart, a complication that can occur after surgery. He died quietly in his sleep.

One week after his death, a writer from Paris came to interview me. She did not ask me much about Steve or his last days, but rather wanted to know why I had performed the operation knowing there was so much for me to lose.

"I did my best and was satisfied with the operation as a doctor," I told her. "Everyone dies, that is the destiny for life. We must all accept it."

Dr. César Santos Vargas was one of Mexico's most skilled surgeons and performed Steve McQueen's final operation.

Extraordinary care meant telling it straight. Steve McQueen's eyes allowed me nothing less than the truth when I met him in late 1980. He showed me more courage and character in that one day than most do in a lifetime.

Mesothelioma racked McQueen's body with tumors, debilitating him. Doctors in America had diagnosed the famous actor with this rare form of cancer several months earlier. I was called upon to perform a life and death operation to remove the tumors because he sought alternative cancer treatment. He wanted to live.

About a month before the operation, I had received an urgent phone call from a doctor in L.A. He said that he had examined a patient who was very famous and wanted me to fly to L.A. to meet him. It was strange to fly to America for a patient and not even know his name, but I agreed, based on my relationship with the doctor. I was told that a private jet would come to Mexico to pick me up.

I met Steve McQueen the day after I arrived. It was immediately obvious to me that he was at the terminal stage of the cancer. He was seated in a chair with an oxygen mask covering his nose and mouth, clearly in pain. It was a miracle he was still alive. We have a saying in Mexico when someone is at the end of their life that they are "15 minutes to 12" and this is what I told Steve when he asked me about his condition.

Coming Home
Mike Jugan

Peace comes from within. You don't achieve it from being internationally famous, owning big houses, driving fancy cars or having money in the bank. That is the big lesson Steve McQueen taught me in his final days.

I was twenty-five years old and the co-pilot on the flight that took Steve McQueen to El Paso, Texas, for that fateful operation scheduled in Juarez, Mexico. Steve was a true hero to me since my brothers and I grew up motocross racing in Southern California. Any kid who loved racing knew who Steve McQueen was. We all wanted to be like him, riding Husky 250s. I think my dad took us to see *On Any Sunday* about fifty times.

I was working for a small Learjet charter company in Long Beach when we received a call to pick up the "Sam Sheppard" party in Oxnard, California, to fly to El Paso, on November 3, 1980. I was instructed to keep quiet because it was Steve McQueen. While we were waiting on the ramp at Oxnard, a gentleman approached the jet, and having confirmed that we were there for the "Sam Sheppard" party, he introduced himself as the Reverend Billy Graham. At this point, I realized something special was happening. Reverend Graham said Steve would arrive shortly, and soon a camper pulled up next to the jet. A canopy had been arranged over the forward part of the aircraft allowing Steve to board discreetly. He was wearing blue jeans, a T-shirt, and a sombrero and carrying a soda; totally cool. When we were ready to depart, Reverend Graham prayed for Steve, his doctors and the flight. I felt like the Creator of the universe Himself was present.

After takeoff, I went back and talked with Steve for about twenty minutes. He was snacking on crackers and soda. I wanted to discuss motorcycles but he was more interested in the plane, and asked what it was like to fly a Learjet. I told him we climbed out at 5,000 feet per minute and we were cruising at 41,000 feet and about 600 mph. He said with a chuckle, "That's better than my Stearman."

It was a life-changing moment for me. I have often marveled at the chance I was given that day to witness Steve's strength, peace and courage. He was obviously sick; but I could sense that he was bigger than all of it—that he would be back on this jet after the surgery, return to Santa Paula and life would go on. He had a strength and peace about him that I cannot fully describe.

The call came in a few days later that Steve had passed away and that we needed to be in El Paso a.s.a.p. Driving to the airport, all I could think about was how sad this would be for Steve's family and friends.

We had two Learjets flying Steve, Barbara and his doctors back to California. Approaching from the east, we called the Santa Paula Airport and told them that Steve and his family were on board and we would do a low fly-by. I remember when we reduced speed, full flaps, gear down and were about 100 feet off the ground, and made our low pass along runway 22, a crowd had gathered outside, waving goodbye to Steve.

We continued to the Ventura County Airport, and some days later his ashes were scattered over the Pacific Ocean by several of his pilot buddies. Steve McQueen was returned to this earth; a dignified and peaceful farewell.

Mike Jugan is a veteran pilot with Alaska Airlines and resides in Gig Harbor, Washington.

The Wayward Son

Jean E. Black

Slater hasn't always embraced Steve McQueen.

I have lived in Slater all my life, and for years there were rumors that Steve had grown up here, had relatives in town, and played with Jackie Giger, his Uncle Claude's step-daughter, as a young boy. There were also rumors that he didn't care much for Slater. In a small town, if someone does not like you—you don't like them back! So there were several decades of, shall we say, harsh feelings toward our famous hometown boy. It's an amazing feat to leave a small town and make it big; however, it's not respected by locals to forget where you came from.

The attitude among the community began to change in March 2007 when the City of Slater extended an olive branch, if not the entire tree, to the McQueen legacy by hosting a festival called "Steve McQueen Days". The idea was the brainchild of a handful of people who pushed hard to reunite the city with their most famous son. City of Slater Assistant Administrator Russell Griffith and Mayor Stephen Allegri embraced the idea.

The locals grumbled and were reluctant to participate. They did not believe that Barbara McQueen, Pat Johnson, Loren Janes and Marshall Terrill—who were invited to be the guests of honor—would entertain the idea of coming to town to celebrate McQueen's life in Slater.

"Nobody from California will come to Slater, especially not Barbara McQueen," they said. But when it was confirmed that the guests had all arrived, they were dumbfounded, especially when more than 2,000 people—the equivalent of Slater's entire population—showed up to see what the fuss was all about. The festival-goers came from other states and from as far away as Japan thanks to an Associated Press story that made the international wires a few days before the big event.

Barbara, Pat, Loren and Marshall not only came, they wooed everyone with their kindness and generosity. Barbara and Marshall signed books for hours on end while Pat and Loren entertained crowds with stories about Steve and their adventures in Hollywood. They also put to rest unfounded rumors that Steve McQueen did not care for Slater.

"Steve didn't hate Slater," Barbara told a spellbound audience. "Steve didn't hate anything, except when he ran out of beer." The crowd ate up her down-home humor, especially when a local asked if it was coincidental that Steve married all brunettes.

"Sure, Steve married all brunettes; but don't forget, he had a lot of blondes in between," Barbara said, which produced howls of laughter. It was then that Slater began its love affair with Barbara McQueen, and in turn, fell in love with her husband all over again.

Slater has finally brought its wayward son home and he has been rightfully honored every year since, most recently, when a highway that runs along the edge of town was named after him.

Jean E. Black is the publisher and editor of the Slater Main Street News, which has been in publication since 1886.

Dreaming I Was Steve McQueen

Dave Supple

Opposite: top left, *The Sand Pebbles;*
top right, *Hell is for Heroes;* middle left,
'The Castle', 1964; bottom left, *Wanted:
Dead or Alive;* bottom right, *Le Mans.*
Below: *The Great Escape.*

I had a dream
I was Steve McQueen,
A big movie star on the silver screen,
Riding my moto without a helmet in Germany,
Facing down the shrewdest poker players in rooms smoky,
Pulling a sophisticated heist on rich New England blue-bloods,
Racing in my Mustang over San Fran's hills from killer hoods,
What a gut wrenchingly exuberant ride it would have been,
Like racing a motorcycle across the stark desert now and then,
Or entering a *Le Mans* race and finishing in the top three
While being a bad black belt in karate meant don't mess with me.

Doin' Steve, even in a dream, wasn't with ease.
How did he make the hard seem like a breeze?
Where would I learn to be so cool?
Doubt it would have been in reform school.
What if I had been abandoned by my dad
And mom gave me up when I was still a lad?
Just like Steve I'd go inside myself someplace deep
And make tough promises that only we two could keep.

When I awoke the woman beside me wasn't a sleek movie star,
And I realized I didn't even know how to race a bike or car
I was just glad Steve left me all those films and the jolts they bring
And a legacy of cool that from hard life emerged the real thing.

*Dave Supple is an open water swimmer, a poet, and a bar owner in San
Francisco. He lives in San Rafael.*

"The King of Cool"

"Life is a Scam"

Steve McQueen, 1930–1980

Photo credits for Steve McQueen: A Tribute to the King of Cool

6	Donna Redden
8	Dave Friedman
10	Kandee Nelson
15	State Historical Society of Missouri
16	Will Smither
17	Marion County Health Department
19	Notley Hawkins (top photo); Veronica Valdez (bottom photos)
19	Veronica Valdez
20-21	Chad Westover
22	Veronica Valdez
23	State Historical Society of Missouri
24	Steve Kiefer
25	Barbara McQueen (bottom)
26-27	Boys Republic
28	Bonhams
29	Boys Republic
30-31	Bonhams
32	Karen Bruno Hornbaker
36-37	John Waggaman
38	Donna Redden
39	Ogunquit Playhouse
41	Donna Redden
43	Brian O'Mahony; Janet Conway (inset photo)
47-48	Donna Redden
50	Max Poultney
51	Max Poultney; Kandee Nelson (inset photo)
53	Donna Redden
55	Bonhams
56-60	Donna Redden
62-64	Donna Redden
67	Donna Redden
68	Karen Bruno Hornbaker
70	Edward Quinn (top photo); United Press International (bottom photo); Bonhams (memorabilia)
71	Barbara McQueen
72-73	Donna Redden
75	Donna Redden
76	Andrew Antoniades (posters)
78	Donna Redden (top and left); Karen Bruno Hornbaker (right)
79	Donna Redden (left); Karen Bruno Hornbaker (right)
82	Karen Bruno Hornbaker
84-85	Donna Redden
86	Elisabeth Osborn (photos); Bonhams (memorabilia)
88-90	Elisabeth Osborn
92	Karen Bruno Hornbaker
97	Karen Bruno Hornbaker
99-100	Bud Ekins; Bonhams (memorabilia)
103-104	Donna Redden (top photos); Jack Dieterich (bottom photos)
106	Photofest
107	RM Auctions
112	Karen Bruno Hornbaker (photos); Bonhams (letter)
118	Donna Redden (inset photo)
120	Karen Bruno Hornbaker
121	Donna Redden (top); Karen Bruno Hornbaker (bottom)
122-123	Donna Redden
124	Donna Redden
125	Motor Trend (second photo)
126-130	Donna Redden (photo); Bonhams (memorabilia)
132	Jean E. Black
141-143	Bonhams (memorabilia); Marshall Terrill (contact sheet)
146	John Norris (left inset photo)
148	Karen Bruno Hornbaker (top and bottom right)
150	Donna Redden
152-153	Donna Redden
155	Robert Relyea (photos and document)
156	Donna Redden
160-161	Kandee Nelson
164	Donna Redden
165	Bonhams (memorabilia)
166	Ed Donovan (photo); Bonhams (memorabilia)
168	Donna Redden
174	Karen Bruno Hornbaker
176	Karen Bruno Hornbaker
179	Donna Redden
182	Liz Ingersoll
183-185	Donna Redden
191	Donna Redden (top and bottom); Karen Bruno Hornbaker (middle)
194	Donna Redden
195	Photofest
196	Donna Redden (left photo); Kandee Nelson (right photo)
198	Richard George
199	Kandee Nelson
200-201	Jeff Gamble
202	Bonhams
203	Richard George (bottom photo)
204-205	Richard George
206	Richard George (photo); Chad Westover (helmet)
207	Motor Trend
208	Daniel Robin (letter)
209	Bonhams
210	Kandee Nelson (top photo); Donna Redden (bottom photos)
211	Bonhams
213	Donna Redden
215	Bonhams (left); Karen Bruno Hornbaker (photo)
216-217	Al Satterwhite
219	Photofest
224	John Klawitter (memorabilia)
225-226	Richard George (photo); John Klawitter (letter)
227	Photofest
227	Richard George; John Klawitter (letter)
228-229	Barbara McQueen; Bonhams (memorabilia)
230	Barbara McQueen (memorabilia)
231-233	Donna Redden
234-235	Kent Twitchell
238	Barbara Leigh
242	John Allen (memorabilia)
246-247	Katy Haber
248	Steve Smith
249	Andrew Antoniades
250-251	Kent James
253	Marshall Terrill (memorabilia)
259	Beth Davey (right photo)
262	Pat Johnson
263	Barbara McQueen
264	Bonhams
265	Andrew Antoniades
268	Richard Baker
270	Richard Baker
272	Photofest
273-274	Barbara McQueen
276	Barbara McQueen; RM Auctions (memorabilia)
278	Bud Ekins
279	Bonhams
280	Bruce Meyer
282	Donna Redden
283	Barbara McQueen
284-285	Gary Davis
286	John Plumlee
288	Bonhams
289	Phil Parslow
292-294	Barbara McQueen
296-302	Barbara McQueen
303	Barbara McQueen (top photo); Kealoha Rosecrans (bottom three photos)
305	Linda Minty
306	Barbara McQueen
307	Mike Schults
308-327	Barbara McQueen; Bonhams (memorabilia)
328	Dave Friedman
330	Barbara McQueen; Bonhams (memorabilia)
332	Barbara McQueen (top left); Glenn Pierce (bottom three)
333	Glenn Pierce
334-339	Barbara McQueen; Bonhams (memorabilia)
340	Mike Dewey (top photo); Barbara McQueen (bottom photo)
342	Barbara McQueen
343	Veronica Valdez (top photo); Bonhams (memorabilia)
344-350	Barbara McQueen
351-355	Dave Friedman
356-357	Barbara McQueen
358-359	Dave Friedman
360-361	Barbara McQueen
361	Rick Penn-Kraus
362	Rick Penn-Kraus (top photo); Dave Friedman (bottom photo)
364-365	Rick Penn-Kraus
366-367	Dave Friedman
368	Barbara McQueen; Bonhams (memorabilia)
369	Bonhams
370-373	Barbara McQueen; Brant Clinard (Bible)
375-376	Barbara McQueen
377	Jean E. Black
378	Karen Bruno Hornbaker (middle left, bottom left)